CULTURE, POLITICS AND SPORT: BRITAIN IN THE 20TH CENTURY

Bitesize Britain

Author
Paul A Leverell

Publisher
TDP Publishing

Copyright © 2023 TDP Publishing

All rights reserved

No part of this book may be reproduced, or stored in a retrieval system, or transmitted in any form or by any means, electronic, mechanical, photocopying, recording, or otherwise, without express written permission of the publisher.

ISBN: 9798850211561 (paperback)
ISBN: 9798850215255 (hardback)

Cover design by: the Design Partnership

Content

Note from the Author	7
1900s: Stars of Music Hall and Social Reform	9
1910s: Modernism, World War and Suffrage	41
1920s: Flapper Culture and Reconstruction	81
1930s: Political Turbulence and BBC Television	111
1940s: Rationing and Parliamentary Coalitions	143
1950s: Youth Culture and a Cup Final	177
1960s: British Invasion and The Kings Road	212
1970s: Inflation and the Three Day Week	245
1980s: Deregulation and Privatisation	275
1990s: Britpop and The Third Way	307

Note from the Author

I am not a professional historian and have no training or qualifications as a writer unless you count an O-Level in English Language and an O-Level in English Literature studied for at my grammar school in Essex in the late 1970s and early 1980s. I am a Social History enthusiast.

The concept of "Bitesize Britain" is to offer bite sized and digestible chunks of social history that delve into Britain in the 20th century. In this edition, I cover the cultural, political, and sporting landscapes of each decade from the dawn of the new century to the eve of the new millennium. It is of course not possible to include every important event and character of the 20th century, I have included the ones that I have found interesting during my research, hopefully, you will find them enjoyable to read about. I hope that the book will bring back some memories, inform you of some events and characters that you did not know about and maybe inspire you to begin your own research into the social history of Britain.

I am aware that I use "Britain" throughout and that this is not the politically correct term. I use "Britain" as shorthand in the early chapters for "United Kingdom of Great Britain and Ireland" and latterly "United Kingdom of Great Britain and Northern Ireland". I hope this shorthand does not offend anybody, although I can already imagine all of the pedants scribbling away leaving comments and reviews about my lack of understanding of "British" history.

I have tried to ensure that all the facts and dates in this work are accurate. However, as 98% of my research has been conducted on the internet you should blame Google for any errors you might find.

1900s
Stars of Music Hall and Social Reform

The year 1900 marked an important period of transition and progress for Britain. The nation was experiencing significant social, cultural, and technological changes that would shape its trajectory for the 20th century. At the dawn of the new century, Britain was at the height of its power as a global empire. The British Empire spanned across the world, covering vast territories and diverse populations. This global influence brought both prosperity and challenges to the nation. Industrialisation and technological advancements had transformed Britain into a leading industrial and economic powerhouse. The country's manufacturing sector thrived, fuelled by innovations in machinery and production techniques. Industries such as textiles, coal mining, steel, and shipbuilding were flourishing, driving economic growth and urbanisation.

Popular culture during the early 1900s was still heavily influenced by the Victorian era, characterised by conservative values and societal norms. However, as the decade progressed, new cultural movements and changes in society began to emerge. The suffragette movement, advocating for women's rights and suffrage, gained momentum during this time. Women began challenging traditional gender roles and actively participated in political and social debates, paving the way for future feminist movements. Music in the 1900s encompassed a range of genres, reflecting the diverse tastes of the population. Classical music continued to be popular, with composers such as Edward Elgar and Gustav Holst making significant contributions to the British musical landscape. However, the emergence of popular songs and music hall performances also gained popularity. Music halls became a hub for entertainment, featuring performances of comedic acts, vaudeville shows, and live music, catering to a wide range of audiences. Literature and art in the 1900s saw the rise of new movements and influential works. The aesthetic movement of the late 19th century continued to influence the arts, emphasising beauty, individualism, and art for art's sake. Notable authors like Arthur Conan Doyle, H.G. Wells, Rudyard Kipling and George Bernard Shaw made significant contributions to literature, challenging societal conventions and exploring complex themes.

The Liberal Party, under the leadership of figures like Henry Campbell-Bannerman and later H.H. Asquith, championed social reforms and introduced policies to address issues such as poverty, education, and working conditions. The Labour Representation Committee, later known as the Labour Party, was formed in 1900, representing the interests of the working-class population and advocating for workers' rights. The political landscape was marked by debates over social welfare, the role of the state, and the rights of workers.

Sport in Britain during the 1900s experienced notable developments and the establishment of enduring institutions. Football continued to grow in popularity, with the establishment of the Football League in 1888. Notable football clubs such as Manchester United and Chelsea were founded during this period. Cricket also remained a prominent sport, with the Ashes series between England and Australia capturing public attention. The period between 1900 and 1909 also witnessed the emergence of international sporting events. The 1908 London Olympic Games were held in Britain. It was a significant event that showcased the country's ability to host a global sporting spectacle. The Olympics brought together athletes from different nations and provided a platform for sporting excellence and international cooperation.

******

Music hall, also known as variety entertainment, emerged in the mid 19th century as a form of popular entertainment that combined elements of comedy, music, and variety acts. By the early 20th century, it had become a thriving industry, with music halls scattered across the urban centre of Britain. These venues ranged from opulent theatres to small, working class establishments, catering to a diverse audience. Some famous music halls, such as the London Pavilion and the Hippodrome, became iconic symbols of the era. The stars of the music hall were its performers, who captivated audiences with their talent, wit, and charisma. During the 1900s, renowned acts such as Marie Lloyd, Vesta Tilley, and George Robey reigned supreme. Marie Lloyd, known for her saucy songs and irreverent humour, was a favourite among working-class audiences. Vesta Tilley, on the other hand, gained fame for her performances as a male impersonator, captivating audiences with her gender-bending portrayals. George Robey was a master of comic timing, entertaining audiences with his humorous monologues and catchy songs.

These performers brought a sense of escapism to the lives of their audience members, who often hailed from lower socio economic backgrounds. Music hall offered an affordable form of entertainment, allowing people to forget their everyday troubles and immerse themselves in laughter and song. The atmosphere in music halls was lively and boisterous, with audiences enthusiastically participating by singing along, clapping, and heckling performers.

Beyond its role as entertainment, music hall reflected the social and political climate of the time. The Edwardian era, which spanned from 1901 to 1910, was a period of significant social change and upheaval. Music hall acts often incorporated political satire and commentary, using humour to critique the ruling classes and shed light on issues such as women's suffrage and labour rights. Performers like Marie Lloyd and Vesta Tilley became symbols of female empowerment, challenging traditional gender norms through their bold and unconventional performances. However, the golden age of music hall in Britain began to wane towards the end of the decade. The rise of new forms of entertainment, such as early cinema and radio, posed a challenge to the traditional music hall format.

******

The Education Act of 1902, also known as the Balfour Act, aimed to reform and improve the education system in England and Wales. It established a framework for local control, compulsory education, and improved funding. While it brought about important changes, it also led to debates and concerns over issues such as religious influence and the balance between state and local control of education. The Act established local education authorities (LEAs) across England and Wales. LEAs were responsible for overseeing and managing education at the local level, including the provision and funding of schools.

The Act aimed to bring together the various types of schools under a unified system. It abolished the School Boards that had been established by the Education Act of 1870 and transferred their responsibilities to the LEAs. Voluntary schools, which were primarily affiliated with religious organisations, were allowed to continue but became eligible for financial support from local rates. LEAs were given the authority to levy rates to finance education, and both voluntary and board schools received financial assistance from local taxes. Education was made compulsory for children aged 5 to 13, setting the foundation for the establishment of a universal elementary education system and established a system of school inspections to ensure standards of education. The Act recognised the need for secondary education and encouraged the establishment of secondary schools. LEAs were given the power to assist in providing secondary education but were not mandated to do so. There was a significant impact on church schools, particularly those associated with the Church of England. It led to increased state control and financial support but also raised concerns regarding the potential erosion of religious influence.

******

Cricket remained a quintessentially British sport, with matches played in idyllic settings across the country. The Ashes series of 1903-04 holds a special place in cricket history as it was a defining moment for both England and Australia. In a stunning turn of events, the English cricket team, led by the astute Plum Warner, achieved a remarkable victory over their Australian counterparts This tour marked the first instance where the

Marylebone Cricket Club (MCC) took charge of organising and sponsoring an overseas tour representing England. The English side, considered underdogs by many, defied all odds and emerged triumphant, winning the five test series by a margin of 3-2.

The opening Test at Sydney Cricket Ground set the stage for an enthralling contest. Australia, after winning the toss, elected to bat first. It was the indomitable MA Noble who rose to the occasion, scoring a magnificent 133 runs. However, the English bowler EG Arnold displayed great skill and determination, claiming 4 wickets for 76 runs. Australia was eventually bowled out for 285 runs. In response, England unleashed an extraordinary debutant, R.E. "Tip" Foster, who etched his name in the annals of cricket history. Foster scored a staggering 287 runs, establishing a world record for the highest individual Test innings by a debutant. With his remarkable performance, Foster propelled England to a mammoth total of 577 runs. Australia, led by the talented VT Trumper's unbeaten 185, fought valiantly but fell short, succumbing to the English bowling prowess led by W Rhodes, who claimed 5 wickets for 94 runs. The match concluded with England triumphing by 5 wickets, signalling their determination to reclaim the Ashes. Moving on to the second Test at Melbourne Cricket Ground, England once again won the toss and elected to bat. JT Tyldesley emerged as the star performer for England, falling agonisingly close to a century with 97 runs to his name. Australia's WP Howell exhibited superb bowling skills, taking 4 wickets for 43 runs. England managed to reach a respectable total of 315 runs. In response, Australia's batting lineup crumbled under the relentless bowling of W Rhodes, who claimed a remarkable 7 wickets for 56 runs. The Australian team was bowled out for a paltry 122 runs. England's second innings featured another impressive display by Tyldesley, who scored 62 runs, supported by Rhodes' 8 wickets for 68 runs. Australia's resistance faltered, and they were dismissed for a mere 111 runs. England secured a resounding victory by 185 runs.

The action shifted to Adelaide Oval for the third Test, where Australia won the toss and elected to bat. VT Trumper dazzled the crowd with a masterful innings of 113 runs. However, EG Arnold's excellent bowling, with 3 wickets for 93 runs, restricted Australia to 388 runs. England's response was led by GH Hirst, who scored a gritty 58 runs. Australian spinner H Trumble showcased his skills, claiming 3 wickets for 49 runs. England fell short with a total of 245 runs. Australia's second innings featured an outstanding century by SE Gregory, scoring 112 runs. BJT Bosanquet's bowling efforts, with 4 wickets for 73 runs, could not prevent Australia from setting a target of 278 runs for England. Despite PF Warner's valiant innings of 79 runs, AJY Hopkins' 4 wickets for 81 runs dashed England's hopes. Australia emerged victorious, triumphing by a commanding margin of 216 runs.

The fourth Test, once again held at Sydney Cricket Ground, witnessed England winning the toss and electing to bat. AE Knight's unbeaten 70 runs, aided by MA Noble's 7 wickets for 100 runs, propelled England to a total of 249 runs. Australia's first innings featured a commendable knock of 47 runs by RA Duff, but EG Arnold's bowling brilliance restricted them to a mere 131 runs. England's second innings saw TW Hayward's half-century, scoring 52 runs, while A Cotter claimed 3 wickets for 41 runs. Australia's chase faltered, and they were dismissed for 171 runs. BJT Bosanquet's sensational bowling performance of 6 wickets for 51 runs guided England to a convincing victory by 157 runs. The final Test took place at Melbourne Cricket Ground, with Australia winning the toss and electing to bat. VT Trumper emerged as Australia's highest scorer, contributing 88 runs. However, LC Braund's exceptional bowling display, claiming 8 wickets for 81 runs, restricted Australia to 247 runs. In reply, England's batting lineup struggled against A Cotter's impressive spell of 6 wickets for 40 runs, resulting in their dismissal for a mere 61 runs. Australia's second innings was led by H Trumble's devastating bowling, taking 7 wickets for 28 runs, ensuring England's pursuit of a target of 356 runs ended abruptly with a total of 101 runs. Australia sealed a comprehensive victory by 218 runs.

This Ashes series of 1903-04 will be remembered as a watershed moment in cricket history. England's triumph against all odds showcases the true essence of the sport, where determination and skill can conquer even the mightiest opponents. The series witnessed several individual performances of exceptional brilliance, with records being shattered and new stars emerging. The MCC's decision to appoint Plum Warner as captain proved to be a masterstroke, as his leadership and strategic acumen guided England to a memorable victory.

******

In 1903, Emmeline Pankhurst and her daughters, Christabel and Sylvia, founded the Women's Social and Political Union (WSPU), also known as the suffragettes. While women did not gain the right to vote during this specific period, the suffrage movement made significant strides towards achieving its goal, setting the stage for further advancements in the following decade. The roots of the women's suffrage movement in Britain can be traced back to the mid-19th century, with pioneers like Millicent Fawcett and Lydia Becker laying the foundation for future activism.

The suffrage movement experienced internal divisions during this period. While the suffragettes pursued more militant tactics, the suffragists, led by Millicent Fawcett and the National Union of Women's Suffrage Societies (NUWSS), pursued a peaceful and constitutional approach, advocating for suffrage through lobbying, petitions, and public campaigns. The suffragettes employed direct action and civil disobedience to demand attention and action from the government. Their tactics included public demonstrations, hunger strikes, and acts of vandalism such as breaking windows and arson. The suffragettes adopted the slogan "Votes for Women" as their rallying cry. They organised numerous public meetings, marches, and protests across the country to raise awareness about women's disenfranchisement and the need for political equality. The disruptive tactics and confrontations with the authorities attracted significant media coverage. Newspapers reported on their activities, resulting in heightened public awareness of the suffrage movement and its objectives.

The suffrage movement faced considerable opposition from various sectors of society, including politicians, the press, and anti-suffrage organisations. Many argued that granting women the right to vote would disrupt traditional gender roles and undermine the social order. In 1910, the Liberal government, led by Prime Minister H.H. Asquith, introduced a series of Conciliation Bills aimed at granting limited suffrage to women. Although these bills ultimately failed to pass, they marked a shift in the political landscape and increased parliamentary discussion on women's suffrage.

******

The decade marked a notable period in the life and career of Sir Arthur Conan Doyle, the renowned British author best known for his creation of the iconic detective character, Sherlock Holmes. During this time, Conan Doyle's literary pursuits, personal experiences and social contributions showcased his versatility and influence in the realms of literature and public life. At the turn of the century, Conan Doyle's Sherlock Holmes stories had already gained immense popularity, captivating readers with their intricate mysteries and the brilliant deductive reasoning of the detective himself. However, in 1903, Conan Doyle made a controversial decision that shocked his avid readers and the literary world as a whole, he killed off Sherlock Holmes in the story "The Final Problem". The news of Holmes' demise caused an uproar among fans, who mourned the loss of their beloved character. In response to the public outcry, Conan Doyle faced immense pressure to revive Holmes, which he eventually did in 1905 with the publication of "The Adventure of the Empty House", revealing that Holmes had survived his supposed death.

Conan Doyle's literary output during this period extended beyond the adventures of Sherlock Holmes. He continued to explore different genres and themes, showcasing his versatility as a writer. In 1902, he published "The Hound of the Baskervilles", a Sherlock Holmes novel set before Holmes' apparent demise. The novel, set in the eerie moors of Dartmoor, captured readers' imaginations with its atmospheric setting and complex mystery. "The Hound of the Baskervilles" remains one of Conan Doyle's most popular and enduring works. In addition to his fiction writing, Conan Doyle ventured into the realm of historical fiction with his novel "Sir Nigel", published in 1906. Set during the Hundred Years' War, the book follows the adventures of a young English knight. Inspired by Conan Doyle's fascination with medieval history, "Sir Nigel" showcases his ability to captivate readers with his storytelling prowess beyond the realm of detective fiction. Conan Doyle's literary contributions during this period were not limited to his works. In 1902, he founded the literary magazine "The Strand", which became immensely popular for its publication of Sherlock

Holmes stories. The magazine introduced readers to a new format of serialised fiction, featuring captivating illustrations and engaging narratives. The success of "The Strand" further solidified Sherlock Holmes' status as a cultural phenomenon and established Conan Doyle as one of the leading figures in British literature.

******

Through his science fiction novels, social commentaries, and non-fiction writings H.G. Wells continued to captivate readers with his visionary ideas and thought-provoking narratives. Wells' exploration of scientific and social themes, coupled with his active involvement in public life, solidified his position as a leading figure in British literature and intellectual circles. Wells continued to produce a remarkable body of work that reflected his innovative ideas, visionary imagination, and keen observations of the social and scientific developments of the era. At the turn of the century, Wells had already established himself as a leading figure in the genre of science fiction with the publication of his groundbreaking novels, such as "The Time Machine" and "The War of the Worlds". In the early 1900s, he continued to expand his literary horizons by exploring new themes and experimenting with different narrative styles. In 1900 Wells published "The First Men in the Moon", a captivating tale that imagines a journey to the moon and explores themes of human exploration, colonisation, and the clash of civilisations. The novel showcased Wells' ability to blend scientific speculation with social commentary, creating thought-provoking narratives that resonated with readers.

During this period, Wells also ventured beyond the realms of science fiction. In 1900, he published "Love and Mr. Lewisham", a social novel that delved into themes of love, marriage, and the pursuit of individual happiness. The book reflected Wells' interest in exploring the complexities of human relationships and the impact of societal norms on personal fulfillment. In addition to his fiction writing, Wells engaged in extensive non-fiction work, contributing to public discourse on various social and political issues. He published works like "Anticipations", where he speculated about the future of society, and "A Modern Utopia", in which he presented his vision of an ideal society. Wells' non-fiction writings showcased his intellectual curiosity and his desire to shape the world through his ideas and observations.

******

At the turn of the century, Rudyard Kipling had already established himself as a prominent writer, known for his evocative poetry and stories that captured the spirit of the British Empire and its colonies. In the early 1900s, he continued to draw inspiration from his experiences in India, where he had spent a significant portion of his life. Kipling's works during this period often portrayed the complexities of colonialism, exploring the relationships between the colonisers and the colonised, and reflecting on the impact of imperialism on both parties.

One of Kipling's notable works from this period is the collection of short stories titled "Plain Tales from the Hills". These stories provided an intimate portrayal of life in British India, capturing the diverse experiences and challenges faced by individuals living in a colonial setting. The collection showcased Kipling's skill in depicting the nuances of the social, cultural, and political dynamics of the time. In addition to his exploration of colonial themes, Kipling's writings during this period also included works that appealed to younger audiences. In 1901, he published "Kim", a novel set in India that follows the adventures of an orphaned Irish boy who becomes embroiled in espionage. "Kim" remains one of Kipling's most celebrated works, combining elements of adventure, coming-of-age, and cultural exploration.

Kipling was a staunch supporter of the British Empire and its imperialistic policies, which garnered both praise and criticism. His poem "The White Man's Burden" encapsulated his perspective on the responsibilities of the British Empire in civilising and guiding other nations, a view that was contested by many. Despite his controversial views on imperialism, Kipling's contributions to literature were widely recognised and celebrated during this period. In 1907, he was awarded the Nobel Prize in Literature, making him the first English-language writer to receive this prestigious honour. The prize acknowledged his exceptional storytelling abilities, his mastery of language, and his ability to create vivid and memorable characters.

******

George Bernard Shaw, on the other hand, experienced a period of great productivity and influence during the 1900s. Shaw, a playwright, critic, and social reformer, was known for his thought-provoking plays that challenged social norms and conventions. He used his writing to explore social, political, and economic issues of his time.

In the early 1900s, Shaw's plays reflected his evolving political beliefs and his interest in socialistic ideas. Works such as "Major Barbara" and "Man and Superman" tackled themes such as capitalism, class struggle, and women's rights. Shaw's plays were characterised by witty dialogue, sharp satire, and a deep understanding of human nature. His ability to blend humour with social commentary made his works both entertaining and thought-provoking. During this period, Shaw's plays were performed by renowned theatre companies, including the Royal Court Theatre and the Royal Shakespeare Company. His work gained recognition not only in Britain but also internationally. Shaw's influence extended beyond the stage, as he was actively involved in political and social debates. He was a prominent member of the Fabian Society, a socialist organisation that sought to achieve social justice through gradual reform.

******

The Old Age Pensions Act of 1908 was a pioneering piece of social legislation that aimed to alleviate poverty and provide a basic level of support for elderly individuals who had little or no income in their old age. It represented a significant step towards the establishment of a more comprehensive social security system in the United Kingdom, setting the precedent for future welfare reforms. The Act laid the groundwork for subsequent advancements in pension schemes and contributed to the broader development of social policies focused on providing support and security for vulnerable members of society.

The Act established a system of state funded pensions for individuals who reached a designated age. It provided financial support to elderly citizens who had limited or no means of income in their old age. Unlike previous pension schemes, which required individuals to make contributions during their working lives, the Old Age Pensions Act introduced a non contributory scheme. Eligibility for the pension was based on age and residency criteria, rather than contributions or means testing. The Act initially set the pension age at 70, although it was later lowered to 65 in subsequent years. To qualify for the pension, individuals had to meet residency requirements and have been a resident in the United Kingdom for at least 20 years, with at least 12 of those years immediately preceding the claim. The pension amount was means tested, meaning that the level of income and financial resources of the pensioner was taken into account when determining the amount of pension received. However, the means testing was relatively lenient compared to other assistance programs, allowing a wider range of individuals to qualify for the pension.

The Act allocated funds for the payment of pensions through general taxation. It marked a significant step towards the development of a welfare state, with the state taking responsibility for providing financial support to older citizens.

******

At the beginning of the 20th century, football in Britain was primarily an amateur sport, with clubs formed by enthusiasts and workers from various industries. The Football Association (FA), established in 1863, played a central role in setting the rules and governing the sport. However, as the popularity of football grew, the demand for a more organised and professional approach to the game emerged. In 1885, the FA legalised professionalism, allowing clubs to pay players for their services. This change laid the groundwork for the professionalisation of football in the coming years. By the early 1900s, the shift towards professionalism had gained momentum, leading to the formation of the first professional leagues. In 1888, the Football League was established, comprising 12 teams from the Midlands and the North of England. The league structure brought about regular competitive fixtures and piqued public interest. The Football League expanded over the next decade, adding more teams and divisions, and by the early 1900s, it had become a prominent feature of British football. The decade from 1900 to 1909 witnessed intense competition in the Football League, with several clubs vying for supremacy. The likes of Aston Villa, Sheffield Wednesday, Manchester United (then known as Newton Heath), and Newcastle United emerged as strong contenders, winning multiple league titles and establishing themselves as football powerhouses. The FA Cup, the oldest national football competition in the world, continued to captivate football fans during this period. The tournament attracted teams from various levels of the football pyramid, from amateur clubs to top-tier professional sides. The FA Cup finals of this era witnessed memorable matches and remarkable performances, becoming highly anticipated events in the British sporting calendar. International football also flourished during this decade. The British Home Championship, an annual tournament contested by the national teams of England, Scotland, Wales, and Ireland (later Northern Ireland), provided a platform for intense rivalries. Matches between these nations drew large crowds and showcased the talent of players representing their respective countries. The national teams of the British Isles also ventured beyond their borders to face international opponents. Notably, in 1908, Great Britain (composed of players from England, Scotland, and Wales) won the gold medal in football at the London Olympics. This victory highlighted the prowess of British football on the global stage.

******

Fashion trends in Britain made a transition from the formal and restrictive styles of the Victorian era to more comfortable and relaxed clothing. At the beginning of the 20th century, women's fashion underwent notable changes. The hourglass silhouette that had characterised the late Victorian era gradually gave way to a straighter, more columnar shape. Corsets, which had been tightly laced to achieve a small waist, became less constrictive. Instead, the focus shifted to creating a high-busted, S-shaped silhouette, achieved by the use of padded brassieres and corsetry that emphasised the bust and raised the waistline. In terms of dresses, the popular styles included the "Gibson Girl" aesthetic. Named after the illustrations by Charles Dana Gibson, this look was characterised by high collars, shirtwaists, and long, flowing skirts. Shirtwaists were blouses with buttons down the front, often worn with matching or contrasting skirts. The skirts featured pleats, ruffles, or flounces and were often worn with petticoats to achieve a fuller appearance. Fabrics like cotton, linen, and silk were commonly used for daytime dresses, while evening gowns were made from luxurious materials such as satin, silk, or velvet. Hats were an essential accessory during this period, and women wore a variety of styles. Large-brimmed hats adorned with feathers, ribbons, and flowers were popular for outdoor activities and social events. Wide-brimmed picture hats, often lavishly decorated, added elegance to women's outfits. These hats were often worn tilted at an angle, framing the face and creating a fashionable look.

Men's fashion in the early 1900s remained relatively formal but underwent some subtle changes. Three-piece suits continued to be the norm, consisting of a jacket, waistcoat, and trousers. However, the silhouette became slightly looser and more relaxed compared to the tight-fitting styles of the previous century. The sack coat, a straight-cut, single-breasted jacket, gained popularity during this period. Trousers were high-waisted and often featured cuffs at the bottom. Accessories played a significant role in men's fashion. Bowler hats, also known as derby hats, were a common choice for everyday wear, while top hats were reserved for more formal occasions. Neckties and bow ties were worn with collared shirts, and pocket watches were popular accessories that added a touch of refinement to men's attire. In terms of evening wear, men often donned tailcoats or tuxedos, while women opted for elegant evening gowns. These gowns featured more intricate details, such as lace, beading, and embroidery. Elaborate hairstyles and accessories, including feathers, ribbons, and jewels, complemented the evening looks. The Art Nouveau movement, characterised by flowing lines and natural motifs, found expression in clothing designs. Soft, floral patterns and intricate lacework became popular, reflecting the influence of this artistic style.

******

The Children's Act of 1908 was a significant milestone in the development of child welfare legislation in the United Kingdom. It aimed to protect children from exploitation, improve their living conditions, and ensure their well being. The Act recognised the specific needs and vulnerabilities of children and introduced measures to address these issues. Its provisions for child labour regulation, juvenile justice, prevention and care, and adoption set the foundation for subsequent reforms and advancements in child welfare and protection.

The Act introduced measures to regulate and restrict child labour. It prohibited the employment of children under the age of 12 in industrial occupations and set limits on the hours of work for children aged 12 to 14. Juvenile courts were established to deal with cases involving child offenders. The juvenile courts were intended to provide a more specialised and supportive approach to juvenile justice, focusing on rehabilitation rather than punishment.

The Act introduced probation as an alternative to imprisonment for young offenders. It allowed for the supervision and guidance of young offenders in the community. Additionally, it provided for the establishment of juvenile detention centres, where young offenders could be placed in a more suitable environment. It also recognised the importance of prevention and early intervention in child welfare. It empowered local authorities to intervene in cases where children were deemed to be at risk or in need of care and protection. Local authorities were given the authority to provide support and assistance to families to prevent the need for child removal or intervention.

Voluntary Homes and Inspection: The Act regulated and inspected voluntary homes for children, including orphanages and residential institutions. It aimed to ensure that children placed in these homes were provided with adequate care, education, and protection. Provisions for the legal adoption of children were introduced. It established a legal framework for adoption, ensuring that the welfare and best interests of the child were prioritised in the adoption process.

******

The early 1900s marked a transformative period for tennis, with the sport gaining popularity among both players and spectators. The Wimbledon Championships, first held in 1877, continued to evolve and attract top players from around the world. The tournament maintained its traditional grass court surface, which became synonymous with the elegance and grace of the sport. During this decade, the Wimbledon Championships witnessed the rise of exceptional tennis players who left an indelible mark on the tournament. One such player was Laurence Doherty, who dominated the men's singles competition between 1902 and 1906. Doherty's powerful serve, precise volleys, and tactical play helped him secure five consecutive Wimbledon titles from 1902 to 1906, establishing himself as one of the era's greatest players. Another notable player during this period was Arthur Gore. Gore, known for his finesse and stylish approach to the game, claimed the Wimbledon men's singles title in 1901 and 1908. His skilful shot-making and tactical acumen made him a formidable opponent on the grass courts of Wimbledon.

In the women's singles competition, the Wimbledon Championships saw the emergence of talented players who achieved remarkable success during this decade. One such player was Blanche Bingley, who won six Wimbledon titles in the 1880s. Although past her prime, Bingley continued to participate in the tournament during the early 1900s and reached the final in 1901, showcasing her enduring passion for the sport. The period also witnessed the rise of Dorothea Douglass Chambers, commonly known as Dorothea Lambert Chambers. She made her mark at Wimbledon, winning the women's singles title a remarkable seven times between 1903 and 1914. Chambers' powerful game, characterised by her strong forehand and imposing presence at the net, earned her a place among the tournament's all-time greats. The Wimbledon Championships of this era also experienced the growth of international participation. Players from countries such as the United States, Australia, and France began to make their presence felt at the tournament, adding a global flavour to the competition. These international players brought new styles and tactics, enriching the diversity of the game and contributing to the global appeal of Wimbledon.

Beyond the players, the Wimbledon Championships underwent infrastructure improvements during this period. The All England Lawn Tennis and Croquet Club, the organising body of the tournament, made efforts to enhance the facilities and spectator experience. The Centre Court, the tournament's main show court, underwent renovations, including the installation of a permanent stand, improving the overall ambiance of the Championships.

******

The cinema industry was still in its infancy, early films were short, silent productions, typically lasting only a few minutes. These films were often shown as part of variety shows or alongside other forms of entertainment, such as magic shows, musical performances, or vaudeville acts. The content of these films ranged from documentary like footage of everyday life to fictional narratives and comedic sketches. Movie theatres of the time were often small, modest venues. Initially, films were screened in temporary spaces, such as fairgrounds or empty storefronts, where makeshift screens and seating arrangements were set up. As the popularity of moving pictures grew, purpose-built cinemas began to emerge, designed specifically for film screenings.

These cinemas were typically single-screen venues, featuring a stage and a seating area, with the screen located at the front. One of the pioneering figures in the British cinema industry during this period was Charles Urban. Urban was an American-born producer and distributor who played a significant role in the development and expansion of the film industry in Britain. He established his own film production company and opened theatres, known as "Kinemacolor Theatres", which specialised in showcasing films using the Kinemacolor process, an early method of colour cinematography.

As the popularity of cinema grew, so did the demand for longer and more sophisticated films. Filmmakers began experimenting with narrative storytelling, developing more complex plots and characters. In 1903, the first British narrative film, "The Great Train Robbery", was released, setting the stage for the future of filmmaking in the country. The film industry also saw advancements in filmmaking techniques, such as the introduction of synchronised sound and the use of special effects. Audiences flocked to movie theatres to experience the magic of moving pictures. Moviegoing became a popular pastime for people from all walks of life, attracting a diverse range of audiences. Ticket prices were generally affordable, making movies accessible to a wider population. The cinema experience was often accompanied by live musical performances, with pianos or small orchestras providing the soundtrack to accompany the silent films.

Despite the growing popularity of cinemas, they faced opposition from various quarters. Some members of the public, particularly from more conservative circles, expressed concerns about the impact of movies on morality and social behaviour. There were calls for censorship and regulations to ensure that the content shown in cinemas was suitable for public consumption.

******

The growing strength of trade unions and the establishment of the Labour Party laid the foundation for increased political representation and improved rights and protections for workers. The period witnessed significant growth in trade union membership and influence, particularly in sectors such as mining, textiles, and transportation. This growth was driven by various factors, including worsening working conditions, low wages, and a desire for collective bargaining power.

In 1900, The Labour Representation Committee (LRC) was established as a political party to represent the interests of the working class. It was formed by various trade unions, socialist organisations, and individuals advocating for labour rights and progressive reforms. The LRC aimed to secure the direct representation of labour interests in the British Parliament. It sought to elect Members of Parliament (MPs) who would advocate for working-class issues, such as better wages, improved working conditions, and social reforms. The LRC evolved into the Labour Party in 1906, following successful electoral campaigns that saw the election of several MPs representing the working-class movement. The Labour Party aimed to give a political voice to the trade union movement and promote social democracy.

The growth of trade unions and the labour movement led to increased demands for union recognition and collective bargaining rights. Workers sought the ability to negotiate wages, working conditions, and employment terms collectively rather than individually. The trade union movement and the Labour Party advocated for social reforms during this period. They campaigned for measures such as better working hours, improved workplace safety, the abolition of child labour, and the introduction of minimum wages. The Trade Disputes Act of 1906, also known as the Taff Vale judgment reversal act, was a significant piece of legislation in Britain that aimed to address the negative consequences of a legal ruling known as the Taff Vale case. In 1901, the Taff Vale Railway Company won a landmark legal case against the Amalgamated Society of Railway Servants (ASRS), a trade union. The ruling held the union liable for damages caused by a strike, enabling employers to seek financial compensation for losses incurred during industrial disputes. The Trade Disputes Act reversed the Taff Vale judgment and provided legal immunity to trade unions involved in peaceful disputes. It prohibited employers from seeking damages from trade unions for economic losses resulting from industrial action.

The Act protected trade union funds from being used to pay legal damages arising from trade disputes. It prevented employers from seizing union funds to recover compensation for damages incurred during strikes or other industrial actions. The Act also explicitly legalised peaceful picketing, ensuring that trade union members could engage in picketing activities without facing legal repercussions.

The Trade Disputes Act of 1906 was a significant development for trade unions in the United Kingdom. It addressed the concerns raised by the Taff Vale case, which had weakened trade unions' legal protections and financial resources. The Act restored some of the power and influence of trade unions, providing them with greater legal security in conducting strikes and other forms of industrial action. It also established a legal framework that recognised the importance of collective bargaining and peaceful protest in labour disputes.

******

At the turn of the 20th century, golf was already a well-established sport in Britain. The country boasted a rich tradition of golf, with several prestigious golf clubs scattered across its landscapes. These clubs provided facilities for enthusiasts to play the game and served as centres for organising tournaments and fostering camaraderie among golfers. The Open Championship, one of the oldest and most prestigious golf tournaments in the world, continued to captivate golf enthusiasts during this decade. The tournament was contested by professional and amateur golfers alike, with players from Britain and beyond competing for the coveted Claret Jug. The Open Championship of this era witnessed remarkable performances, creating memorable moments in golf history. One of the standout players during this period was Harry Vardon. Vardon, known for his exceptional skill and innovative grip technique, dominated the golfing scene. He won The Open Championship six times between 1896 and 1914, including victories in 1899 and 1903. Vardon's success and influence helped popularise the sport and elevate its status in Britain. Another influential figure during this decade was James Braid. Braid was a highly skilled player and renowned golf course architect. He won The Open Championship five times between 1901 and 1910, further solidifying his place among the top golfers of the time. Braid's contributions to golf course design left a lasting legacy, as many of his creations continue to be enjoyed by golfers today. The period also witnessed advancements in golf equipment and course design. Innovations such as the rubber cored ball and the hickory shafted club had a significant impact on the game, allowing players to achieve greater distances and control. Golf course architects began to incorporate strategic elements into their designs, challenging players with hazards, bunkers, and undulating greens.

******

The period marked the early stages of radio broadcasting in Britain, as the technology advanced and the foundations for what would become a revolutionary medium of communication were laid. During this time, radio experimentation and development were taking place, setting the stage for the future of broadcasting in the country. At the turn of the century, wireless telegraphy, which allowed for the transmission of telegraph signals without the need for physical wires, was a rapidly developing technology. Inventors and scientists around the world were exploring the possibilities of wireless communication, and Britain was at the forefront of these advancements. Pioneering figures such as Guglielmo Marconi, Oliver Lodge, and John Ambrose Fleming made significant contributions to the field.

In 1896, Marconi successfully transmitted wireless signals across the English Channel, demonstrating the potential for long-distance wireless communication. This achievement sparked interest and enthusiasm among scientists and inventors in

Britain. Marconi's experiments paved the way for further developments in wireless telegraphy and set the stage for the eventual emergence of radio broadcasting. During the early 1900s, wireless telegraphy was primarily used for point-to-point communication, such as ship-to-shore communication or military purposes. However, some individuals saw the potential for wireless transmission to reach a broader audience. One notable pioneer in this regard was Reginald Fessenden, a Canadian-born inventor and engineer who conducted experiments in wireless transmission.

In 1906, Fessenden made history by conducting the first radio broadcast of voice and music. From his experimental station in Massachusetts, he transmitted a short program that included him playing the violin and reading a Bible passage. Although Fessenden's broadcast was not heard in Britain, it sparked further interest in the possibilities of wireless communication and laid the groundwork for future developments. In 1909, the General Post Office (GPO) granted the first experimental broadcasting license to Marconi's Wireless Telegraph Company. This license allowed Marconi to conduct experiments in broadcasting audio signals, including music and speech. Despite the progress made during this period, radio broadcasting as a mass medium was still in its infancy. The technology and infrastructure required for widespread radio broadcasting were yet to be fully realised. The focus was primarily on wireless telegraphy and point-to-point communication rather than broadcasting to a general audience.

******

The Labour Exchanges Act of 1909 aimed to address unemployment and labour market inefficiencies by establishing a system that facilitated the matching of job seekers with available job opportunities. It recognised the importance of job registration, information dissemination, and guidance in improving employment outcomes. The Act reflected a growing recognition of the need to support and enhance labour market efficiency. The Act authorised the establishment of Labour Exchanges, which were government-run employment agencies. These exchanges acted as intermediaries between job seekers and employers, facilitating the placement of workers into suitable employment. Job seekers were now required to register at the Labour Exchanges, providing information about their skills, qualifications, and work preferences. The exchanges then endeavoured to match registered workers with suitable job vacancies based on their skills and the requirements of employers. The Act also aimed to assist employers in finding suitable workers for their job vacancies. Employers could approach the Labour Exchanges to advertise job openings and seek assistance in recruiting workers.

The Act emphasised the importance of providing timely and accurate information about job vacancies. Labour Exchanges collected and disseminated information on available job opportunities to registered job seekers, thereby improving the efficiency of the job market. The services provided by the exchanges were initially free of charge, with funding primarily coming from government sources.

******

Athletics gained popularity as well, with the Amateur Athletic Association (AAA) organising various track and field events. The London Olympics of 1908 marked an important moment in British sporting history they were originally scheduled to take place in Rome, Italy. However, due to the eruption of Mount Vesuvius in 1906, the Italian government had to redirect its resources to the recovery efforts, and the Games were eventually relocated to London. It was the first time that the Olympics were hosted by the United Kingdom.

British athletes participated enthusiastically in the Games, showcasing their skills and competitive spirit across a range of sports. The event took place from 27th April to 31st October 1908 and featured a total of 22 sports, including athletics, swimming, cycling, boxing, tennis, and more. Britain had a team of 676 competitors in 24 sports. In terms of medal count, Great Britain emerged as the top performing nation, securing the highest number of medals overall. British athletes won a total of 146 medals, including 56 gold, 51 silver, and 39 bronze. This remarkable achievement solidified Britain's dominance in the sporting arena during that era. One of the standout performances by a British athlete at the 1908 Olympics was that of Henry Taylor, a swimmer. Taylor claimed three gold medals in the pool, winning the men's 400m freestyle, the men's 1500m freestyle, and the men's 4x200m freestyle relay. His exceptional swimming prowess and victories were celebrated by the home crowd.

In the field of athletics, Great Britain also had notable achievements. Wyndham Halswelle, a British athlete, won gold in the men's 400m race. This event is particularly remembered for its controversial finish. Halswelle's American competitor, John Carpenter, was disqualified for obstructing Halswelle during the race, leading to a rerun of the event. Halswelle eventually emerged victorious in the rerun, earning him a place in Olympic history. The 1908 London Olympics also marked the introduction of the Olympic medal ceremony, where winning athletes were presented with gold, silver, and bronze medals on a podium. This iconic tradition continues to be a significant part of the Olympic Games to this day.

******

The Housing and Town Planning (Housing of the Working Classes) Act of 1909 represented a significant step in addressing the housing needs of the working classes and improving living conditions. It provided local authorities with new powers, financial resources, and standards to tackle housing problems, including slum clearance, housing provision, and urban planning. This Act aimed to improve housing conditions for the working classes by providing local authorities with powers and resources to address housing issues. It allowed local authorities to undertake slum clearance and demolition of unsanitary and overcrowded housing. The Act also authorised local authorities to construct new housing for the working classes. It provided financial assistance and grants to local authorities to facilitate the construction of affordable housing, particularly in areas with housing shortages or where existing housing was deemed unfit for habitation. Minimum standards for housing construction and maintenance were outlined. It set out requirements for ventilation, lighting, sanitation, and overall habitability of the houses built for the working classes. Local authorities were responsible for enforcing these standards.

The Act granted local authorities the power of compulsory purchase, enabling them to acquire land for housing development or slum clearance, even if the landowners were unwilling to sell. This power helped facilitate urban redevelopment and the creation of new housing areas. Although the primary focus of the Act was housing, it also included provisions related to town planning. It encouraged local authorities to prepare town planning schemes to guide future development, including the layout of streets, open spaces, and the coordination of public amenities.

******

The early 1900s witnessed the birth of motor racing as a sport in Britain. At the start of the 20th century, motor racing was still in its infancy, with the sport being more of an exhibition than a formal competition. However, the allure of speed and the excitement of the emerging technology captured the imagination of enthusiasts and drew crowds of spectators. In 1902, the Gordon Bennett Cup, an international motor race, was held in Britain for the first time. The race took place in the English county of Kent and featured a challenging circuit that tested the drivers' skills and the reliability of their vehicles. The event attracted top drivers from different countries, and the victory went to Selwyn Francis Edge, driving for the Napier team, marking an early triumph for British motor racing.

Another notable event during this period was the establishment of the Brooklands circuit in 1907. Located in Weybridge, Surrey, Brooklands became the first purpose built motor racing track in the world. The circuit featured banked turns and a long straight, allowing drivers to achieve high speeds. Brooklands quickly became a centre for motor racing and testing, attracting both British and international competitors. During this decade, British automobile manufacturers played a crucial role in the development of racing cars. Companies such as Napier, Wolseley, and Sunbeam produced powerful and innovative vehicles that competed in various races. These manufacturers used motor racing as a platform to showcase their engineering capabilities and gain recognition in the automotive industry. One of the most significant achievements in British motor racing during this period was the establishment of the Isle of Man TT (Tourist Trophy) race. In 1907, the first Isle of Man TT race was held, featuring motorcycle racing on public roads. The event gained popularity and continued to grow, eventually becoming one of the most prestigious motorcycle races in the world. Although motor racing was still a relatively niche sport during this decade, it attracted a dedicated following of enthusiasts and captured public attention. The speed and excitement of the races appealed to both spectators and participants, fuelling the growth and evolution of the sport.

******

At the turn of the 20th century, the British Empire was the most extensive empire in the world, covering vast territories across continents. Britain's imperial possessions included India, Canada, Australia, New Zealand, parts of Africa, and numerous colonies and territories. The late 19th and early 20th centuries witnessed the "Scramble for Africa", during which European powers, including Britain, competed to acquire territories in Africa. Britain sought to expand its influence and control in Africa through colonial acquisitions and protectorates, often driven by economic interests, resource exploitation, and strategic considerations. The Boer Wars fought between Britain and the Boer Republics in South Africa (Transvaal and Orange Free State), took place during this period. The conflicts were primarily driven by British interests in the region's mineral resources, particularly gold and diamonds. The wars resulted in a British victory and the eventual establishment of British control over the region.

In the early 1900s, tensions between Britain and Germany escalated, primarily due to imperial ambitions and competition for economic dominance. The German naval expansion and the development of its fleet challenged British naval supremacy, leading to increased militarisation and an arms race between the two nations. In 1904, Britain and France signed the Entente Cordiale, a diplomatic agreement aimed at resolving colonial disputes and promoting cooperation between the two powers. The agreement allowed Britain to focus its attention on potential conflicts with Germany and solidified its alliance with France. Britain's foreign policy in Asia was shaped by its rivalry with Russia, known as the "Great Game". Both powers sought to expand their influence and control in Central Asia, including regions such as Afghanistan and Persia (modern-day Iran), due to geopolitical and strategic interests. Britain engaged in diplomatic efforts to maintain a balance of power and secure alliances to protect its imperial interests. It sought to maintain friendly relations with other major powers, such as the United States and Japan, while navigating the complexities of European politics. Britain focused on maintaining a powerful navy as a means to protect its imperial interests and project its influence globally. The Royal Navy played a crucial role in safeguarding trade routes, protecting colonies, and projecting British power around the world.

1910s
Modernism, World War and Suffrage

The 1910s were a tumultuous and transformative period in British history, marked by significant political, social and cultural changes. Politically, the 1910s witnessed a shift in power and the rise of the Labour Party as a prominent force. The Liberal Party, led by Prime Minister H.H. Asquith, implemented several social reforms, including the National Insurance Act of 1911, which introduced health and unemployment insurance. However, political tensions were on the rise, and the decade was marked by debates over issues such as Irish Home Rule and women's suffrage.

The outbreak of World War I in 1914 had a profound impact on Britain. The nation mobilised for war, and the conflict led to significant changes in society and the economy. The war effort required the participation of millions of people, leading to a shift in gender roles and an increase in female employment in traditionally male dominated industries. The war also brought devastation and loss, with millions of lives lost and the country grappling with the physical and emotional aftermath.

The suffrage movement, advocating for women's right to vote, gained momentum during the 1910s. The suffragettes, led by figures like Emmeline Pankhurst, employed militant tactics to draw attention to their cause. Their activism included hunger strikes, protests, and acts of civil disobedience. The Representation of the People Act of 1918 granted voting rights to certain women over the age of 30 and paved the way for further progress towards gender equality. Labour struggles were another defining feature of the 1910s. Workers across various industries, such as mining and transportation, demanded better working conditions, fair wages, and the right to unionise. Strikes and labor disputes were common, often resulting in violent clashes with authorities. The most notable labour conflict of the decade was the Dublin Lockout of 1913, where workers protested against poor working conditions and unfair treatment.

The cultural landscape of the 1910s reflected the tensions and changes of the time. The emerging modernist movement in literature, art, and architecture challenged traditional conventions. Writers like Virginia Woolf, T.S. Eliot, and James Joyce pushed boundaries with their experimental styles and themes. In art, the Vorticist movement, led by Wyndham Lewis, embraced industrialisation and geometric forms, reflecting the changing industrial society. The war also had a profound impact on the cultural and artistic scene. It influenced literature with works such as Wilfred Owen's powerful war poetry, which depicted the horrors of trench warfare. Artists captured the impact of the war through paintings and sculptures, with the emergence of war artists documenting the conflict firsthand. The war also influenced the development of cinema, with propaganda films and documentaries shaping public opinion and conveying the realities of the war.

The 1910s also witnessed societal divisions and conflicts. Class distinctions were pronounced, and the gap between the wealthy elite and the working class widened. The social unrest and demands for change led to the growth of socialist and communist ideologies, as well as the rise of trade unions and political movements advocating for workers' rights. The end of the 1910s marked a turning point in British history. The war came to an end in 1918, and the country faced the challenges of post-war reconstruction and the reintegration of soldiers into civilian life. The effects of the war, both physical and emotional, continued to reverberate through society, and the scars of the conflict were deeply felt.

******

Transportation was revolutionised in the 1910s with the widespread adoption of automobiles and the expansion of road networks. The mass production of cars, such as the Model T by Henry Ford, made them more affordable and accessible to the general public. This led to a transformation in transportation patterns, as people could now travel greater distances and explore new areas. The automobile also brought about changes in social dynamics and leisure activities, as families could embark on road trips and explore the countryside.

Another notable technological advancement was the development of aviation. The Wright brothers successfully flew the first powered airplane in 1903, and by the 1910s, aviation was gaining traction. British aviators like Claude Grahame-White and Thomas Sopwith made significant contributions to the field. The growing popularity of aviation sparked public fascination, and air shows and exhibitions attracted large crowds. The advent of aviation not only revolutionised travel but also played a role in the defence industry and the military during World War I.

Communication also underwent a revolution with the widespread adoption of telephones and the expansion of telephone networks. Telephones became more common in homes and businesses, allowing for faster and more direct communication over long distances. This advancement brought people closer together and facilitated more efficient business transactions. Additionally, the telegraph continued to be widely used for long-distance communication, connecting people across the country and even internationally.

The decade also witnessed significant progress in the field of entertainment technology. Cinemas became more widespread, providing a new form of mass entertainment. Silent films were projected on large screens, captivating audiences and offering a visual spectacle. The popularity of cinema grew rapidly, and it became a prominent form of cultural expression and storytelling. The emergence of cinema as a popular entertainment medium had a profound impact on popular culture and influenced the development of narrative storytelling and visual aesthetics.

The phonograph, invented by Thomas Edison, also gained popularity during this time. It allowed people to listen to recorded music and speeches in their own homes, expanding access to cultural and educational content. The phonograph influenced music consumption and distribution, leading to the emergence of the recording industry and the growth of popular music. In daily life, technological advancements in the 1910s improved efficiency and convenience. Electrical power became more widely available, replacing gas lighting in homes and businesses. Electric appliances, such as refrigerators and washing machines, alleviated some of the burdens of household chores. The increasing availability of electricity also enabled the growth of industries and contributed to urbanisation and industrialisation.

******

The early part of the decade marked the rise of women's football as an organised sport in Britain. Inspired by the popularity of the men's game, women formed their own teams and began participating in matches. This growing interest in football among women reflected a desire to challenge societal norms and demonstrate their athletic abilities. During World War I, as a large number of men were enlisted in the military, women played an increasingly vital role in the workforce. Women working in munitions factories and other war-related industries formed football teams known as munitions teams or factory teams. These teams provided an outlet for physical activity, camaraderie, and recreation during their limited leisure time. Munitions teams gained significant popularity and recognition, attracting enthusiastic crowds. The matches they played were not only a source of entertainment but also served as fundraising events for war-related charities. Football became a means of bringing communities together and boosting morale during the challenging wartime period. Women's football matches drew substantial crowds, reflecting the growing interest and support for the sport. Spectators, including both men and women, flocked to stadiums to watch these matches, demonstrating a willingness to embrace women's participation in football. Some of the most notable matches included encounters between munitions teams from different regions or factories. These matches showcased the skills, competitiveness, and determination of women on the football field, challenging preconceived notions about women's athletic abilities.

The popularity of women's football also brought about changes in societal attitudes. Some segments of the population embraced the sport and recognised women's right to participate in football, applauding the display of athleticism and team spirit. Women footballers gained recognition for their talent and dedication to the game.

However, not everyone supported the idea of women playing football. Some individuals, including some members of the Football Association (FA), held traditional views that deemed football unsuitable for women. Concerns were raised about the physical demands of the game and the potential impact on femininity. The controversy surrounding women's football culminated in 1921 when the FA officially banned women's teams from playing matches on FA affiliated grounds. This decision, which lasted until the 1970s, severely hindered the growth and development of women's football in Britain. Despite the subsequent ban on women's football, the 1910s marked an important milestone in the history of the sport. Women's football teams and players demonstrated their skills, resilience, and passion for the game, challenging societal norms and perceptions of women's capabilities.

******

Following the end of World War I in 1918, football gradually resumed its normalcy. The Football League recommenced for the 1919-1920 season. However, the war had left its mark on the football landscape. Some clubs faced financial difficulties due to the loss of revenue and the challenges of rebuilding their squads. However, new clubs also emerged, with Chelsea and Arsenal joining the Football League during this period.

The post-war era saw a renewed sense of enthusiasm for football. The sport played a crucial role in bringing communities together and restoring a sense of normalcy after the turmoil of the war. Football stadiums once again became vibrant gathering places, where supporters cheered on their teams with renewed passion. Football's impact extended beyond the boundaries of the game itself. It became a symbol of national identity and pride. International matches, such as the British Home Championship, held great significance for the nations involved. These tournaments fostered a sense of unity among England, Scotland, Wales, and Ireland (later Northern Ireland), and fuelled healthy rivalries. In addition to its cultural impact, football also had economic implications. The sport generated revenue through ticket sales, merchandise, and advertising, providing a boost to local economies. Football clubs became an integral part of their communities, supporting local businesses and providing employment opportunities.

******

The decade marked a significant turning point for the Liberal Party, as it embraced a new progressive agenda centred on social reform. This period saw the party transform, shifting from its traditional laissez-faire approach to a more interventionist role in addressing social issues and inequality. The early 20th century presented a backdrop of socio-economic challenges that laid the foundation for the Liberal Party's shift towards social reform. Industrialisation and urbanisation had led to widespread poverty, inadequate housing, poor working conditions, and social inequality. Progressive movements in other countries, such as the United States, also influenced British political thought and set the stage for change. What is more, the rise of the labour movement and trade unions, combined with the emergence of progressive intellectuals and social activists, exerted pressure on political parties to address the urgent social issues facing the working class. The rise of social reform within the Liberal Party was driven by influential figures who championed progressive policies. One such figure was David Lloyd George, who served as Chancellor of the Exchequer from 1908 to 1915. Lloyd George played a pivotal role in implementing social reforms, focusing on issues such as poverty, healthcare, and education. Another prominent figure was Winston Churchill, who held various ministerial positions during this period and was a strong advocate for social welfare. His support for progressive policies helped shape the Liberal Party's agenda and contributed to the rise of social reform. One of the landmark achievements of the Liberal Party that effected the decade was the introduction of the People's Budget in 1909. Proposed by David Lloyd George, this budget aimed to address social inequality by introducing a series of tax reforms to redistribute wealth and fund social programs.

The budget proposed higher taxes on the wealthy, including an increase in inheritance taxes and the introduction of a supertax on high incomes. The additional revenue generated was used to fund measures such as old-age pensions, improved housing, and expanded healthcare and education services. The Liberal Party's commitment to social reform extended to various sectors, resulting in a range of significant legislative measures. One notable reform was the National Insurance Act of 1911, which provided financial protection against sickness and unemployment for workers. This marked a crucial step towards a comprehensive social insurance system in Britain. The Liberals also enacted the Shops Act of 1912, which aimed to regulate working hours and improve conditions for retail workers. Additionally, reforms in the area of housing sought to address the appalling living conditions of the urban poor. The Liberal Party's embrace of social reform in the 1910s had a profound and lasting impact on British society. The introduction of social welfare measures improved the living conditions of the working class and provided a safety net against economic insecurity. These reforms also laid the foundation for the establishment of the modern welfare state in Britain. The principles of social justice and state intervention to alleviate poverty and promote equality became deeply ingrained in the political discourse and shaped the policies of subsequent governments.

******

The early part of the decade still embraced traditional music hall performances, but the advent of cinema brought a new and accessible form of mass entertainment. Cinema in 1910s Britain underwent a transformative period, both in terms of its technological advancements and its impact on society. The decade witnessed the rapid growth and popularity of cinema as a form of mass entertainment, with the medium becoming increasingly accessible to the general public.

The transition from silent films to films with synchronised sound had not yet occurred, and the medium relied solely on visual storytelling. However, there were improvements in camera techniques, film stock, and editing methods, enabling filmmakers to create more sophisticated and visually appealing works. British cinema of the 1910s was dominated by the genre of the "cinema of attractions". These films focused on spectacle, novelty, and visual effects, aiming to captivate and entertain audiences. Many of these early films featured slapstick comedy, trick shots, and special effects, often drawing inspiration from the popular music hall tradition. One of the most prominent figures in British cinema of the 1910s was Charles Chaplin. Originally from England, Chaplin rose to international fame during this decade. He began his career in the United States, where he joined the Keystone Studios and created his iconic character, "The Tramp". Chaplin's films, such as "The Kid" and

"The Gold Rush", blended physical comedy with social commentary, showcasing his unique ability to evoke both laughter and pathos. Although his most significant contributions were made in the 1920s, Chaplin's early work in the 1910s set the stage for his subsequent success.

Other notable British filmmakers of the 1910s included Cecil Hepworth and G.A. Smith, who were pioneers in the early years of British cinema. Hepworth was known for his innovative approach to storytelling and visual effects, while Smith experimented with techniques such as time-lapse photography and reverse motion. Their contributions to the medium helped shape the direction of British cinema.

The First World War had a major impact on British cinema during this period. The conflict presented both challenges and opportunities for the film industry. Many filmmakers turned their attention to creating propaganda films that aimed to boost morale and support the war effort. These films depicted heroic soldiers, patriotic themes, and anti-German sentiment. Notable examples include "The Battle of the Somme" (1916), a documentary-style film that portrayed the realities of trench warfare and became one of the most successful films of the era. While the war influenced the content of many films, it also disrupted the production and distribution of movies. The scarcity of resources and restrictions imposed during the war limited the ability of filmmakers to create and screen films. However, the demand for entertainment during this time led to the establishment of "kinema" or "kinematograph" theatres, which became popular gathering places for people seeking respite from the challenges of the war.

In addition to the impact of the war, the 1910s also witnessed the emergence of film censorship and regulation in Britain. The British Board of Film Censors (later known as the British Board of Film Classification) was established in 1912 to ensure that films complied with moral and social standards. This regulatory body had the authority to censor or ban films deemed inappropriate or offensive, reflecting the concerns of the time regarding the influence of cinema on society.

******

It was during this decade that the Suffragette movement gained significant momentum and attracted widespread attention. The suffragettes, led by figures such as Emmeline Pankhurst and her daughters Christabel and Sylvia, adopted a more militant approach to campaigning. Their organisation, the Women's Social and Political Union (WSPU), employed direct action tactics, including protests, demonstrations, and acts of civil disobedience, to demand voting rights for women. The Conciliation Bill of 1911 became a focal point in the suffrage struggle during the 1910s. Proposed by private members of Parliament sympathetic to the cause, the bill aimed to grant limited suffrage to women. However, it faced significant opposition, particularly from the House of Lords, which vehemently opposed extending voting rights to women. The rejection of the Conciliation Bill by the House of Lords prompted an escalation of suffragette activism. Protests intensified, leading to arrests, hunger strikes, and force-feeding of imprisoned suffragettes. These acts of resistance garnered public attention and sympathy for the suffrage cause.

The outbreak of World War I in 1914 brought a temporary pause to the suffrage movement as suffragettes redirected their efforts towards supporting the war effort. Organisations like the Women's Social and Political Union suspended their militant activities and focused on activities such as nursing, munitions work, and fundraising. However, the war also created opportunities for suffragettes to demonstrate their capabilities and contributions. Women's involvement in the war effort, both on the home front and in various roles previously dominated by men, highlighted their capability, dedication, and necessity in society. These contributions played a crucial role in shifting public opinion and challenging traditional gender norms. The militant tactics employed by suffragettes during the 1910s drew both support and criticism. While some condemned their methods, arguing that they undermined the cause, others saw their radical actions as necessary to draw attention to the inequality and injustice faced by women. Acts of civil disobedience, such as the destruction of property, disrupted public spaces, and sparked debates about the suffrage movement. The suffragettes' determination and resilience in the face of opposition and repression helped to galvanise support and raised awareness about the urgent need for women's political recognition.

The struggle for women's suffrage in 1910s Britain left a lasting legacy on the country's political landscape and the fight for gender equality. The achievements of the suffragettes paved the way for further advancements in women's rights and participation in politics. The Representation of the People Act 1918 marked the beginning of women's formal inclusion in the political process. Subsequent acts, such as the Equal Franchise Act of 1928, granted women the right to vote on equal terms with men, further solidifying their political rights.

The suffrage movement of the 1910s also had broader societal implications. It challenged traditional gender roles and norms, empowering women to assert their rights and demand equality in all aspects of life. The suffragettes' fight for political recognition was intertwined with their struggle for social, economic, and legal rights, laying the groundwork for future feminist movements and shaping the feminist agenda of the 20th century. Moreover, the suffrage movement in Britain inspired and influenced similar movements around the world. The determination and tactics of the suffragettes served as a model for activists in other countries who sought to secure women's right to vote and achieve gender equality. The struggle for women's suffrage in 1910s Britain was a momentous period characterised by intense activism, resilience, and sacrifice. The suffragettes, through their militant tactics and unwavering commitment, challenged societal norms, influenced public opinion, and forced the government to recognise the urgency of women's political rights. The movement's achievements culminated in the passage of the Representation of the People Act 1918, which granted limited suffrage to women and marked a significant step towards gender equality in the political sphere.

******

The county cricket system, with teams like Yorkshire, Lancashire, and Surrey, drew large crowds and intense rivalries. Matches were eagerly anticipated, and cricket grounds became focal points for communities, fostering a sense of identity and shared experiences. Cricket's social significance extended beyond the sport itself. Matches provided opportunities for social gatherings, picnics, and family outings. The sport became a symbol of national identity and an expression of traditional English values, promoting camaraderie and fair play. International cricket played a crucial role in the 1910s, with England's national team competing against other cricketing nations. The Ashes, the historic cricket series played between England and Australia, had a significant impact on cricket and its popularity in 1910s Britain.

The Ashes contests of the 1910s captivated cricket fans on both sides of the globe. The rivalry and intensity of the matches further elevated the significance of the series, turning it into one of the most anticipated events in cricket. The success of the Ashes series during this period had a profound impact on the growth of cricket in Britain. The contests captured the public's imagination, and spectators eagerly followed the progress of each match through newspapers and radio broadcasts. The series helped to solidify cricket's position as the national sport and contributed to the sport's enduring popularity.

World War I brought significant disruptions to cricket in Britain with the suspension of county cricket and international matches during the war years. However, cricket played an important role in raising morale and supporting the war effort. Soldiers played cricket in the trenches and on the home front, providing a sense of normalcy and camaraderie amid the chaos of war. Matches were organised to raise funds for war-related causes, and cricketing equipment was sent to soldiers overseas, reflecting the sport's contribution to the war effort. Following the end of World War I, cricket gradually resumed its place in British society. The 1919 season marked the return of county cricket, with teams rebuilding their squads and resuming competitive matches. Cricket's resurgence in the post-war era was accompanied by changes in the game itself. The introduction of new tactics, increased focus on batting technique, and innovations in bowling styles brought a fresh dynamism to cricket, captivating both players and spectators.

******

Literature continued to evolve, reflecting the changing social and political landscape. The modernist movement, which had started to gain momentum before the war, continued to flourish writers like Virginia Woolf, T.S. Eliot, and James Joyce. These writers made significant contributions to modernist literature and transformed the literary landscape of the time.

Virginia Woolf, born on 25th January 1882, in London, was a key figure in the Bloomsbury Group, an influential circle of writers, intellectuals, and artists. Woolf's works are known for their innovative narrative techniques, stream-of-consciousness writing, and exploration of the inner lives and experiences of her characters. In the 1910s, Woolf published her first novels, "The Voyage Out" and "Night and Day", which established her as a writer of great talent and originality. Woolf's writing challenged traditional narrative structures and delved into the complexities of human consciousness and perception. Her novels often focused on the inner lives of her characters, capturing their thoughts, emotions, and subjective experiences.

T.S. Eliot, born on 26th September 1888, in St. Louis, Missouri, but later became a British citizen, was a seminal figure in modernist poetry. Eliot's poetry is characterised by its complexity, allusiveness, and incorporation of various literary and cultural references. In the 1910s, Eliot published his influential poem, "The Love Song of J. Alfred Prufrock", which marked a departure from traditional poetic forms and themes. "The Love Song of J. Alfred Prufrock" is a dramatic monologue that explores themes of alienation, social anxiety, and the struggle for self-identity in the modern world. Eliot's fragmented and multi-layered language, along with his incorporation of literary allusions and cultural references, challenged conventional poetic forms and opened up new possibilities for poetic expression.

James Joyce, born on 2nd February 1882, in Dublin, Ireland, is widely regarded as one of the most innovative and influential writers of the 20th century. Joyce's works, including his masterpiece "Ulysses" and his collection of short stories "Dubliners", pushed the boundaries of narrative and language. In the 1910s, Joyce was experimenting with different narrative techniques and exploring themes of identity, sexuality, and the relationship between the individual and society. "Dubliners" is a collection of interconnected stories that depict various aspects of life in Dublin, capturing the struggles, frustrations, and limitations experienced by its characters. Joyce's use of vivid imagery, realistic dialogue, and meticulous attention to detail created a vivid portrayal of Dublin and its inhabitants, while his exploration of the inner lives of his characters hinted at the psychological complexities beneath the surface.

Writers like D.H. Lawrence, E.M. Forster, and H.G. Wells embodied this changing attitude towards authority and tradition. They delved into themes such as sexuality, psychology, and the impact of social constraints on personal freedom. Their novels offered a critical examination of the rigid social structures that had been reinforced during the Edwardian era and advocated for a more open-minded and liberated society. D.H. Lawrence's works during the years 1910 to 1919 were characterised by his bold exploration of human psychology, sexuality, and societal constraints. He challenged traditional values and conventions, pushing the boundaries of literary expression. Lawrence's ability to capture the complexities of human relationships and his lyrical prose contributed to his enduring legacy as a significant figure in 20th-century literature. During this period, D.H. Lawrence published several notable works that showcased his distinctive style and thematic exploration. In 1911, he published "Sons and Lovers", a semi-autobiographical novel that delved into the complexities of human relationships and the impact of family dynamics. The novel explores the intense emotional and psychological struggles of its protagonist, Paul Morel, as he navigates his relationships with his mother and various romantic interests. "Sons and Lovers" is known for its psychological depth, rich character development, and exploration of themes such as sexuality, class, and personal freedom. 1915 saw Lawrence publish "The Rainbow", a novel that faced controversy upon its release due to its explicit portrayal of sexuality. The book explores the lives of three generations of the Brangwen family, examining their struggles with societal expectations, sexuality, and the search for personal fulfillment. "The Rainbow" challenged traditional norms and moral conventions of the time, leading to its suppression and eventual banning for a period. In 1915, Lawrence published "The Lost Girl", a novel that delves into themes of gender, social class, and personal identity. The story follows Alvina Houghton, a young woman who breaks free from her small-town constraints and embarks on a journey of self-discovery. "The Lost Girl" explores the tension between societal expectations and individual desires, highlighting the struggle for autonomy and fulfillment.

During the First World War, Lawrence's literary output was influenced by the tumultuous times. In 1916, he published "Women in Love", a novel that further explores the themes of human relationships and sexuality. The book focuses on the lives of two sisters, Ursula and Gudrun, and their relationships with two men. "Women in Love" delves into the complexities of love, desire, and the impact of war on personal relationships. The novel is known for its intense psychological exploration, lyrical prose, and its critique of the societal constraints placed on individuals.

******

British athletics experienced significant growth, attracting participants and spectators alike. Notable athletes achieved remarkable feats, establishing themselves as celebrated figures in the athletic community. The period also witnessed progress in women's athletics, breaking down gender barriers. Athletics had a positive impact on society, promoting physical fitness, fostering community spirit, and providing entertainment. While

World War I disrupted the sport temporarily, athletics played a role in maintaining soldiers' fitness during the war.

The 1910s witnessed the emergence of several notable British athletes who left a lasting impact on the sport. These athletes achieved remarkable feats and set records, becoming celebrated figures in the athletic community and beyond. Harold Abrahams, who later gained fame through the film "Chariots of Fire", competed in the 100 meters and 200 meters events. He became the Amateur Athletics Association (AAA) champion in the 100 meters in 1919. Albert Hill, an outstanding middle-distance runner, won gold medals in the 800 meters and 1,500 meters events at the 1920 Olympic Games in Antwerp. His achievements in the 1910s established him as one of the leading British athletes of the time.

The decade marked a period of growing recognition and participation in women's athletics. Although women's athletic competitions were still relatively limited, there was progress in breaking down barriers and challenging traditional gender roles. In 1919, the Women's Amateur Athletic Association (WAAA) was founded, providing a platform for women athletes to compete and showcase their abilities. Women's athletics events, including sprints, hurdles, high jump, and long jump, were held at various competitions. Notable female athletes of the time included Mary Lines, who won the WAAA championships in the 100 yards, 220 yards, and long jump events. She became a prominent figure in women's athletics and played an important role in paving the way for future generations of female athletes.

******

Britain had an impressive team of 274 athletes competing in 16 sports and finished as the second most successful nation in terms of medal count at the Stockholm 1912 Olympic Games. British athletes earned a total of 41 medals, including 10 gold, 15 silver, and 16 bronze. Athletics was one of the standout disciplines for British athletes at the Stockholm Olympics. Arnold Jackson claimed gold in the 1500 meters, displaying remarkable endurance and tactical skill in middle-distance running. The British men's team triumphed in the 4x400-meter relay, securing the gold medal and highlighting their teamwork and speed.

British athletes also made their mark in other sports disciplines. British tennis player Charles P. Dixon and Edith Hamman won the gold medal in the mixed indoor singles event and Edith Hamman the gold in the Women's' Indoor Singles. There were also medals in Rowing, Shooting, Swimming, Cycling, Fencing, Diving and Gymnastics. Britain's performance at the Stockholm 1912 Olympic Games had a significant impact on the nation's sporting landscape. The impressive medal tally showcased the strength and depth of British athletes across multiple disciplines. The achievements of athletes like Wally Kinnear, and Arnold Jackson brought recognition and honour to the nation. Britain's performance at the Stockholm 1912 Olympic Games was outstanding, securing the nation's place as the second most successful country in terms of medal count.

******

The outbreak of World War I in 1914 created a sense of national crisis that led to a temporary suspension of political divisions. The British government, under Prime Minister Herbert Asquith, formed a coalition that included members from both the Liberal and Conservative parties. This coalition aimed to unite the nation in the face of external threats and coordinate wartime efforts. The war also brought about a sense of patriotism and national unity among the British public. Political parties and suffrage movements initially set aside their differences to support the war effort. This unity, however, began to erode as the war progressed and challenges mounted.

The demands of wartime necessitated significant government control and intervention in various aspects of society. The British government implemented measures such as censorship, rationing, and price controls to manage resources and maintain public order. The state's expanded role during the war laid the groundwork for the later expansion of the welfare state and the notion of government intervention in social and economic affairs. The war presented political challenges and divisions within the government and between political parties. The handling of the war effort, including issues such as conscription, military strategy, and the management of resources, led to debates and disagreements among political leaders. These divisions within the government and the strains caused by the war created opportunities for new political forces to emerge. One such force was the Labour Party, which capitalised on the discontent among the working class and the failures of the traditional Liberal and Conservative parties. The Labour Party, advocating for workers' rights and social reform, gained traction and began to challenge the established political order.

The war exposed the failures of laissez-faire capitalism and led to a growing disillusionment with pre-war political structures. The war experience and the hardships endured by the population fostered a sense of social solidarity and a demand for greater government intervention. The war also contributed to the rise of socialist and pacifist movements, challenging the prevailing nationalist and imperialist ideologies. The experience of widespread suffering and loss prompted a reevaluation of political values and the pursuit of more equitable and peaceful societies. The war had a lasting impact on the relationship between the government and its citizens. The expanded role of the state during the war led to an expectation of government intervention in social and economic affairs, laying the groundwork for the establishment of the welfare state in the subsequent years. It challenged traditional political alliances and paved the way for the emergence of new political forces. The Labour Party, with its focus on workers' rights and social reform, gained momentum and began to rival the dominance of the traditional Liberal and Conservative parties.

The Treaty of Versailles, signed in 1919, reshaped the geopolitical landscape and led to the reconfiguration of alliances and power dynamics. Britain's role as a global power underwent significant changes, and its political priorities shifted in response to the new international order.

******

The outbreak of World War I had a profound impact on literature and art. Writers and poets, such as Wilfred Owen, Siegfried Sassoon, and Rupert Brooke, depicted the horrors of trench warfare and the loss of innocence in their works. Through their poignant and powerful poetry, these writers captured the harrowing realities of war, expressed their personal experiences and emotions, and provided profound insights into the human condition during one of the most devastating conflicts in history.

Wilfred Owen, born on 18th March 1893, in Shropshire, England, is widely regarded as one of the greatest war poets. Owen began writing poetry at a young age, but it was during his service as a soldier in World War I that he found his true poetic voice. Owen enlisted in the army in 1915 and was later commissioned as a second lieutenant. He experienced firsthand the horrors of trench warfare, including the use of chemical weapons, and was diagnosed with shell shock. It was during his treatment for shell shock that he met another influential poet of the time, Siegfried Sassoon, who became his mentor and friend.

Owen's poetry reflects his personal experiences and his desire to convey the truth about the realities of war. His works expose the brutality, futility, and psychological toll of combat. Owen's poems are characterised by vivid and visceral imagery, detailed descriptions, and a careful attention to sound and rhythm. They often explore the themes of the loss of innocence, the dehumanising effects of war, and the psychological trauma experienced by soldiers. One of Owen's most celebrated poems is "Dulce et Decorum Est". Published posthumously, the poem vividly depicts a gas attack and the excruciating suffering endured by soldiers. Owen's use of graphic imagery and sensory details creates a haunting portrayal of the horrors of war. The poem concludes with a powerful condemnation of the glorification of war and the false notion that it is honourable to die for one's country.

Bent double, like old beggars under sacks,
Knock-kneed, coughing like hags, we cursed through sludge,
Till on the haunting flares we turned our backs
And towards our distant rest began to trudge.
Men marched asleep. Many had lost their boots
But limped on, blood-shod. All went lame; all blind;
Drunk with fatigue; deaf even to the hoots
Of tired, outstripped Five-Nines that dropped behind.

Gas! Gas! Quick, boys!–An ecstasy of fumbling,
Fitting the clumsy helmets just in time;
But someone still was yelling out and stumbling
And flound'ring like a man in fire or lime...
Dim, through the misty panes and thick green light,
As under a green sea, I saw him drowning.

> *In all my dreams, before my helpless sight,*
> *He plunges at me, guttering, choking, drowning.*
>
> *If in some smothering dreams you too could pace*
> *Behind the wagon that we flung him in,*
> *And watch the white eyes writhing in his face,*
> *His hanging face, like a devil's sick of sin;*
> *If you could hear, at every jolt, the blood*
> *Come gargling from the froth-corrupted lungs,*
> *Obscene as cancer, bitter as the cud*
> *Of vile, incurable sores on innocent tongues,–*
> *My friend, you would not tell with such high zest*
> *To children ardent for some desperate glory,*
> *The old Lie: Dulce et decorum est*
> *Pro patria mori.*

Siegfried Sassoon, born on 8th September 1886, in Kent, England, is another influential poet associated with World War I. Sassoon came from a privileged background and initially embraced the patriotic fervour that swept through Britain at the outbreak of the war. However, his experiences on the front lines transformed his perspective, and he became increasingly critical of the war and its leaders. Sassoon's poetry reflects his disillusionment and his desire to expose the truth about the devastating effects of war. Sassoon's early war poetry displays a more traditional style, characterised by romanticism and idealism. However, as his disillusionment grew, his poetry became more biting and satirical, directly criticising the authorities and the conduct of the war. In 1917, Sassoon wrote a public declaration against the war, which earned him the reputation of a war protester. Instead of facing a court-martial, he was sent to a military hospital for treatment of his alleged shell shock, where he met and influenced Wilfred Owen. One of Sassoon's most well-known poems is "The Hero". The poem satirises the glorification of war and the heroic ideals associated with it. Sassoon challenges the idea of valorising soldiers who sacrifice their lives on the battlefield, emphasising the tragedy and waste of young lives cut short. "The Hero" calls attention to the discrepancy between the patriotic rhetoric and the harsh reality of war, highlighting the dissonance between public perception and the experiences of soldiers.

Rupert Brooke, born on 3rd August 1887, in Warwickshire, England, was a poet who gained fame for his idealistic and patriotic portrayal of war. Unlike Owen and Sassoon, Brooke's poetry reflects the early optimism and romanticism that characterised the pre-war period. He volunteered for the navy at the outbreak of World War I but died of an infection in 1915 before seeing active combat. Despite his short life, Brooke's poetry had a significant impact on the perception of war and patriotism during the early years of the conflict. Brooke's most famous poem is "The Soldier". Written in 1914, the poem expresses a patriotic and idealistic view of war. It portrays the sacrifice of a soldier who dies fighting for his country as an honourable and noble act. "The Soldier" presents a romanticised vision of war, depicting a soldier's connection to his homeland and the belief that his death will contribute to a greater cause.

The poem resonated with many at the time, capturing the prevailing sentiment of the early stages of the war. While Brooke's poetry differs in tone and perspective from that of Owen and Sassoon, it is important to note his influence on the portrayal of war during World War I. His idealised and patriotic vision of sacrifice and duty reflected the initial sentiments and motivations of many young men who enlisted in the early stages of the conflict. However, as the war progressed and the realities of trench warfare became apparent, the poetry of Owen and Sassoon would come to dominate the literary landscape.

******

Tennis enjoyed a surge in popularity, captivating the attention of players and spectators alike. The sport became synonymous with sophistication and leisure, attracting participants from various social classes. Tennis clubs and courts became vibrant gathering places, offering opportunities for socialising and friendly competition. Tennis also played a role in breaking down social barriers. Mixed doubles matches allowed men and women to compete together, challenging traditional gender roles. The sport provided a platform for social interaction and fostered a sense of community among players and spectators.

The decade witnessed the rise of several iconic tennis players who left a lasting impact on the sport. Players such as Anthony Wilding, Suzanne Lenglen, Kitty McKane, and Bill Johnston became household names, captivating audiences with their skills and style of play. Rivalries between these players added excitement and drama to the sport. The rivalry between Anthony Wilding and Norman Brookes, known as the "Big Four", enthralled spectators and elevated the level of competition. The rivalry between Suzanne Lenglen and Dorothea Lambert Chambers in the women's game showcased the growing prominence of women in tennis.

International competitions played a significant role. The Davis Cup, established in 1900, continued to gain prestige and became a highly anticipated event. The competition brought together national teams, including Britain, the United States, Australia, and France, creating intense rivalries and fostering national pride. The Davis Cup matches captivated tennis fans, who closely followed the performances of their respective countries. The competition showcased the depth of talent and the growing international nature of the sport. The success of British players, particularly in the early part of the decade, contributed to the popularity and prominence of tennis in Britain.

******

The visual arts also underwent significant transformations during the 1910s. The artistic movements that had emerged before the war, such as Cubism and Futurism, continued to influence British artists, resulting in the development of Vorticism, a uniquely British avant-garde movement. Led by artists like Wyndham Lewis and David Bomberg, Vorticism embraced the machine age, fragmentation, and dynamic energy. It celebrated the modern urban experience and rejected the conventions of traditional representation. In addition to the avant-garde movements, the 1910s also saw a renewed interest in the traditional craftsmanship and design of the Arts and Crafts movement, a design and decorative arts movement that emerged in the late 19th century as a response to industrialisation. While the movement had its roots in the late Victorian era, the 1910s saw a shift in focus and a growing recognition of the need to adapt to changing social and artistic circumstances.

The Arts and Crafts movement emphasised the importance of craftsmanship, handwork, and the integration of art into everyday life. It sought to revive traditional craftsmanship and promote the use of high-quality materials, while also challenging the dehumanising effects of mass production. The movement encompassed a range of artistic disciplines, including architecture, furniture design, textile arts, and ceramics. In the early 1910s, the Arts and Crafts movement began to experience a decline in its original ideals and aesthetic principles. The movement's founders, such as William Morris and John Ruskin, had focused on the celebration of hand craftsmanship and the rejection of industrialisation. However, by the 1910s, there was a growing realisation that the movement needed to adapt to new artistic trends and the changing social landscape.

One of the significant developments in the 1910s was the emergence of the so-called "New Art" movement or the "Modern Style". This new approach to design and aesthetics was influenced by international Art Nouveau and the emerging modernist movements. The Modern Style embraced simpler forms, a more abstract aesthetic, and a focus on industrial materials. It challenged the traditional Arts and Crafts emphasis on hand craftsmanship and favoured mass production techniques. Despite this shift, the Arts and Crafts movement continued to have a lasting impact on the arts and design scene in 1910s Britain. The movement's principles were still influential, particularly in architecture and interior design. Many architects and designers embraced the ideals of simplicity, functionality, and the integration of art into everyday life.

One notable figure in the 1910s British Arts and Crafts movement was Archibald Knox, a designer and teacher associated with the Celtic Revival movement within the Arts and Crafts movement. He was known for his distinctive designs inspired by Celtic motifs, which he applied to a variety of objects, including metalwork, jewellery, and ceramics.

******

The Representation of the People Act 1918 emerged from a confluence of factors, including the suffrage movement, the impact of World War I, and changing social attitudes. Prior to the Act, the British electoral system was characterised by significant restrictions, including limited suffrage for men and a complete exclusion of women. However, the suffrage movement, which had gained momentum in the late 19th and early 20th centuries, laid the groundwork for electoral reforms. The act introduced several key provisions that significantly expanded the electorate. It extended the franchise to nearly all men over the age of 21, regardless of property ownership, and granted the vote to women over the age of 30 who met certain property qualifications. The Act also removed many existing restrictions and provided additional seats in Parliament for densely populated urban areas. What is more, the Act introduced proportional representation for the first time in British electoral history. This change aimed to ensure fairer representation and mitigate the influence of gerrymandering, enhancing the democratic nature of the electoral process.

The Representation of the People Act 1918 marked a major breakthrough for women's suffrage. Although the Act did not grant full voting rights to women on equal terms with men, it represented a significant step forward. The Act enfranchised around 8.4 million women, which was almost 40% of the total adult female population in Britain at the time. It created a precedent and laid the foundation for subsequent reforms that eventually granted women full voting rights in 1928.

The Act also had a transformative effect on women's political participation and representation. It allowed women to stand for election to the House of Commons, leading to the election of the first female Members of Parliament in 1918. Although the number of women elected was initially limited, it marked a crucial breakthrough in breaking down gender barriers in politics. The Representation of the People Act 1918 had profound political and social implications. The expansion of the franchise brought about a significant shift in political power. It broadened the electorate and allowed a greater diversity of voices to be heard, leading to a more representative democracy. The Act also led to changes in political campaigning strategies, as politicians had to appeal to a larger and more diverse electorate. The Act's provisions, marked a significant departure from the restrictive electoral practices of the past. It recognised the need for a more inclusive and representative democracy, reflecting the changing societal attitudes towards political participation and social progress.

******

Nancy Astor married Waldorf Astor, an American-born British politician and member of the prominent Astor family. When Waldorf inherited his father's peerage and became Viscount Astor, Nancy automatically became Viscountess Astor. This position in the British aristocracy allowed her to participate in the political scene and eventually run for Parliament. In 1919, following the passage of the Representation of the People Act, which extended voting rights to some women, Nancy Astor successfully contested the by-election for the constituency of Plymouth Sutton. Her election to Parliament made headlines and generated immense public interest due to her gender and the significance of the milestone. Nancy Astor's election was not without challenges and controversy. She faced opposition from traditionalists who believed that women should not hold political office. Astor's campaign drew attention to issues affecting women and families, emphasising social welfare and public health reform. She was also a vocal advocate for temperance, promoting the cause of alcohol prohibition.

As a Member of Parliament, Astor used her platform to address various social issues and advocate for women's rights. She was an active participant in debates and discussions, often challenging traditional viewpoints and advocating for progressive reforms. Astor worked towards improving living conditions for the working class, promoting women's suffrage, and advancing social welfare legislation. Astor's tenure in

Parliament was marked by her spirited personality and willingness to speak her mind. Her presence in the House of Commons, where she was often the only woman, brought a new perspective and dynamic to the traditionally male-dominated institution. While her outspokenness sometimes garnered criticism, it also earned her respect and admiration as a powerful and influential figure. Nancy Astor's election to Parliament opened doors for other women to follow in her footsteps. Her presence challenged societal norms and paved the way for increased female representation in British politics. Although her election did not immediately lead to significant legislative changes, it marked a symbolic victory for women's rights and set a precedent for women's participation in the political process.

******

Brass bands had a strong presence in communities across the country, providing entertainment and cultural enrichment. They played a wide range of music, including popular tunes, classical compositions, and marches, and their performances were highly anticipated events. Brass bands in the 1910s consisted of various brass instruments, such as trumpets, cornets, trombones, tubas, and French horns, along with percussion instruments like drums and cymbals. They were often associated with industrial areas and mining communities, where they played a significant role in social and cultural life. Brass bands were also affiliated with workplaces, churches, and local organisations, fostering a sense of camaraderie and identity. During the decade, brass bands continued to perform traditional and popular music. They played arrangements of classical compositions by composers like Edward Elgar and John Philip Sousa, showcasing their technical skill and musicality.

The National Brass Band Championships, held annually since 1900, were a highlight of the brass band calendar. These events brought together bands from different regions, allowing them to demonstrate their talent and compete for recognition. In addition to competitions, brass bands performed at various events, including parades, festivals, and public gatherings. They entertained audiences with their lively and precise performances, creating a festive and celebratory atmosphere. Brass bands were especially popular during holidays and community celebrations, where they played patriotic songs and uplifting tunes.

******

In the 1910s, the Conservative Party was one of the major political parties in Britain. Led by Andrew Bonar Law and later by Stanley Baldwin, the party was in power for most of the decade. The Conservative Party of the 1910s was marked by a commitment to traditional values and social hierarchy. They were opposed to radical changes in society and politics, and generally favoured a gradualist approach to reform. The party was particularly popular among the upper classes, who saw it as a defender of their interests. One of the major challenges faced by the Conservative Party in the 1910s was the rise of the Labour Party. The Labour Party represented the growing working-class movement, and its policies aimed to improve the conditions of the working class. The Conservative Party opposed many of these policies, seeing them as a threat to the existing social order.

Another major issue facing the Conservative Party in the 1910s was the question of Ireland. Ireland was then a part of the United Kingdom, and there was growing discontent among Irish nationalists who sought independence. The Conservative Party generally favoured maintaining the union between Great Britain and Ireland, but they were divided over how to address the Irish question. The Conservative Party's stance on economic and social issues in the 1910s was largely influenced by their belief in limited government intervention and a commitment to free-market principles. They advocated for lower taxes, reduced government spending, and a laissez-faire approach to the economy. The party saw economic prosperity and individual initiative as key drivers of progress and social stability. In terms of social policy, the Conservative Party held conservative views on issues such as morality, family values, and social order. They generally opposed radical social reforms and sought to maintain traditional social structures. This included support for the established Church of England and the preservation of aristocratic privileges.

During World War I, the Conservative Party played a crucial role in the wartime government. The aftermath of World War I brought about significant political and social changes. The Conservative Party faced new challenges as the country grappled with post-war reconstruction and social unrest. The party's response to these challenges varied, with some conservatives advocating for a more interventionist approach to address social inequality and economic instability, while others remained committed to traditional conservative values.

******

The influence of jazz began to make its way into Britain during the decade. Jazz, characterised by its improvisation and syncopation, brought a new level of vibrancy and spontaneity to music. It was influenced by African American musical traditions and found popularity in the United States, eventually spreading to Europe. In Britain, jazz music was initially heard through recordings and performances by American jazz musicians. However, British musicians soon began to embrace the genre and incorporate jazz elements into their compositions. Jazz bands started to emerge, and the music became more prominent in dance halls, clubs, and social gatherings. The influence of ragtime and jazz can be seen in the works of British composers and musicians of the time. Pioneering British jazz musicians, such as Billy Arnold and Jack Hylton, played a crucial role in popularising the genre in Britain. They formed jazz ensembles and performed in clubs and theatres, introducing audiences to the lively and energetic sounds of jazz music.

The impact of jazz extended beyond the music itself. The genres influenced dance styles, with popular dances like the Charleston and the Black Bottom incorporating jazz rhythms and movements. Jazz music also had a cultural and social impact, representing a departure from the traditional music of the Victorian era and reflecting the changing attitudes and spirit of the modern age.

******

Classical music in 1910s Britain was a vibrant and diverse genre that reflected the changing cultural and artistic landscape of the time. It was a period of transition and innovation, with composers exploring new musical styles and pushing the boundaries of traditional classical music. Edward Elgar was one of the most prominent composers of the era. His compositions, such as the "Enigma Variations" and the "Pomp and Circumstance Marches", captured the essence of British patriotism and national identity. Elgar's music was often characterised by lush orchestration, emotional depth, and a strong melodic sense.

Ralph Vaughan Williams emerged as a leading figure in British classical music during the 1910s. He drew inspiration from folk melodies and English landscapes, incorporating them into his compositions. His works, such as the "Fantasia on a Theme by Thomas Tallis" and the "London Symphony", showcased a distinctively British musical language.

The influence of impressionism, as pioneered by French composers like Claude Debussy and Maurice Ravel, extended to British composers of the time. They were inspired by the atmospheric and evocative qualities of impressionist music and incorporated these elements into their compositions. The works of Frederick Delius, influenced by impressionism, gained recognition during this period. The 1910s saw the emergence of modernist and avant-garde movements in classical music. Composers like Arnold Schoenberg and Igor Stravinsky were pushing the boundaries of tonality and form, challenging traditional conventions. Although these avant-garde styles had a more significant impact on the European classical music scene, their influence was also felt in Britain, sparking discussions and debates among composers and musicians.

Opera and ballet were significant components of the classical music scene in 1910s Britain. Opera companies, such as the Royal Opera House, presented productions of both traditional and contemporary works. British composers, including Benjamin Britten and Gustav Holst, made contributions to opera and ballet, infusing their compositions with British themes and sensibilities. Chamber music, characterised by its intimate and small-scale nature, remained an essential part of the classical music repertoire. String quartets, piano trios, and other chamber ensembles performed works by both British and international composers. Chamber music recitals provided opportunities for musicians to showcase their virtuosity and interpretative skills. The emergence of recordings and phonographs in the early

1900s had a significant impact on the music industry and culture in Britain.

They allowed for the widespread dissemination of music, making it more accessible to a wider audience. People could now listen to their favourite songs and artists in the comfort of their own homes, leading to a surge in demand for recorded music. This helped to popularise music and expand its reach beyond traditional concert halls and music halls. With the ability to capture and manipulate sound, composers and producers could experiment with different recording techniques and create new sounds. Recordings and phonographs also facilitated the commercialisation of music. Record labels and music publishers could now produce and distribute music on a large scale, leading to the emergence of a commercial music industry. This allowed for the monetisation of music, creating new opportunities for artists and musicians. It also lead to the rise of celebrity culture. Popular artists and performers could now reach a wider audience, leading to a surge in their popularity and fame.

******

Born out of the labour movement and fuelled by the growing discontent among the working class, the Labour Party provided a new voice and political platform for workers' rights, social reform, and economic justice. The origins of the Labour Party can be traced back to the late 19th century, with the rise of trade unions and the labour movement. The working class, faced with poor working conditions, low wages, and limited political representation, sought a political vehicle to advocate for their rights and interests.

The formation of the Independent Labour Party (ILP) in 1893, under the leadership of Keir Hardie, marked an important step towards the creation of a distinct political organisation for the working class. The ILP focused on social reform, trade unionism, and independent working-class representation. The Representation of the People Act 1918, which extended the right to vote to more segments of the population, including working-class men and some women, created favourable conditions for the Labour Party's electoral success. This act paved the way for the party to secure parliamentary seats and establish itself as a viable political force. In the general election of 1918, the Labour Party won 63 seats in the House of Commons, signalling a breakthrough for the party and solidifying its position as the primary representative of the working class.

World War I had a significant impact on the emergence of the Labour Party. The war created socio-economic instability and exposed the harsh realities faced by the working class. The demands of wartime production, coupled with the sacrifices made by workers, heightened the sense of injustice and inequality, leading to increased support for the Labour Party's agenda. Moreover, the war disrupted traditional political alliances, paving the way for new political forces to emerge. The Labour Party benefited from the growing disillusionment with the traditional Liberal and Conservative parties, which were seen as failing to adequately address the needs and aspirations of the working class.

The Labour Party's emergence brought the issues of social justice, equality, and worker empowerment to the forefront of British politics. It challenged the traditional class divisions and power structures, paving the way for a more egalitarian society. The party's focus on social justice and workers' rights helped redefine the political discourse and shaped subsequent political agendas. The Party's emergence also influenced other political movements and parties. It prompted the Liberal Party to adopt more progressive policies, leading to the rise of social reform within their ranks. However, the Labour Party faced challenges and internal divisions in its early years. The party had to navigate various ideological factions and balance the demands of trade unions, socialists, and moderates within its ranks. These tensions sometimes hindered the party's ability to present a unified front and affected its electoral performance.

******

Boxing had a significant following, with many notable British boxers achieving fame during the 1910s. Prominent names like Bombardier Billy Wells and Ted "Kid" Lewis captured the public's imagination. Bombardier Billy Wells, born William Thomas Wells, was a prominent British heavyweight boxer who had a successful career during the early 20th century. Wells began his professional boxing career in 1911 and quickly made a name for himself as a powerful and hard-hitting fighter. Standing at 6 feet 3 inches tall and weighing around 190 pounds, he possessed a sturdy build and possessed a formidable punch. One of Wells' most notable achievements came in June 1913, when he faced off against the legendary French boxer Georges Carpentier in a bout for the European Heavyweight Title.

Although Wells lost the fight by a knockout in the 4th round, he gained immense popularity and respect for his valiant effort against Carpentier, who was considered one of the best fighters of his time. Despite the loss to Carpentier, Wells continued to have a successful career. He fought numerous bouts against prominent opponents and earned a reputation as a tough and durable fighter. He had a unique style characterised by his powerful right hand and a strong chin that allowed him to withstand heavy blows. Wells' most significant victory came on 16th December 1912, when he faced British boxer Iron William Hague at the National Sporting Club in Covent Garden. Wells knocked out Glover in the 6th round of 20 to claim the British heavyweight title, a significant accomplishment in his career.

Ted "Kid" Lewis, born Gershon Mendeloff on 24th October 24 1893, in Whitechapel, London, was a British Jewish boxer who had a highly successful boxing career during the early 20th century. He is widely regarded as one of the greatest British boxers of all time. Lewis began his professional boxing career in 1909 at the age of 15 and quickly gained recognition for his exceptional skills and ring intelligence. He earned the nickname "Kid" due to his youthful appearance and relatively young age when he started his career. Throughout his career, Lewis primarily fought as a welterweight and later moved up to the middleweight division. He possessed exceptional technical abilities, a strong defence, and excellent counter-punching skills. Lewis was known for his strategic approach to boxing, relying on his superior ring craft and defensive skills to outwit his opponents. One of Lewis' most significant achievements came on 31st August 1915, when he defeated Jack Britton to claim the world welterweight title. The fight took place in Boston and Lewis won to become the first British boxer to win a recognised world title in the United States. He successfully defended the title multiple times throughout his career. Lewis engaged in several high-profile fights during his career, facing some of the best boxers of his era. He had a notable rivalry with Jack Britton, with the two fighters meeting in a total of 20 bouts and 224 rounds of boxing, including their world title clash. The rivalry between Lewis and Britton is considered one of the greatest in boxing history.

******

The 1916 Easter Rising in Ireland was initially unsuccessful but its aftermath ignited a wave of political and nationalist sentiment in Ireland and within Britain itself. The British government's heavy-handed response, including the execution of rebel leaders, sparked public outrage and increased support for Irish independence. The Easter Rising galvanised the nationalist movement in Ireland and led to the rise of Sinn Féin, a political party advocating for Irish self-determination. Sinn Féin's demands for an independent Irish republic gained significant support, challenging the status quo and shifting the focus of the Irish question in British politics. The question of Irish Home Rule, the demand for self-government within the United Kingdom, had been a contentious issue in British politics for decades. The Irish Home Rule movement gained momentum during the 1910s, with the Liberal Party under Prime Minister H.H. Asquith making efforts to pass Home Rule legislation. However, the prospect of Irish Home Rule and the growing nationalist sentiment in Ireland caused political divisions within Britain. The Conservative Party, led by Andrew Bonar Law, strongly opposed Home Rule and formed alliances with Unionist forces in Ireland to resist its implementation. These divisions within political parties and the wider political landscape had a significant impact on British politics during the period.

The events surrounding the Easter Rising played a pivotal role in the erosion of the Liberal Party's dominance in British politics. The Liberal Party, traditionally seen as the party of Home Rule, faced internal divisions over the issue. The failure to enact Home Rule legislation and the perceived mishandling of the Irish situation damaged the party's credibility and led to a decline in support. Meanwhile, the rise of Sinn Féin and its call for Irish independence attracted significant attention and support in Ireland. The growing popularity of Sinn Féin further marginalised the Liberal Party's position and challenged the existing political order.

The Easter Rising and the Irish Home Rule movement resulted in the emergence of new political alignments in British politics. The Conservative Party, with its opposition to Home Rule, formed alliances with Unionist forces in Ireland, establishing a closer relationship between Unionism and the Conservative Party. The rise of Sinn Féin and the growing nationalist sentiment also led to the emergence of alliances between Irish nationalists and sympathetic British politicians. This alliance-building process contributed to the formation of a broader coalition that sought to challenge the established political parties and advocate for Irish independence.

The events surrounding the Easter Rising and the Irish Home Rule movement forced a reevaluation of British imperial policies and the governance of Ireland. The failures in addressing Irish grievances and the increasing demands for Irish self-determination prompted a reassessment of Britain's colonial policies and raised questions about the sustainability of the British Empire. The Irish nationalist movement and the events of the 1910s exposed the contradictions within the British imperial project. The call for Irish self-government resonated with other nationalist movements within the empire, leading to increased demands for independence and self-determination from other colonial territories.

1920s
Flapper Culture and Reconstruction

The 1920s, often referred to as the "Roaring Twenties", was a transformative period in British history. After the devastation of World War I, the nation experienced significant social, political, and cultural changes. The war had taken a toll on the country, both physically and emotionally, with many lives lost and communities shattered. The government focused on reconstruction and the healing of war wounds, which led to the establishment of the British Legion, an organisation dedicated to supporting veterans and their families.

Politically, the decade saw a power shift. The Labour Party gained momentum and made significant strides, even though it did not hold power at the national level. The Conservative Party, under the leadership of Stanley Baldwin, dominated the political landscape. The era witnessed the first women to take seats in Parliament, with Nancy Astor becoming the first female MP in 1919. However, despite some progress, women still faced significant barriers to achieving political representation. Economically, the 1920s brought a period of relative prosperity. The country experienced a post-war boom, with industries such as manufacturing, mining, and textiles thriving. The end of the war stimulated consumer demand, leading to increased production and rising living standards. The automotive industry, in particular, saw significant growth, with car ownership becoming more accessible to the middle class.

Culturally, the 1920s witnessed a sense of liberation and modernity. The war had shattered traditional values, and a new generation emerged, eager to embrace change. The "Flapper" culture became popular, symbolising the newfound freedom and independence of young women. Flappers challenged social norms with their short hair, bold fashion choices, and active participation in social and cultural events. Jazz music, originating from America, captured the spirit of the era and became immensely popular. Literature and art flourished during the 1920s. Writers such as Virginia Woolf, T.S. Eliot, and D.H. Lawrence continued to make significant contributions to modernist literature. The Bloomsbury Group, a collective of intellectuals and artists, including Woolf and economist John Maynard Keynes, became influential in shaping cultural discourse. In the art world, the Vorticist movement, led by Wyndham Lewis, celebrated modernity and technology through abstract and geometric forms. The 1920s also saw advancements in technology and entertainment. The introduction of the radio brought news, music, and entertainment directly into people's homes, connecting the nation in new ways. Broadcasting became increasingly popular, with the establishment of the British Broadcasting Company in 1922, which later became the British

Broadcasting Corporation (BBC). Theatres and cinemas became popular entertainment venues, and the film industry saw significant growth, with Charlie Chaplin emerging as a global star. Socially, the 1920s brought a shift in traditional gender roles and social expectations. Women gained more freedom, challenging Victorian-era conventions. They embraced new opportunities for education and employment, and the "New Woman" emerged as a symbol of female empowerment. The 1928 Equal Franchise Act granted women aged 21 and over the right to vote on equal terms with men. However, it is important to note that these changes were primarily experienced by urban, middle-class women, while many working-class women still faced significant challenges and inequality and most women's roles were still largely defined by traditional expectations of marriage and motherhood.

******

After the end of World War I, the British government had to shift its focus from wartime production to rebuilding the economy, demobilising the armed forces, and addressing the social and economic consequences of the conflict. One of the primary challenges was the conversion of war industries to peacetime production. During the war, industries such as munitions, armaments, and shipbuilding had expanded significantly to meet the demands of the military. With the end of hostilities, the government had to reorient these industries towards civilian production. This involved scaling back production, retraining workers, and diversifying industrial output to meet the demands of the civilian market. The demobilisation of soldiers and the scaling back of industries led to a rise in unemployment. The government had to address the social and economic consequences of unemployment through various measures.

These included providing unemployment benefits, introducing public works programs to create employment opportunities, and encouraging retraining and relocation of workers to industries with higher demand.

The end of the war brought increased demands for housing as soldiers returned home and families sought accommodation. The government initiated housing schemes and programs to address the shortage of affordable housing. Infrastructure development, such as road construction, electrification, and the expansion of public transport, was also a priority to support economic growth and improve living conditions. The 1920s brought economic challenges, including inflation, fluctuating commodity prices, and trade disruptions. These challenges required careful management of monetary policy, including controlling inflation, managing interest rates, and addressing the balance of trade issues. The government aimed to strike a balance between economic stability and promoting growth. The agricultural sector faced particular challenges during the transition to peacetime production. Agricultural productivity had increased during the war due to government intervention and increased demand. However, the post-war period saw declining prices, reduced government support, and competition from imports. The government implemented policies to support farmers, including subsidies, research programs, and market interventions.

The war disrupted global trade and led to significant government intervention in the economy. The government aimed to restore a market-driven economy and reduce state control. This involved scaling back wartime regulations, removing price controls, and facilitating the transition to a free market economy. The return to a gold standard for the currency, which occurred in 1925, was also an important step towards stabilising the economy and encouraging international trade. Rebuilding international trade relationships was crucial for Britain's economic recovery. The government engaged in negotiations to restore pre-war trade agreements, resolve war debts, and address reparations owed to Britain by defeated countries. These efforts were aimed at stimulating export industries and regaining access to international markets.

******

The 1920s marked a significant era for football in Britain, as the sport experienced remarkable growth and transformation. The Football League, established in 1888, continued to evolve during this decade, shaping the foundation of modern professional football and leaving a lasting impact on the sport. The 1920s witnessed a surge in popularity and commercialisation of football in Britain. The aftermath of World War I brought a renewed sense of national pride and enthusiasm for the sport. The public's appetite for football grew exponentially, and stadiums filled with passionate supporters every match day.

During this decade, the Football League expanded, with the addition of new clubs and the formation of additional divisions. The top-tier league, known as the First Division, continued to showcase some of the finest football talent in the country. Prominent teams such as Burnley, Liverpool, Arsenal, Manchester United, Everton and Huddersfield emerged as powerhouses, captivating fans with their skill and flair. The 1920s also witnessed the rise of legendary players who left an indelible mark on the sport. Names like Dixie Dean, George Camsell, and Alex James became household names, revered for their goal-scoring prowess and technical brilliance. These players became idols for aspiring footballers and inspired a generation with their performances on the pitch. However, the decade was not without its challenges. Football faced the aftermath of the First World War, which disrupted the sport and had a profound impact on the clubs and players. Many footballers served in the war, and some even lost their lives. The sport had to rebuild itself and adapt to the post-war reality. Financial stability was a significant concern for many clubs in the 1920s. The escalating costs of running a professional football club, coupled with the economic uncertainties of the time, created financial hardships for some teams. However, the formation of a more structured and organised Football League system helped address some of these challenges. The 1920s also marked the advent of broadcasting football matches on the radio. The first game broadcast on the new BBC service was on 22nd January 1927 when Arsenal drew 1-1 with Sheffield United. This development significantly contributed to the sport's popularity, as fans across the country could now follow their favourite teams and players from the comfort of their own homes. The radio broadcasts brought the excitement of football to a wider audience and further fuelled the growth of the sport.

The Football Association Challenge Cup, commonly known as the FA Cup, remained a prestigious tournament. In 1923, the iconic Wembley Stadium was opened, becoming the home of English football and hosting FA Cup Finals. The FA Cup Final in 1923 is famously known as the "White Horse Final" and was held on 28th April 1923, at Wembley Stadium. The match was contested between Bolton Wanderers and West Ham United. The final is called the "White Horse Final" because of the presence of a white horse named Billie on the pitch. It was brought in to help control the crowd, which was estimated to be over 200,000 spectators. The match itself ended in a 2-0 victory for Bolton Wanderers. David Jack opened the scoring for Bolton in the second half, and Jack Smith added a second goal to secure the win. This victory made Bolton Wanderers the first club to win the FA Cup at Wembley Stadium. The attendance at the 1923 FA Cup Final remains a record for any football match in England.

The high number of spectators, combined with the historic significance of the match being the first FA Cup final at Wembley, contributed to its iconic status in football history.

******

Britain had a successful campaign at the 1920 Olympics in Antwerp winning a total of 42 medals, including 14 gold, 15 silver, and 13 bronze from a team of 234 competitors competing in 21 sports. Notable British athletes included Albert Hill, who won gold in both the 800 meters and 1,500 meters events, and Harry Edward, who secured bronze medals in the 100m and the 200m. British boxers had a successful outing as well, winning six medals, including two gold, one silver, and three bronze. Harry Mallin won gold in the lightweight division, while Ronald Rawson secured gold in the heavyweight division.

The British rowing and cycling teams had dominant performances, winning a total of two rowing medals and five cycling medals including gold for Thomas Lance and Harry Ryan in the Tandem event. British tennis players achieved considerable success, winning six medals, including two gold, three silver, and one bronze. Oswald Turnbull and Maxwell Woosnam won the gold medal in the men's doubles event and Kathleen McKane and Winifred McNair in the women's doubles event.

******

The aftermath of World War I had a profound impact on British literature. Many writers who experienced the horrors of war firsthand sought to express their disillusionment, grief, and a sense of loss through their works. The war shattered the ideals of progress and stability, leading to a questioning of traditional values and a reevaluation of the role of literature in society.

Detective fiction gained popularity during the 1920s, with writers like Agatha Christie and Dorothy L. Sayers captivating readers with their intricate plots and memorable characters. Agatha Christie, often referred to as the "Queen of Crime", began her writing career in the 1920s and quickly gained popularity with her captivating plots and skillful storytelling. Her most famous detective character, Hercule Poirot, made his debut in her novel "The Mysterious Affair at Styles". The book introduced readers to the eccentric and brilliant Belgian detective, marking the beginning of a series of Poirot novels that would span several decades. Christie's cleverly crafted mysteries, filled with red herrings and unexpected twists, enthralled readers and solidified her reputation as a master of the genre. One of Christie's most well-known works, "Murder on the Orient Express", exemplifies her ability to create intricate and suspenseful narratives. The novel follows the investigation led by Hercule Poirot after a murder takes place on the famous Orient Express train. Christie's attention to detail and her ability to weave together multiple threads of the story have made this novel a classic of detective fiction.

Dorothy L. Sayers was another prominent crime writer of the 1920s, known for her series of detective novels featuring the character Lord Peter Wimsey. Sayers brought a unique blend of wit, intelligence, and social commentary to her works, making them stand out in the genre. Her first Lord Peter Wimsey novel, "Whose Body?", introduced readers to the aristocratic detective and set the stage for a series of clever and engaging mysteries. Sayers's novel "Strong Poison" marked a significant development in her writing career. It introduced Harriet Vane, a strong and independent female character who becomes Lord Peter Wimsey's love interest. Sayers defied traditional gender roles and expectations by portraying Vane as an intelligent and capable woman who plays an active role in solving crimes. This progressive depiction of women in crime fiction was groundbreaking at the time and contributed to Sayers's enduring legacy. Both Agatha Christie and Dorothy L. Sayers brought their unique styles and storytelling techniques to the crime fiction genre. While Christie's focus was primarily on the intricate plotting and unexpected twists, Sayers incorporated social commentary and explored deeper themes within her works. Their novels not only entertained readers with their mysteries but also offered insightful glimpses into the social fabric and cultural nuances of 1920s Britain.

The 1920s saw the emergence of new poetic movements, the exploration of innovative forms and themes, and the rise of influential poets who left a lasting impact on the literary landscape. One of the most influential poets of the 1920s was W.B. Yeats. Although his career began in the late 19th century, Yeats continued to produce notable works during this decade. His poetry reflected his interest in Irish mythology, the occult, and the cyclical nature of history. Yeats's collection "The Tower" delved into themes of aging, mortality, and the complexities of human relationships. His evocative language and lyrical style resonated with readers, making him one of the most celebrated poets of the time.

The 1920s also saw the emergence of the Georgian poets, a group of poets characterised by their focus on traditional forms and their celebration of the English countryside. Led by figures like Rupert Brooke, Edward Thomas, and Siegfried Sassoon, the Georgian poets sought to revive a sense of Englishness and pastoral beauty in their works. Their poetry, often marked by its accessibility and romanticised portrayal of nature, offered a contrast to the experimental nature of modernist poetry. The influence of war was still palpable in the poetry of the 1920s. War poets like Wilfred Owen, who tragically died during World War I, continued to be revered for their poignant and powerful verses that captured the horrors of war. Owen's posthumously published collection, "The Poems of Wilfred Owen", brought attention to the realities of trench warfare and the psychological toll it took on soldiers. His direct and vivid language, along with his compassionate portrayal of the suffering and sacrifice of soldiers, made a lasting impact on subsequent generations of poets.

******

The coalition government, which consisted of the Conservative and Liberal parties, had been in power during the war. However, there was growing discontent over issues such as war weariness, economic challenges, and the handling of the Irish question. The Conservative Party, under the leadership of Andrew Bonar Law, withdrew from the coalition, citing dissatisfaction with Prime Minister David Lloyd George. The split within the coalition set the stage for a new political landscape and the emergence of a stronger Conservative Party.

The 1922 general election, held on 15th November, saw the Conservative Party emerge as the dominant political force. The party campaigned on a platform of stability, law, and order, appealing to a nation recovering from the war and seeking a return to normalcy. The Conservatives won a landslide victory, securing 344 seats out of the total 615 in the House of Commons. The election marked a significant decline for the Liberal Party. The party suffered from internal divisions and the fallout from the coalition government. It lost a considerable number of seats, winning only 62 in the election. Labour made significant gains, winning 142 seats, and becoming the second-largest party in Parliament for the first time. The election marked a turning point in Labour's journey towards becoming a major political player. After the general election, the Conservative

Party formed a government under the leadership of Andrew Bonar Law. However, internal divisions within the party, particularly over the issue of tariff reform and protectionism, created a challenging political environment. These divisions and the Prime Ministers' health resulted in Bonar Law's resignation in May 1923 and Stanley Baldwin being asked by King George V to form a government. During this period, Britain faced an economic crisis, including high unemployment rates and industrial unrest. The government's response to these challenges and its handling of economic policies faced criticism and further added to the political instability. The economic crisis heightened the urgency to find a stable solution through another election.

******

The 1923 general election, held on 6 December 1923, resulted in a hung parliament, with no single party having a majority. The Conservative Party, under Stanley Baldwin, formed a minority government, but it faced challenges in dealing with economic issues, industrial unrest, and foreign policy concerns. As a result, Baldwin's government resigned, and the Labour Party, led by Ramsay MacDonald, was invited to form a government with the support of the Liberal Party. During its brief tenure, the first Labour government implemented significant social and welfare reforms. It focused on addressing the needs of the working class and disadvantaged groups.

The first Labour government faced challenges in foreign policy, particularly regarding relations with the Soviet Union. The government pursued diplomatic recognition of the Soviet Union, which was controversial and faced opposition from some quarters. This decision reflected Labour's desire for international cooperation and a more balanced approach to foreign relations. The government faced economic challenges during its tenure.

Inflation and unemployment rates were high, and industrial unrest persisted. The government attempted to address these issues through measures such as the Unemployment Insurance Act, which increased unemployment benefits, and the restoration of wage councils to protect workers' rights. The first Labour government faced numerous challenges and internal divisions. Its reliance on support from the Liberal Party made it vulnerable to shifting political dynamics. The government fell in October 1924 after a vote of no confidence. Nonetheless, the first Labour government laid the foundation for future Labour Party policies and achievements, particularly in the areas of social welfare and worker rights.

******

The general election held on 29th October 1924 took place after a short-lived Labour government, which had been in power since January 1924. The Labour government, led by Ramsay MacDonald, faced challenges and criticism, particularly regarding its foreign policy decisions. The Labour Party campaigned in this election on a platform of social reforms, workers' rights, and a focus on improving the conditions of the working class. During their previous time in government, they had implemented some significant policies, including the Wheatley Housing Act and the Widows', Orphans', and Old Age Contributory Pensions Act. However, they faced criticism for their foreign policy approach and concerns over Soviet influence. The Conservative Party, led by Stanley Baldwin, positioned itself as the party of stability, law, and order. They criticised the Labour government's foreign policy decisions, particularly their recognition of the Soviet Union, and focused on economic issues, promising to address unemployment and restore confidence in the economy.

The Liberal Party, led by Herbert Samuel, campaigned on a platform of free trade and individual liberties. They sought to appeal to moderate voters and positioned themselves as a centrist alternative to the more polarised Labour and Conservative parties.

The 1924 general election resulted in a significant victory for the Conservative Party. They secured 412 seats out of the total 615 in the House of Commons, giving them a comfortable majority. The Labour Party won 151 seats, becoming the main opposition party, while the Liberal Party secured only 40 seats. The 1924 general election marked a shift in the political landscape. The Conservative Party's victory brought them back to power after a brief period of Labour rule. It also demonstrated the volatility of British politics during this time, with rapid changes in the balance of power. The election had significant implications for foreign policy. The Conservative government, led by Stanley Baldwin, pursued a more conservative and cautious approach compared to the previous Labour government. They adopted a more traditional foreign policy stance, reversing the recognition of the Soviet Union and maintaining a more conservative approach towards international affairs.

******

Cricket held its traditional status as a cherished sport in Britain. County cricket matches and Test matches against international teams, particularly Australia, attracted large crowds. Notable cricketers of the time, such as Jack Hobbs and Herbert Sutcliffe, achieved legendary status. The Ashes series between England and Australia continued to be a highly anticipated event. The Ashes are named after a satirical obituary published in 1882, stating that English cricket had died and "the body will be cremated, and the ashes taken to Australia".

During the 1920s, there were two Ashes series held in Britain. The Ashes series in 1921 was closely contested and ended in a 1-1 draw, with four matches played. England won the first Test at Nottingham, while Australia emerged victorious in the second Test at Lord's. The final two matches ended in draws. Notable performances included Warwick Armstrong's all-round brilliance for Australia and Jack Hobbs' batting heroics for England.

Australia won the 1926 series 1-0, with five matches played. The first Test at Nottingham was drawn, and Australia won the second Test at Lord's. The remaining three Tests ended in draws. A standout player in this series was England's Jack Hobbs, who scored a double century in the first Test and had a remarkable overall batting performance.

******

The 1920s saw the expansion of cinema as a popular form of entertainment for the masses. Movie theatres, often called cinemas or picture houses, became increasingly prevalent in towns and cities across the country. The growth of purpose-built cinemas allowed for a more immersive movie-going experience, with larger screens, comfortable seating, and improved projection technologies. However, cinema attendance during the 1920s was not limited to urban areas. Mobile cinemas, known as "cinemotor vans", traveled to rural areas, bringing films to communities that had limited access to movie theatres. These traveling cinemas played a crucial role in making cinema a popular form of entertainment for people from all walks of life. One of the notable developments in British cinema during the 1920s was the transition from silent films to sound. In 1927, the American film "The Jazz Singer" was released, which featured synchronised sound sequences. This breakthrough technology, known as "talkies", revolutionised the film industry worldwide.

British filmmakers quickly embraced the new technology, and British audiences eagerly embraced sound films. With the advent of sound, British filmmakers began producing their own talkies, leading to the establishment of major film studios. Companies such as Gaumont-British, British International Pictures (BIP), and Gainsborough Pictures emerged as influential players in the British film industry. These studios produced a range of genres, including comedies, dramas, musicals, and literary adaptations, catering to the diverse tastes of audiences.

Comedies played a significant role in British cinema during the 1920s. Comedic duos like Stan Laurel and Oliver Hardy, collectively known as Laurel and Hardy, rose to fame with their slapstick humour and endearing characters. Their short films, such as "Putting Pants on Philip" and "Big Business", delighted audiences and continue to be cherished today. The 1920s also witnessed the emergence of notable British filmmakers who made significant contributions to cinema. Alfred Hitchcock, often regarded as one of the greatest directors in film history, began his career in the 1920s. His early silent films, such as "The Lodger: A Story of the London Fog", showcased his mastery of suspense and innovative storytelling techniques. British cinema in the 1920s also saw adaptations of literary works, bringing classic novels to the silver screen. Notable adaptations include "Oliver Twist" directed by Frank Lloyd, based on Charles Dickens's novel, and "The Hound of the Baskervilles" directed by Maurice Elvey, featuring the iconic detective Sherlock Holmes. While Hollywood dominated the international film market, British cinema in the 1920s showcased the country's unique cultural and artistic sensibilities. British filmmakers focused on portraying distinct British settings, characters, and societal issues, giving British cinema its own identity.

******

The 1920s witnessed the continued emergence of motor racing as a thrilling spectator sport. The Brooklands circuit in Surrey became a prominent venue for high-speed racing events, attracting enthusiasts and leading drivers of the time. The British Grand Prix in 1926 was a significant motor racing event that took place on 7th July 1926, at Brooklands. The race was part of the 1926 World Manufacturers' Championship, an early predecessor to the Formula One World Championship that started in 1950. The 1926 British Grand Prix featured a field of 11 cars, representing various manufacturers of the time. The race was held over a distance of 110 laps, covering a total of approximately 308 miles on the Brooklands circuit. The circuit was a banked oval track, known for its high speeds and challenging conditions.

The race was won by French driver Louis Wagner, who was driving a Delage 155B. Wagner completed the 110 laps in a time of 4 hours, 18 minutes, and 11 seconds, with an average speed of around 71.75 mph. This victory marked the first and only British Grand Prix win for Wagner. It's worth noting that the term "British Grand Prix" was not commonly used at the time. The 1926 race is retrospectively recognised as the British Grand Prix by historians, as it was the first major international motor race held in Britain and had a significant impact on the development of motorsport in the country.

******

Flapper culture in Britain during the 1920s was a vibrant and revolutionary movement that challenged traditional gender norms and social conventions. The term "flapper" was used to describe young women who adopted a modern and unconventional lifestyle. One of the defining features of flapper fashion was the transformation of women's clothing silhouettes. Flapper dresses were characterised by their loose and straight shapes, in contrast to the fitted and corseted styles of the past. These shift dresses, often made of lightweight fabrics such as silk or chiffon, hung straight down from the shoulders and had dropped waistlines. The absence of defined waistlines allowed for greater comfort and ease of movement, reflecting the flappers' desire for freedom. Flapper dresses were typically knee-length or slightly shorter, which was considered scandalously short for the time. The shorter hemlines allowed women to showcase their legs, challenging traditional notions of modesty. This shift in skirt length was a direct response to the changing roles and attitudes of women, as they became more active participants in sports, dancing, and other social activities. Another iconic feature of flapper fashion was the use of geometric shapes and bold patterns. Art Deco designs, characterised by their symmetrical lines and stylised motifs, influenced the patterns and embellishments found on flapper dresses. Popular patterns included zigzags, chevrons, and geometric shapes that added a sense of modernity and sophistication to the garments. Flappers also embraced the bobbed hairstyle, which became a symbol of their rebellious spirit. The traditional long and elaborate hairstyles of the past were replaced with short, cropped cuts that required minimal styling. The bobbed hairstyle was seen as a symbol of liberation and modernity, reflecting the flappers' desire to break away from traditional feminine ideals.

Accessories played a significant role in completing the flapper look. Long strands of pearls, often referred to as "ropes", were a popular accessory and were worn in multiple layers for a dramatic effect. Feathered headbands, cloche hats, and decorative hairpieces were also commonly worn to add flair to the overall ensemble. T-strap or Mary Jane-style shoes with low heels were preferred for their comfort and suitability for dancing. Makeup also underwent a transformation during the flapper era. Women started to experiment with bolder and more dramatic makeup looks. Darkened eyebrows, smoky eyes, and deep red or plum coloured lips were popular choices. These makeup styles emphasised the flappers' desire to challenge societal norms and express their individuality.

Flappers challenged traditional gender roles by participating in activities previously considered exclusive to men. They embraced new forms of entertainment, such as dancing the Charleston, which became synonymous with the flapper culture. Jazz music played a significant role in the flapper movement, with its lively rhythms and energetic spirit capturing the essence of the era. Flappers were associated with a carefree and hedonistic lifestyle. They frequented jazz clubs and dance halls, where they socialised, danced, and enjoyed the nightlife. They were often depicted as rebellious and adventurous, engaging in behaviours such as smoking, drinking, and casual dating, which were considered unconventional for women at the time. The emergence of the flapper culture was also influenced by broader social and political changes of the era. The First World War had brought about significant shifts in society, as women had taken on roles traditionally reserved for men while they were away at war. This experience led to a sense of empowerment and a desire for greater independence among women.

The flapper movement was not without its critics. Traditionalists viewed flappers as a threat to societal norms and traditional values. They believed that the behaviours and attitudes of flappers represented a decline in moral standards. The media often portrayed flappers as rebellious and immoral, perpetuating stereotypes and moral panic. However, the flapper culture also had a positive impact on women's liberation. Flappers challenged societal expectations and paved the way for greater gender equality and opportunities for women in the years to come. They embraced a sense of individualism and independence, demanding their right to pursue education, careers, and personal fulfillment beyond the domestic sphere.

******

The BBC was founded in 1922 as a private company with a public service remit. Its primary objective was to provide unbiased news, educational programming, and cultural content to the British public. The BBC's formation was in response to the demand for a centralised and regulated broadcasting system that could serve the public interest. Initially, the BBC operated as a consortium of private radio manufacturers and wireless retailers. It established a network of radio transmitters across the country to ensure nationwide coverage. These transmitters enabled the broadcasting of radio programs to a growing number of listeners who owned radio receivers. The BBC's early programming consisted of a diverse range of content. It included news bulletins, talks, educational lectures, live music performances, and cultural programs. The BBC's emphasis on impartial news reporting and educational content helped to foster a sense of trust and credibility among the British public. In 1927, the BBC was granted a Royal Charter, which transformed it into a public corporation known as the British Broadcasting Corporation. The Royal Charter solidified the BBC's commitment to serving the public interest and provided a framework for its operations and governance.

The 1920s saw significant advancements in radio technology, which further enhanced the BBC's ability to reach wider audiences. The introduction of more powerful transmitters, improvements in audio quality, and the expansion of the broadcasting network allowed the BBC to broadcast to more listeners across the country. One of the landmark events of the 1920s was the first live radio broadcast of the British monarch. In 1923, King George V delivered a Christmas message that was transmitted across the country, marking the beginning of a tradition that continues to this day with the Queen's annual Christmas message.

The BBC's programming during the 1920s reflected the cultural, social, and political climate of the time. It featured live music performances, including orchestral concerts and popular dance music, which brought entertainment into people's homes. Radio dramas and comedy shows entertained audiences, while talks and lectures provided educational content. The BBC also played a role in the promotion of British culture and literature. It featured readings of classic literature, interviews with prominent writers, and discussions on literary topics. This helped to foster a sense of national identity and pride in British literary heritage.

However, it is important to note that the BBC's programming in the 1920s was limited, broadcasting hours were restricted and programming choices were often dictated by technical limitations and financial constraints.

******

The Bolshevik Revolution in Russia in 1917 had a profound effect on British politics in the 1920s. The revolution, which led to the establishment of the Soviet Union, brought about a radical transformation in Russia's political, economic, and social systems that had a huge impact on British politics during that period. The establishment of a communist government in Russia raised concerns among the political establishment in Britain. There was a prevailing fear that the revolutionary ideals and communist ideology might spread to other countries, including Britain. The British government and mainstream political parties viewed communism as a threat to the existing capitalist system and the social order, which led to increased vigilance against left-wing movements. The fear of communism led to a period of heightened anti-communist sentiment in Britain. The government and intelligence agencies monitored and investigated communist organisations and individuals suspected of being sympathetic to the Bolshevik cause. The state enacted laws and measures to curb the influence of communism, such as the notorious "Red Scare" trials of 1921, which targeted left-wing activists. The aim was to counter any potential radicalisation and prevent the spread of communist ideas within the country. The revolutionary events in Russia heightened debates about the role of the working class, social inequality, and the feasibility of socialism in Britain. Influenced by the Bolshevik example, the British labour movement experienced ideological shifts and internal divisions, with some factions advocating for more radical socialist positions. The Revolution played a role in the split within the British Labour Party during the 1920s. The revolution, with its emphasis on workers' power and class struggle, had a significant impact on socialist thinkers within the party. The more radical elements were drawn towards the revolutionary ideals of the Bolsheviks, while others sought a more moderate and reformist path. This ideological divide eventually led to the formation of the Communist Party of Great Britain (CPGB) in 1920, separate from the Labour Party. The emergence of the Soviet Union influenced British foreign policy during the 1920s. The British government faced the challenge of dealing with a new communist state that posed ideological and geopolitical challenges.

The British authorities adopted policies aimed at containing the perceived threat of Soviet expansionism while maintaining diplomatic relations. This led to a delicate balance of engagement and containment in dealing with the Soviet Union.

The 1920s were also a crucial phase in Britain's management of its vast colonial empire. International events, such as the Amritsar Massacre on 13th April 1919 and the emergence of nationalist movements in India and other colonies, intensified debates on colonial governance and calls for greater self-rule. The international backdrop of decolonisation and anti-colonial sentiment influenced British politics, forcing discussions on imperial policies, reforms, and the future of the empire.

******

The Olympic Games of 1924 were held in Paris, France. Britain sent a team of 267 athletes in 18 sports and had a successful campaign winning a total of 34 medals, including nine gold, thirteen silver, and twelve bronze. Harold Abrahams emerged as a standout athlete, winning gold in the men's 100 meters event and silver in the 4x100 meters relay. Eric Liddell won gold in the 400m and took bronze in the 200m. The British rowing team continued their strong performance, winning two gold medals. Harold Abrahams was born on 15th December 1899, in Bedford, England, Abrahams emerged as a sporting legend, not only for his remarkable achievements on the track but also for his unwavering spirit and enduring legacy. Abrahams' journey towards athletic greatness began during his time at Repton School, where he discovered his natural talent for sprinting. He honed his skills under the guidance of his dedicated coach, Sam Mussabini, whose unconventional training methods and innovative techniques played a pivotal role in shaping Abrahams' career. In 1920, Abrahams earned a place at the University of Cambridge, where he studied law at Gonville and Caius College. He became a prominent member of the university's athletics team, representing Cambridge in various track events. Abrahams' speed and agility were unparalleled, and he quickly established himself as one of the country's most promising sprinters. However, it was the 1924 Paris Olympics that would define Abrahams' legacy. Despite facing numerous obstacles and fierce competition, he proved himself to be an indomitable force on the track. Abrahams made history by winning the gold medal in the 100-meter sprint, becoming the first British athlete to achieve such a feat. His victory was immortalised in the critically acclaimed film "Chariots of Fire", which showcased Abrahams' unwavering determination and relentless pursuit of excellence. Beyond his athletic achievements, Abrahams was a true gentleman, admired for his integrity and sportsmanship. He firmly believed in fair play and advocated for amateurism in sports. Abrahams was a strong advocate for ethical competition his commitment to sportsmanship left an indelible mark on the sporting community, inspiring generations of athletes to strive for greatness with honour and integrity. Following his retirement from competitive athletics, Abrahams continued to contribute to the world of sports in various capacities. He served as a journalist, providing insightful commentary and analysis on athletics events. Abrahams also became a respected sports administrator, advocating for the rights of athletes and working towards improving the infrastructure of British sports. Abrahams' passion for sports extended beyond track and field. He was an avid supporter of football and served as the chairman of the British Amateur Athletics Board. Abrahams' leadership and dedication helped elevate the standards of British athletics, leaving a lasting impact on the sport. In addition to his sporting achievements, Abrahams was an accomplished academic and lawyer. He pursued a successful legal career, specialising in employment law. Abrahams' determination and intellect propelled him to become a leading figure in his field, respected for his knowledge and expertise. Harold Abrahams' unwavering spirit, dedication, and integrity make him a true sporting icon.

His achievements on the track, coupled with his contributions to sportsmanship and athletic administration, have left an indelible mark on the world of athletics. Abrahams' story reminds us that greatness is not merely defined by medals and records but by the values and principles we uphold as individuals. He will forever be remembered as a champion on and off the track, an embodiment of the Olympic spirit.

Born on 16th January 1902, Eric Liddell showed exceptional athletic prowess from a young age. He was known for his incredible speed and determination on the track. His faith in God also played a significant role in shaping his life and athletic career. During the 1924 Olympics, Liddell faced a dilemma. As a devout Christian, he believed that Sunday should be a day of rest and worship. However, his best event, the 100 meters, was scheduled to take place on a Sunday. Liddell made the difficult decision to withdraw from the 100 meters, even though it was his best chance for a gold medal. Undeterred, Liddell shifted his focus to the 400 meters race. The distance was longer than his specialty, but he embraced the challenge. The race was highly anticipated, and Liddell's commitment to his faith became a topic of discussion and admiration among both athletes and spectators. On 11th July 1924, the day of the 400 meters final, Liddell lined up alongside other world-class runners. The pressure was intense, but Liddell ran with determination and strength. With every stride, he showcased his remarkable speed and endurance. In a stunning display of athleticism, Liddell sprinted across the finish line, winning the gold medal with a new Olympic record time of 47.6 seconds. His victory was celebrated with tremendous enthusiasm, and Liddell became a symbol of inspiration for many. Liddell's success at the 1924 Olympics did not end with the 400 meters. He also competed in the 200 meters race, where he won a bronze medal, Harold Abrahams finished 6th. Although he did not secure the same level of success as in the 400 meters, his achievements showcased his versatility as an athlete. Eric Liddell's story at the 1924 Olympics transcended mere athletic achievement. His unwavering commitment to his faith, his integrity, and his sportsmanship left a lasting impression on the world. Liddell's life continued to inspire others even after his Olympic triumph, as he later became a missionary in China and dedicated his life to helping others.

******

Vanessa Bell and the Bloomsbury Group were influential figures in the British art and intellectual scene during the 1920s. They were part of a circle of artists, writers, and intellectuals who challenged traditional artistic and societal norms, leaving a lasting impact on British culture.

Vanessa Bell, born in 1879, was a British painter and interior designer. She was the sister of Virginia Woolf, a renowned writer and member of the Bloomsbury Group. Bell was known for her bold use of colour and her innovative approach to composition. Her style evolved over the years, transitioning from post-impressionism to a more abstract and modernist approach. Vanessa Bell, along with her sister Virginia Woolf, Roger Fry, Clive Bell, Duncan Grant, and other prominent artists and writers, formed the core of the Bloomsbury Group. They sought to challenge established artistic and societal norms by embracing modernist ideas, including Post-Impressionism and Cubism. The group held regular gatherings, known as "Thursday Evenings", where members engaged in lively discussions on art, literature, and philosophy.

One of the significant contributions of Vanessa Bell and the Bloomsbury Group was their exploration of interior design and decoration. They believed that art should not be limited to the canvas but should extend into every aspect of daily life. Bell, along with Grant, created innovative and avant-garde interior designs, incorporating bold colours, abstract patterns, and unconventional furniture arrangements. Their designs were seen as a fusion of art and everyday life, challenging traditional notions of domesticity and aesthetics. Vanessa Bell's paintings during the 1920s showcased her evolving artistic style. She moved away from traditional representation and embraced a more abstract and modernist approach. Her works often featured flattened forms, bold colours, and simplified compositions. Bell's paintings captured the essence of modern life, reflecting the changing societal attitudes and the influence of the modernist movement.

Surrealism also made its mark in Britain during the 1920s. Artists such as Eileen Agar and Paul Nash explored dreamlike and subconscious imagery, drawing inspiration from the works of the Surrealist movement founded in France. Surrealist art often combined realistic and fantastical elements, creating a sense of mystery and the irrational. The 1920s also saw the rise of the British avant-garde movement. Artists such as David Bomberg and Christopher Nevinson experimented with a range of styles, including Cubism and Futurism, and tackled themes of urbanisation, technology, and the effects of war. Their works reflected the social and political changes of the time, as Britain grappled with the aftermath of World War I and the industrial revolution.

In addition to these modernist movements, traditional forms of art continued to be practiced during the 1920s. The Royal Academy of Arts in London maintained its influence, showcasing works by established artists and providing a platform for more conservative artistic styles. The art scene in Britain during the 1920s was not limited to painting and sculpture. The influence of modernist ideas extended to other art forms, including design, photography, and architecture.

******

The Irish question had been a longstanding issue, with tensions between Britain and Ireland dating back centuries. The desire for independence gained momentum during the late 19th and early 20th centuries, fuelled by factors such as cultural nationalism, resentment towards British rule, and aspirations for Irish autonomy. The general elections in Ireland during the 1920s were crucial in shaping the path towards independence. In 1918, Sinn Féin achieved a landslide victory, securing an overwhelming majority of seats in Ireland. However, instead of taking their seats in the British Parliament, the Sinn Féin members established their own parliament, known as Dáil Éireann, proclaiming Irish independence. The British government responded with a heavy-handed approach, dispatching military forces to suppress the growing independence movement. This led to a period of intense conflict and violence known as the Irish War of Independence (1919-1921). The conflict resulted in widespread casualties and destruction, as well as the implementation of martial law.

To resolve the issue, negotiations took place between British and Irish representatives. The culmination of these negotiations was the signing of the Anglo-Irish Treaty in December 1921. The treaty led to the establishment of the Irish Free State, a self-governing dominion within the British Empire. While the treaty fell short of complete independence and satisfied neither side entirely, it represented a significant step forward. However, the treaty also sparked division within Ireland. The treaty's provisions, particularly the creation of the Irish Free State as opposed to a fully independent republic, caused a split in the nationalist movement. This division led to the Irish Civil War (1922-1923), pitting pro-treaty forces against anti-treaty forces.

******

Boxing in Britain during the 1920s experienced significant growth and popularity. The decade witnessed the emergence of several notable British boxers who made their mark both nationally and internationally. In 1929, the British Boxing Board of Control (BBBofC) was established to regulate and govern professional boxing in Britain. The BBBofC introduced rules and regulations, implemented safety measures, and provided structure to the sport. "Kid" Lewis, a Jewish fighter from London, became the world welterweight champion in 1915 and held the title until 1922. He was a popular and respected boxer during the 1920s. There was also Jimmy Wilde known as the "Mighty Atom", Wilde was a flyweight boxer who held the world title from 1916 to 1923. He was highly regarded for his exceptional speed and knockout power and Benny Lynch, a Scottish boxer, who emerged in the late 1920s and early 1930s. He became the world flyweight champion in 1935, but his career spanned both the 1920s and 1930s. The 1920s witnessed several memorable domestic rivalries that captivated boxing fans in Britain. One notable rivalry was between Jimmy Wilde and Eugene Criqui, a French boxer. Wilde and Criqui faced each other multiple times, with Criqui eventually defeating Wilde to win the world flyweight title in 1923. Boxing matches in the 1920s often took place in renowned venues such as the National Sporting Club in London and the Stadium in Liverpool. These venues attracted large crowds and played a significant role in the growth and popularity of boxing in Britain. The 1920s also saw the emergence of British heavyweight boxers who garnered attention and acclaim. While no British heavyweight boxers held world titles during the decade, fighters like Joe Beckett and Tom Gibbons gained recognition for their performances in the ring.

******

Art Deco, a distinctive and influential art and design style, had a significant impact on Britain in the 1920s. This modernist movement, characterised by its sleek lines, geometric shapes, and luxurious materials, permeated various aspects of British culture, from architecture and interior design to fashion and visual arts. Art Deco architecture flourished, particularly in urban areas. Prominent examples include the iconic London Underground stations designed by Charles Holden, which showcased geometric forms and decorative details. The Battersea Power Station in London is another notable Art Deco landmark. The style's streamlined and symmetrical designs, often incorporating bold geometric patterns and motifs, were employed in both commercial buildings and residential structures. Art Deco influenced various forms of visual arts in Britain during the 1920s. Painters, such as Tamara de Lempicka and Edward McKnight Kauffer, embraced the style in their artworks, employing geometric shapes, vibrant colours, and a sense of modernity. Art Deco also influenced graphic design, with its bold typography, simplified forms, and striking compositions. Posters, advertisements, and book covers often incorporated Art Deco elements. It also had a significant impact on jewellery design in Britain during the 1920s. The style favoured geometric shapes, symmetrical designs, and the use of colourful gemstones. Platinum and white gold were preferred metals, providing a sleek and modern look. Pieces often featured intricate filigree work, angular forms, and step-cut gemstones, reflecting the geometric motifs of the Art Deco style.

1930s
Political Turbulence and BBC Television

Britain in the 1930s was a period marked by significant social, economic, and political challenges. It was a time of transition and turbulence as the nation grappled with the aftermath of World War I and the Great Depression. Britain, heavily reliant on international trade, was hit hard by the collapse of the global financial system. Unemployment soared, reaching its peak in 1933 with around 2.5 million people out of work. The government responded with various relief measures and public works programs to alleviate the suffering, but the economic recovery was slow.

Politically, the 1930s was a decade of significant change. The Labour Party, led by Ramsay MacDonald, won the general election in 1929, forming the country's first-ever Labour government. However, the party faced internal divisions and struggled to tackle the economic crisis effectively. MacDonald's decision to form a National Government in 1931, a coalition including members from different parties, caused a split in the Labour Party and led to its decline in popularity. The rise of fascism in Europe also had an impact on Britain during this period. The British Union of Fascists (BUF), led by Sir Oswald Mosley, gained attention with its calls for authoritarianism, protectionism, and anti-Semitism. Mosley's rallies and marches, including the notorious Battle of Cable Street in 1936, created social unrest and sparked counter-demonstrations by anti-fascist groups such as the Communist Party and Jewish organisations.

In terms of cultural trends, the 1930s saw a mix of nostalgia for the pre-war era and a growing interest in modernity. Art Deco, an artistic style characterised by sleek lines and geometric patterns, became popular in architecture and design. The era also witnessed the rise of the "bright young things ", a group of young socialites known for their extravagant parties and rebellious behaviour.

Despite the economic challenges, the 1930s saw some notable achievements in science and technology. Sir Frank Whittle developed the concept of the jet engine, laying the foundation for modern aviation. The BBC's television service, the world's first regular television service, was launched in 1936. These advancements reflected Britain's ongoing commitment to innovation and scientific progress. The 1930s also witnessed significant social changes. The status of women in society continued to evolve, as they gained increased access to education and employment opportunities. The working-class population faced numerous challenges during the decade. The severe unemployment and poverty experienced by many led to widespread discontent. Industrial strikes and protests were common, as workers demanded better wages and improved working conditions. The Jarrow March of 1936, in which unemployed shipyard workers marched from Jarrow to London to highlight the impact of unemployment, became a symbol of the hardships faced by many during this period.

******

The 1930s saw a surge in film production in Britain, with numerous studios and production companies emerging. Major studios such as British International Pictures (BIP), Gaumont British, and Associated British Picture Corporation (ABPC) dominated the industry. These studios produced a wide range of films, including dramas, comedies, musicals, and literary adaptations. The 1930s witnessed advancements in film technology, including the widespread adoption of sound in British cinema. "Talkies" or sound films became the norm, enabling filmmakers to incorporate dialogue, music, and sound effects into their productions. This technological shift opened up new storytelling possibilities and expanded the range of genres and narratives explored. Musicals became increasingly popular during the 1930s, providing escapist entertainment for audiences during the Great Depression. Talented actors, singers, and dancers, such as Jessie Matthews and Gracie Fields, gained fame through their performances in British musicals. Films like "Evergreen" and "Shipmates O' Mine" showcased lavish song and dance numbers, offering a glamorous and uplifting experience for viewers. British cinema of the 1930s drew heavily from literary sources. Many notable novels and plays were adapted into films, bringing beloved characters and stories to the screen. Films like "Pygmalion" based on George Bernard Shaw's play and "Goodbye, Mr. Chips" based on James Hilton's novel were critically acclaimed and resonated with audiences. The 1930s also showcased the comedic talents of British actors and actresses. Personalities like George Formby, Will Hay, and Gracie Fields became popular for their humorous performances. Their comedic films provided light-hearted entertainment and brought laughter to audiences. British films of the 1930s received international acclaim and achieved success beyond domestic audiences. Films such as "The 39 Steps" directed by Alfred Hitchcock and "The Lady Vanishes" directed by Hitchcock as well, gained recognition for their suspenseful storytelling and innovative filmmaking techniques.

******

In Britain, the Great Depression led to a sharp decline in industrial production, widespread unemployment, and a collapse in international trade. The country's heavy reliance on exports and its position as a global economic power made it highly vulnerable to the global economic crisis. Industries such as coal mining, shipbuilding, textiles, and steel production were hit hard, leading to factory closures, layoffs, and wage cuts. Unemployment soared during the 1930s. By 1933, over three million people were out of work in Britain, representing more than 20% of the workforce. This had a devastating impact on families and communities, as many struggled to make ends meet and faced poverty and homelessness. The government was ill-prepared to deal with such high levels of unemployment and lacked effective measures to address the crisis. The agricultural sector also suffered, as falling prices and decreased demand for British exports affected farmers. Many rural areas experienced economic hardships, and farmers faced difficulties in repaying their debts and maintaining their livelihoods.

The government's response to the Great Depression initially followed a policy of austerity and balanced budgets. It aimed to maintain the value of the British pound and stabilise the economy through fiscal discipline. However, these measures ended up exacerbating the economic downturn, as reduced government spending and higher taxes further contracted the economy. In 1931, Britain faced a financial crisis, prompting the country to abandon the gold standard. This decision allowed for currency devaluation, making British exports more competitive. It was a significant step towards economic recovery, as it stimulated trade and boosted industrial production.

The Great Depression also had social and political repercussions in Britain. The economic hardships and widespread unemployment fuelled social unrest and led to increased support for radical political ideologies. Extremist movements such as communism and fascism gained some following during this period. In response to the economic crisis, the British government introduced various measures to alleviate the suffering. These included the introduction of unemployment benefits, public works projects, and the establishment of organisations like the National Unemployment Register to provide assistance to the jobless. However, these efforts were limited in scope and effectiveness. It was not until the rearmament programme of the late 1930s, as Britain prepared for the looming threat of World War II, that the country's economy began to recover. Increased government spending on defence and military production helped stimulate employment and economic activity, eventually leading to a gradual exit from the Great Depression.

******

England's cricket team, under the leadership of Douglas Jardine, emerged victorious in the highly controversial Bodyline series against Australia in the winter of 1932-33. The tour, organised by the Marylebone Cricket Club (MCC), included five Test matches in Australia, with England claiming The Ashes by a margin of four games to one. The first Test, a timeless match held at the Sydney Cricket Ground, witnessed England's dominance as they secured a resounding 10-wicket victory over Australia. Winning the toss, Australia elected to bat but could only muster a total of 360 runs in their first innings. Stan McCabe provided the only significant resistance, scoring an unbeaten 187 runs. England's Harold Larwood showcased his bowling prowess, claiming five wickets for 96 runs. In response, England displayed a commanding performance, led by Herbert Sutcliffe's remarkable knock of 194 runs. Their innings total reached a formidable 524 runs. Tim Wall was the pick of the Australian bowlers, taking three wickets for 104 runs. Facing a deficit of 164 runs, Australia crumbled in their second innings, succumbing to Harold Larwood's relentless pace bowling. They were dismissed for a mere 164 runs, resulting in a comprehensive victory for England. Jardine's side sealed the match by 10 wickets, with Herbert Sutcliffe and the Nawab of Pataudi comfortably chasing down the required one run.

The second Test at the Melbourne Cricket Ground saw Australia bounce back, securing a 111-run victory over England. After winning the toss, Australia elected to bat and posted a total of 228 runs in their first innings. Jack Fingleton top-scored with 83 runs, while Bill Voce took three wickets for 54 runs. In reply, England struggled against Australia's bowling attack and could only manage 169 runs, with Herbert Sutcliffe contributing 52 runs. Bill O'Reilly starred for Australia, claiming five wickets for 63 runs. In their second innings, Australia found their rhythm with Donald Bradman's unbeaten century (103 runs). Wally Hammond took three wickets for 21 runs, but Bradman's resilience ensured Australia reached a total of 191 runs. Chasing a target of 251 runs, England faltered against O'Reilly's spin, and they were bowled out for 139 runs, conceding victory to Australia.

The third Test at Adelaide Oval became synonymous with the controversial Bodyline tactics employed by England. The match witnessed heated exchanges and physical injuries. England, after winning the toss, elected to bat and scored 341 runs in their first innings. Maurice Leyland top-scored with 83 runs, while Tim Wall took five wickets for 72 runs. In reply, Australia could only manage 222 runs, with Bill Ponsford contributing 85 runs. Gubby Allen was the standout bowler for England, claiming four wickets for 71 runs. England continued their dominance in the match, posting a mammoth total of 412 runs in their second innings, with Wally Hammond leading the charge with 85 runs. Bill O'Reilly took four wickets for 79 runs. Chasing an improbable target of 532 runs, Australia faltered and were dismissed for 193 runs, handing England a commanding victory by 338 runs.

The fourth Test, held at The Gabba in Brisbane, witnessed England's triumph by six wickets. Australia won the toss and elected to bat, posting a total of 340 runs in their first innings. Vic Richardson top-scored with 83 runs, while Harold Larwood took four wickets for 101 runs. In response, England put up a strong fight, led by Herbert Sutcliffe's knock of 86 runs. Bill O'Reilly was the pick of the Australian bowlers, claiming four wickets for 120 runs. Australia's second innings saw them struggle, managing a mere 175 runs, with Len Darling contributing 39 runs. Gubby Allen's three wickets for 44 runs restricted the Australian batsmen. Chasing a target of 176 runs, England reached their goal comfortably, with Maurice Leyland's unbeaten 86 guiding them to victory.

The fifth and final Test at the Sydney Cricket Ground witnessed a strong performance from both teams' middle orders. Australia won the toss and elected to bat, posting a competitive total of 435 runs in their first innings. Len Darling top-scored with 85 runs, while Harold Larwood claimed four wickets for 98 runs. In reply, England responded strongly, with Wally Hammond scoring a brilliant century (101 runs). Philip Lee took four wickets for 111 runs. Australia's second innings witnessed a collapse, courtesy of Hedley Verity's spin bowling. Donald Bradman's valiant 71 runs were not enough to save Australia, as they were bowled out for 182 runs. Set a target of 165 runs, England comfortably reached their goal, winning the match by eight wickets. Wally Hammond, once again, played a crucial role, scoring 75 runs. The Bodyline series of 1932-33 will be remembered as one of the most controversial and fiercely contested Ashes battles in cricket history. The tactics employed by the England team, led by Douglas Jardine, sparked intense debate and discord. Despite the controversy, England emerged triumphant, winning the series 4-1. The performances of players such as Herbert Sutcliffe, Harold Larwood, and Wally Hammond will be etched in cricket folklore. Australia, though defeated, showcased resilience and fighting spirit throughout the series. The Bodyline era left a lasting impact on the game, leading to changes in bowling regulations and tactics.

******

Football in Britain during the 1930s was marked by intense competition, notable teams, and exceptional players. Despite the backdrop of economic challenges and political tensions, football remained a source of joy and unity for the nation. The achievements, rivalries, and memorable moments of this era continue to be celebrated and form an integral part of the rich history of British football.

The Football League and its top division, the First Division, continued to be the pinnacle of professional football in Britain.

The decade witnessed fierce competition between clubs, and several teams emerged as dominant forces. Arsenal, under the management of Herbert Chapman, showcased exceptional performances during the early part of the 1930s. The club won the First Division title in 1931, 1933, 1934, 1935 and 1938 establishing themselves as one of the strongest teams of the era. Led by talented players such as Alex James, Cliff Bastin, and Ted Drake, Arsenal played an exciting and attacking style of football that captivated fans. The rivalry between Arsenal and Tottenham Hotspur reached its peak in the 1930s. The North London derby captivated fans and created a passionate divide between the two sets of supporters. Matches between the two teams were intense and closely contested, adding to the excitement of the era. Another notable team of the period was Everton. Inspired by the legendary Dixie Dean, Everton were Second Division Champions in 1931, won the First Division in 1932 and the FA Cup in 1933 before winning the First Division again in 1939. Dean, a prolific goal scorer, achieved a remarkable feat by scoring a record-breaking 60 league goals during the 1931-32 league campaign, a record that still stands to this day. His goal-scoring prowess and Everton's success made them a significant force in British football during the 1930s.

The FA Cup, the oldest national football competition in the world, continued to be a prestigious tournament that captured the imagination of football enthusiasts. The 1930s saw several memorable FA Cup finals. In 1932, Newcastle United secured a thrilling 2-1 victory over Arsenal in an exciting final, while in 1934, Portsmouth won their first-ever FA Cup, defeating Manchester United. During the 1930s, the Cup also provided an avenue for underdog stories and surprises as smaller clubs such as West Bromwich Albion, Preston North End, and Sunderland achieved success, proving that anything was possible in the competition. The 1930s also witnessed the growth of football broadcasting and the increasing popularity of radio coverage. The British Broadcasting Corporation (BBC) provided live commentary of matches, bringing the excitement of football to homes across the nation. This development helped to further elevate football's status and increase its popularity. However, the decade was not without its challenges. The economic hardships of the Great Depression affected football clubs, leading to financial struggles for many. Some clubs faced difficulties in attracting spectators, and attendance figures fluctuated during this period. Additionally, the approach of World War II in the late 1930s cast a shadow over football and eventually resulted in the suspension of the Football League during the war years.

******

The 1930s saw a shift from the flapper style of the 1920s to a more feminine and sophisticated silhouette. The waistline returned to its natural position, and garments became more form-fitting, accentuating the curves of the body. Hemlines gradually lengthened, and dresses and skirts often reached mid-calf or ankle length. The 1930s were characterised by the introduction of the bias cut, which involved cutting fabric diagonally to create a clingy and fluid drape. This technique, popularised by designer Madeleine Vionnet, resulted in elegant and figure hugging gowns and evening wear. Draping and pleating techniques were also utilised to create soft and graceful lines. Daytime fashion for women in the 1930s often featured tailored suits with padded shoulders and wide-leg trousers. Matching skirt suits were also popular, often worn with blouses featuring large collars and bow ties. Separates, such as sweaters, blouses, and skirts, were mixed and matched for versatility. Floral prints and geometric patterns were common in day dresses.

Men's fashion in the 1930s moved away from the loose and casual styles of the previous decade. Suits became more structured, with broader shoulders and tapered trousers. Double-breasted suits were popular, often worn with contrasting vests and wide ties. Wide-brimmed fedora hats, brogues, and braces were common accessories. Sportswear became increasingly popular in the 1930s, reflecting a growing interest in outdoor activities. Knitted sweaters, polo shirts, and shorts were worn for tennis, golf, and other leisure pursuits. Beachwear featured one-piece swimsuits, often with halter necklines and modest coverage.

Women's hairstyles in the 1930s were typically long and softly waved, with finger waves and curls framing the face. The bob hairstyle, popularised in the 1920s, evolved into more natural-looking and softer styles. Makeup emphasised a pale complexion with rosy cheeks, defined eyebrows, and bold, rounded lips. The glamorous Hollywood film industry had a significant influence on fashion during the 1930s. Film stars like Jean Harlow and Greta Garbo popularised slinky gowns, fur coats, and elegant accessories, setting trends that were emulated by women across Britain.

******

Unlike some other European countries, such as Italy and Germany, fascism did not gain significant political power in Britain during the 1930s. However, some fascist movements and organisations emerged and garnered some support. The rise of fascism in Britain during this period can be understood within the context of the economic and political challenges faced by the country at the time. The British Union of Fascists (BUF), led by Sir Oswald Mosley, was the most prominent fascist organisation in Britain during the 1930s. Mosley, a former member of the

Labour Party, founded the BUF in 1932 and aimed to unite disparate fascist and nationalist groups under one banner. They advocated for a strong authoritarian government, corporatism, and the suppression of political opponents. Mosley adopted several tactics and symbols associated with Italian and German fascism, such as the use of uniforms, marches, and salutes.

The BUF organised large rallies, known as Blackshirt rallies, which attracted some support. Their propaganda emphasised national unity, protectionism, and the idea of a strong leader who could guide Britain out of the economic crisis. However, the BUF faced opposition from various quarters, including anti-fascist organisations, trade unions, and political parties. One significant event that marked the rise of fascism in Britain was the 1936 Battle of Cable Street. The BUF planned a march through the East End of London, which had a significant Jewish and immigrant population. However, an unprecedented coalition of local residents, anti-fascist organisations, and leftist groups formed a massive counter-demonstration, effectively blocking the march and forcing the BUF to abandon their plans. The Battle of Cable Street is often seen as a turning point in the resistance against fascist movements in Britain.

Fascist movements in Britain faced several challenges that limited their growth. The established political parties, including the Conservatives, Labour, and the Liberal Party, were generally united against fascism and actively opposed the BUF. Moreover, the British political system and democratic traditions, coupled with a strong sense of national identity, provided a counterbalance to fascist ideology. Additionally, fascist movements in Britain were fragmented, lacked strong leadership, and struggled to gain a broad appeal beyond a relatively small number of followers. The BUF's support peaked in the mid-1930s but declined afterward. Mosley's attempts to present himself as a viable alternative to mainstream politics ultimately faltered. The outbreak of World War II in 1939 further marginalised fascist movements in Britain. The country's focus shifted to national unity and the fight against Nazi Germany, leading to the internment of Mosley and other prominent fascists due to their perceived threat to national security.

******

Magazines and newspapers were an important part of popular culture. In the 1930s, Britain had a vibrant publishing industry, with numerous magazines and newspapers catering to various interests and readerships. The Illustrated London News was a prominent magazine in Britain during the 1930s. It was a highly regarded weekly publication known for its extensive use of illustrations, engravings, and photographs to document and report on significant events, both domestic and international. The Illustrated London News was already an established publication, having been founded in 1842. By the 1930s, it had a long history and was recognised as one of the leading illustrated magazines in Britain. The magazine covered a wide range of topics, including news, politics, society, arts, culture, science, and exploration. It provided detailed accounts of major events, historical milestones, and social issues of the time. The magazine extensively covered international events during the 1930s, including the rise of Adolf Hitler and the Nazi Party in Germany, the Spanish Civil War, the lead-up to World War II, and notable political developments in other countries. The Illustrated London News remained influential in shaping public opinion and disseminating information throughout the 1930s. It continued to be a valuable source of news, analysis, and visual representation of significant events and cultural developments.

Picture Post, launched in 1938, brought a new style of photojournalism to Britain. It featured large, high-quality photographs that captured the essence of a story and emphasised the human element. The magazine's photographers, including Bert Hardy, Kurt Hutton, and Bill Brandt, employed innovative techniques and approached their subjects with empathy and a sense of intimacy. Picture Post focused on social documentary photography, using images to tell stories about ordinary people and their lives. The magazine covered a wide range of social issues, including poverty, unemployment, housing conditions, and the impact of World War II. Its powerful photographs brought attention to these issues and fostered public awareness and debate. It excelled at portraying human-interest stories that resonated with readers. It captured everyday life and events, showcasing the emotions, struggles, and triumphs of ordinary individuals. By presenting relatable stories, the magazine fostered empathy and understanding among its audience. Picture Post was accessible to a broad readership. It used a combination of striking visuals, engaging captions, and concise text to convey information effectively. The magazine aimed to bridge the gap between serious journalism and popular appeal, making news and current affairs engaging for a wider audience. Its success and innovative approach influenced other publications both in Britain and internationally. Its visual storytelling style and commitment to social documentary photography inspired a new generation of photojournalists and led to the development of similar magazines elsewhere.

The Strand Magazine was also a popular British publication during the 1930s. It was a monthly magazine that focused on a wide range of topics, including fiction, detective stories, non-fiction articles, and general interest content. It was best known for its publication of fictional works, particularly detective stories. It featured stories by renowned authors, including Sir Arthur Conan Doyle's Sherlock Holmes series, which had originally gained popularity through its serialisation in the magazine. Other famous detectives, such as Agatha Christie's Hercule Poirot and Dorothy L. Sayers' Lord Peter Wimsey, also appeared in its pages. The magazine often serialised popular novels, allowing readers to follow stories in installments. This serialised format provided an ongoing narrative and created anticipation among readers for each new issue. Alongside fiction, The Strand Magazine included a variety of non-fiction articles, essays, and general interest content. It covered topics such as history, travel, science, and current events, providing a diverse range of reading material for its audience.

******

In the 1930s, children's comics played a significant role in the entertainment and reading habits of young readers in Britain. While the comics industry was still developing, several notable children's comics were popular during that time. The Dandy was introduced to the British public on 4th December 1937. It was published as a weekly comic book by D.C. Thomson & Co. Ltd. The first issue featured a mix of comic strips, text stories, puzzles, and activities. It included a variety of comic strips featuring different characters. Some notable characters from the early years included Desperate Dan, Keyhole Kate, Korky the Cat, and Danny and His Magic Camera. These characters became iconic figures of The Dandy and remained popular for many years. The Dandy was known for its lighthearted and humorous content. It provided comic strips that focused on slapstick humour, funny situations, and clever wordplay, catering to the entertainment preferences of young readers. The early issues of The Dandy featured colourful and distinctive artwork. The comic strips were typically drawn in a simple and expressive style that appealed to children. The visual humour played an essential role in engaging readers. Alongside The

Dandy The Beano was first published on 30th July 1938, by D.C. Thomson & Co. Ltd. It was also released as a weekly comic book, offering a mix of comic strips, stories, puzzles, and activities. The Beano introduced us to Dennis the Menace, Minnie the Minx, The Bash Street Kids, Lord Snooty, and Biffo the Bear. The Beano was known for its mischievous and anarchic humour, appealing to children with its irreverent tone. The comic strips often featured characters engaging in pranks, causing trouble, and challenging authority figures. Other popular comics of the time included Film Fun, showcasing comedic stories featuring popular film stars of the era. The Rover, featuring action-packed stories, often with a historical or nautical theme. Mickey Mouse Weekly inspired by the popularity of Walt Disney's animated characters and Radio Fun, capitalising on the growing popularity of radio during the 1930s. These comics, and others provided young readers with engaging stories, colourful artwork, and interactive content. They offered a mix of humour, adventure, and popular characters that resonated with children of the time. Many of these comics continued to flourish and became cherished parts of British comic book history.

******

Edward VIII ascended to the throne in January 1936 after the death of his father, King George V. However, his reign was short-lived and tumultuous. Edward's relationship with an American socialite and divorcée, Wallis Simpson, became a major controversy and source of concern for the government and the British establishment. At the time, the Church of England did not recognise divorce, and it was deemed inappropriate for the King to marry a woman who was divorced. This created a conflict between Edward's desire to marry Wallis Simpson and his position as the head of the Church of England.

The government and Prime Minister Stanley Baldwin, as well as various members of the royal family, expressed their opposition to Edward's marriage plans. They believed that such a marriage would be unacceptable and potentially damaging to the monarchy's reputation. Under mounting pressure, Edward VIII had to make a difficult choice between his love for Wallis Simpson and his role as King. In December 1936, just months into his reign, Edward decided to abdicate in favour of marrying Wallis. His abdication speech was broadcast to the nation, in which he famously declared,

"I have found it impossible to carry the heavy burden of responsibility and to discharge my duties as king as I would wish to do without the help and support of the woman I love".

Edward's abdication led to his younger brother, Albert, Duke of York, ascending the throne as King George VI. This unexpected turn of events thrust George VI into the spotlight, and he became a respected and popular monarch, particularly during World War II. The abdication crisis had significant constitutional implications. It highlighted the monarchy's dependence on public opinion and the importance of adhering to traditional values and expectations. It also demonstrated the power of the government and the establishment in influencing the monarch's decisions.

******

Tennis enjoyed considerable popularity during this period, with the Wimbledon Championships serving as a highlight of the British sporting calendar. The Wimbledon Championships of 1933 marked a significant moment in tennis history with the triumph of Fred Perry. The tournament, held at the All England

Lawn Tennis and Croquet Club, witnessed Perry's breakthrough and his first major victory, setting the stage for his future success in the sport. At the time, Fred Perry was a 19-year-old rising star in British tennis. Although he had shown promise in previous tournaments, his victory at Wimbledon in 1933 would elevate him to new heights and establish him as one of the leading players in the world. The road to the final was not an easy one for Perry. He faced strong opponents and had to navigate through the rounds with determination and skill. In the quarterfinals, Perry overcame French player Christian Boussus in a thrilling five-set match, showcasing his tenacity and mental fortitude. In the semifinals, Perry faced Jack Crawford, an Australian player known for his powerful game. Perry displayed remarkable composure and tactical intelligence, outmanoeuvring Crawford to secure a hard-fought victory and a place in the final.

The final of the 1933 Wimbledon Championships featured Fred Perry against Australian player Jack Bromwich. The match took place on 8th July 1933 and would prove to be a pivotal moment in Perry's career. Perry entered the final with a mix of nerves and excitement, aware of the significance of the opportunity before him. The atmosphere at Centre Court was electric as fans eagerly anticipated the clash between the rising British star and the talented Australian opponent. The match itself was a tense and closely contested affair. Perry demonstrated his athletic prowess, agility, and shot-making abilities, while Bromwich countered with his powerful groundstrokes and relentless determination. The two players engaged in captivating rallies, thrilling the spectators with their skills and competitive spirit. In a hard-fought battle, Perry managed to edge past Bromwich, winning the match in four sets with a scoreline of 6-4, 6-3, 3-6, 6-1. The victory opened the door to a remarkable period of success for him. He went on to win two more consecutive Wimbledon titles in 1934 and 1935.

******

The launch of Penguin Paperbacks in Britain in 1935 was a groundbreaking moment in the history of publishing. Penguin Books, founded by Allen Lane, revolutionised the accessibility and affordability of books, making quality literature available to a wider audience. At the time, the publishing industry predominantly catered to the upper classes, with expensive hardcover books being the norm. Lane recognised the need for affordable and portable books that could reach a broader readership. Inspired by a conversation he had at a train station, Lane decided to create a line of high-quality paperbacks that would cost no more than a pack of cigarettes.

On 30th July 1935, the first ten Penguin titles were released. The distinctive design featured bright orange covers, uniform typography, and a logo of a penguin in the corner. The books were priced at sixpence each, which was significantly cheaper than traditional hardcovers. The initial selection of titles included a range of fiction and non-fiction, covering works by notable authors such as Ernest Hemingway, Agatha Christie, and André Maurois. Penguin aimed to provide a mix of classic and contemporary literature, catering to different tastes and interests.

The launch of Penguin Paperbacks was met with both excitement and skepticism. Some critics doubted the viability of paperbacks, questioning whether readers would be willing to buy books of lower quality and durability. However, Penguin's commitment to high editorial standards and the introduction of new printing techniques helped dispel these concerns. The affordability and portability of Penguin books quickly resonated with the public. They became a popular choice for commuters, students, and the general reading public. Penguin's innovative marketing strategies, such as placing book racks in railway stations, further contributed to its success. Penguin's impact went beyond the publishing industry. By making books more accessible and affordable, they democratised reading and broadened the literary tastes of the general public. Penguin Paperbacks played a significant role in promoting literacy and education, allowing people from all walks of life to access a wide range of literature. In addition to their commercial success, Penguin Books also fostered a sense of cultural and intellectual exchange. The Penguin Specials series, launched in 1937, published works on topical issues, politics, and current affairs. These books provided a platform for critical analysis and encouraged public engagement with important social and political debates.

The launch of Penguin Paperbacks also influenced the design and publishing industry. The uniformity of Penguin's cover design and branding set a new standard for book aesthetics. It showcased the potential for books to be both visually appealing and accessible. The success of Penguin Paperbacks paved the way for other publishers to enter the paperback market. The popularity of paperbacks continued to grow throughout the 20th century, eventually becoming the preferred format for many readers.

******

During the 1930s, the town of Jarrow heavily relied on Palmer's shipyard and the Jarrow steelworks for employment. However, in 1931, Palmer's shipyard closed down, leading to the loss of thousands of jobs. This closure had a devastating impact on the local economy, as the shipyard was the primary source of income for the town. The closure of the shipyard was followed by the closure of the Jarrow steelworks in 1934, which further deepened the unemployment crisis in the area. Jarrow faced an unemployment rate of over 70%, causing immense poverty and desperation among the residents.

In response to these dire circumstances, a group of unemployed shipyard workers, led by local Member of Parliament (MP) Ellen Wilkinson, organised the Jarrow March. On 5th October 1936, around 200 men from Jarrow set off on a 300-mile march to London. The purpose of the march was to draw attention to the desperate conditions in Jarrow and to advocate for government intervention to create jobs and alleviate unemployment. The marchers carried a petition, signed by over 11,000 people, which called for the reopening of the shipyard and the provision of financial aid to the town. As the marchers made their way to London, they gained significant public sympathy and support. The Jarrow March became a symbol of the broader unemployment crisis and economic hardships faced by many working-class communities during the Great Depression. Upon reaching London, the marchers presented their petition to the government but were met with disappointment. The government, led by Prime Minister Stanley Baldwin, declined to provide immediate relief for Jarrow and rejected their demands for job creation measures.

While the Jarrow March did not achieve its immediate goals, it brought national attention to the issue of unemployment and the plight of industrial towns like Jarrow. It highlighted the need for government intervention and influenced subsequent policies aimed at tackling unemployment in the following years.

******

The launch of BBC1, the first television channel of the British Broadcasting Corporation (BBC), was a significant milestone in the history of British television. It marked the beginning of regular programming and brought television into the homes of millions of viewers across the country. BBC1 was officially launched on 2nd November 1936. The launch followed years of experimentation and development in television technology, with the BBC leading the way in broadcasting innovation. The channel's inaugural broadcast featured a mix of live performances, news, and other programming.

One of the key events broadcast on BBC1 during its early years was the coronation of King George VI in 1937. This marked an important moment in the channel's history, as it demonstrated the ability of television to bring major national events directly into people's homes, creating a shared viewing experience. In its early years, BBC1 faced several challenges, including limited programming hours and technical constraints. Broadcasting hours were initially limited to a few hours in the evening, and the channel went off the air during the day. Additionally, the number of television sets in households was relatively low, and there were regional variations in signal reception and availability.

Despite these challenges, BBC1 steadily grew in popularity. The channel offered a range of programming, including news, drama, comedy, variety shows, and sports coverage. It quickly became a central source of entertainment and information for the British public.

******

The Treaty of Versailles, which ended World War I, imposed severe restrictions on Germany's military capabilities. However, in the 1930s, Hitler began rearming Germany, openly defying the provisions of the treaty. Recognising the need to respond to this growing threat, Britain, under the leadership of Prime Ministers Stanley Baldwin and later Neville Chamberlain, gradually shifted its policies and started rearmament efforts.

There were several key aspects to Britain's rearmament and preparation for war during this period.

Britain expanded its military forces, particularly the British Army, Royal Navy, and Royal Air Force (RAF). The size of the armed forces was increased, and new equipment and weapons were developed and deployed. This included modernising the navy by building new battleships, cruisers, and aircraft carriers, as well as expanding the RAF's capabilities with new aircraft. In response to the growing threat of aerial bombing, the government introduced Air Raid Precautions (ARP) measures to protect civilians in the event of an attack. This involved building air raid shelters, establishing warning systems, training air raid wardens, and conducting public awareness campaigns. Alongside ARP, civil defence measures were implemented to ensure the protection and resilience of the civilian population. This included training and organising volunteers for various roles, such as first aid, fire fighting, and emergency response.

Britain's rearmament efforts faced challenges due to economic constraints and the lingering impact of the Great Depression. The rearmament process required significant financial resources and diverted funds from other areas, posing economic difficulties for the country. Despite these challenges, Britain's rearmament and preparation for war in the 1930s reflected a recognition of the growing threat posed by Nazi Germany.

Britain's policy of appeasement towards Germany in the 1930s aimed to avoid another devastating world war by satisfying Hitler's demands and maintaining peace in Europe. As Hitler began to challenge the provisions of the Treaty of Versailles and engage in territorial expansion, Britain initially adopted a policy of non-intervention. The scars of World War I were still fresh, and many British leaders and the general public were reluctant to engage in another conflict.

The appeasement policy was based on several key beliefs and objectives. First, it was believed that Germany had legitimate grievances stemming from the harsh terms of the Treaty of Versailles, and addressing these concerns would reduce Hitler's desire for further aggression. Second, the British government hoped that by accommodating Hitler's demands, it could maintain peace and stability in Europe. The policy of appeasement became more pronounced with the British response to Hitler's remilitarisation of the Rhineland in 1936. Despite the violation of the Treaty of Versailles, Britain chose not to take any significant action, and Chamberlain famously declared that the situation was merely a "storm in a teacup". The British government continued its appeasement policy in the face of subsequent aggressive actions by Germany. When Hitler demanded the annexation of the Sudetenland, a region in Czechoslovakia with a significant ethnic German population, Chamberlain and other European leaders pursued negotiations rather than confrontation. The Munich Agreement of 1938 is often seen as the epitome of appeasement. Chamberlain, along with French Prime Minister Édouard Daladier and Italian leader Benito Mussolini, agreed to Hitler's demands and allowed Germany to annex the Sudetenland. The agreement was based on the belief that appeasing Hitler would lead to peace and stability in Europe. However, Hitler's subsequent invasion of Czechoslovakia in 1939 shattered the illusions of appeasement. It became clear that Hitler's ambitions were not satisfied by appeasement and that his aggressive actions would continue unless met with force.

Britain and France declared war on Germany on 3rd September 1939, two days earlier Germany had invaded Poland. The state of war was announced to the British public in a radio broadcast by Neville Chamberlain at 11.00 am with this statement.

"This morning the British ambassador in Berlin handed the German government a final note stating that unless we heard from them by 11 o'clock that they were prepared at once to withdraw their troops from Poland, a state of war would exist between us. I have to tell you now that no such undertaking has been received, and that consequently this country is at war with Germany".

******

Sir Malcolm Campbell was a British racing driver and land speed record holder who became a legendary figure in the world of motorsports. Born on 11th March 1885, in Chislehurst, Kent, Campbell had a lifelong passion for speed and engineering. He went on to break numerous land speed records during the 1920s and 1930s, becoming a symbol of British daring and innovation. Campbell's interest in speed began at a young age when he witnessed a car race at the Brooklands circuit in Surrey. Inspired by the spectacle, he became determined to pursue a career in motorsports. In 1910, he purchased his first car, a secondhand Talbot, and began participating in various racing events. Despite limited success initially, Campbell quickly gained a reputation for his fearless driving style.

Malcom Campbell became the first person to exceed the 150mph limit in July 1925 at Pendine Sands in Carmarthenshire. In total Sir Malcolm Campbell broke nine land speed records the last of which was in September 1935 when Campbell set a new land speed record of 301.337 mph at the Bonneville Salt Flats in Utah, United States. This was the first time a driver exceeded 300 mph. He used a series of specially designed vehicles, each named "Bluebird ", to break records. These streamlined machines were powered by aircraft engines and featured cutting-edge engineering innovations.

Sir Malcolm Campbell was not only a land speed record holder but also a water speed record holder. He achieved several notable records on the water. He broke the water speed record four times between September 1937 and August 1939 in a Blue Bird hydroplane, on the last occasion reaching 141.74mph on Coniston Water in the Lake District. Campbell's pursuit of speed was not without its risks. He faced numerous challenges and dangers during his record attempts, including mechanical failures, crashes, and even injuries. Despite these setbacks, he remained undeterred and continued to push the boundaries of speed. Beyond his accomplishments as a record-breaking driver, Campbell also played a significant role in promoting and advancing motorsports. He was a charismatic and influential figure, using his fame and success to popularise the sport and inspire future generations of racers.

******

One of the key figures of British literature in the 1930s was George Orwell. His works, such as "Down and Out in Paris and London" and "The Road to Wigan Pier", offered powerful insights into poverty, social inequality, and the working class. Orwell's writings combined journalistic observations with literary techniques, showcasing his commitment to social justice and political awareness. In the realm of fiction, authors like Evelyn Waugh, Graham Greene, and Aldous Huxley made significant contributions. Waugh's satirical novels, including "Decline and Fall" and "A Handful of Dust", depicted the decline of British society and the moral decay of the upper class. Graham Greene's works, such as "Brighton Rock", explored themes of guilt, sin, and Catholicism against the backdrop of a morally ambiguous world. Aldous Huxley's dystopian novel

"Brave New World" presented a chilling vision of a future society controlled by technology and consumerism.

The 1930s also saw the emergence of a group of writers known as the Auden Generation, led by W.H. Auden. Auden's poetry, with its social commentary, reflected the anxieties and political turmoil of the era. His collection "Look, Stranger!" captured the sense of unease and disillusionment prevalent during the time. Dorothy L. Sayers, known for her detective fiction, continued to produce popular works during this decade. Her character Lord Peter Wimsey featured in novels like "Strong Poison" and "Murder Must Advertise", combining elements of mystery, wit, and social commentary. Virginia Woolf, a prominent member of the Bloomsbury Group, continued to push the boundaries of narrative and consciousness in works like "The Waves" and "The Years". Her stream of consciousness style and innovative storytelling techniques challenged traditional literary conventions.

In addition to these individual voices, literary magazines and journals played a crucial role in shaping the literary landscape of the 1930s. The publication of influential literary magazines like "The Criterion" and "The Adelphi" provided platforms for writers to share their works and engage in intellectual debates. These publications fostered a sense of community among writers and facilitated the exchange of ideas.

Overall, British literature in the 1930s was marked by a diversity of voices and a heightened sense of social and political consciousness. From Orwell's social critiques to Auden's poetic reflections and the experimentation of the Bloomsbury Group, writers of this period grappled with the complexities of their time and left a lasting impact on the literary landscape.

******

One prominent artistic movement of the 1930s was the Euston Road School, a group of realist painters who sought to depict everyday life and the urban landscape. Artists such as William Coldstream, Victor Pasmore, and Graham Bell emphasised careful observation, capturing scenes of ordinary people and the changing face of the city. Their work reflected a desire to represent the social realities of the time with honesty and authenticity. Another significant development was the emergence of Surrealism in Britain. Influenced by the ideas of Sigmund Freud and the European Surrealist movement, British artists embraced the exploration of the subconscious and the irrational. The British Surrealists, including artists like Eileen Agar, Edward Burra, and Roland Penrose, produced works that combined dreamlike imagery, symbolic motifs, and elements of surprise and juxtaposition.

Political and social concerns were also reflected in the art of the 1930s. The impact of the Great Depression and the rise of fascism in Europe led to a heightened awareness of class struggles and political activism. The Artists International Association (AIA) was established in 1933 as a platform for politically engaged art, organising exhibitions and fostering dialogue on social and political issues. Artists associated with the AIA, such as Edward Ardizzone and Clifford Rowe, used their art to address issues of social injustice and the rise of totalitarianism.

The 1930s also saw a revival of interest in traditional crafts and design. The Arts and Crafts movement, which originated in the late 19th century, experienced a resurgence as artists and designers sought to reconnect with the handmade and the natural world. The work of Eric Gill, Edward Johnston, and Bernard Leach exemplified this return to craftsmanship, with their focus on typography, calligraphy, and pottery. In addition to these movements, the 1930s also saw the continuation of modernist tendencies in British art. Artists like Ben Nicholson, Barbara Hepworth, and Henry Moore explored abstraction, geometric forms, and the interplay of light and space. They were influenced by continental European movements such as Cubism and Constructivism, which challenged traditional notions of representation and sought to create a new visual language. Furthermore, photography gained recognition as an art form during this period. Pioneering photographers such as Bill Brandt, Angus McBean, and Cecil Beaton explored new techniques, documented social conditions, and captured the spirit of the time through their images. It is important to note that art in the 1930s was not confined to a singular style or ideology. Artists experimented with different approaches and mediums, reflecting the diversity of their experiences and perspectives. The art of the era showcased a range of artistic responses to the changing world, from realism to abstraction, social commentary to the exploration of the subconscious.

******

In the early 1930s, W.H. Auden emerged as a key figure of a group of poets known as the Auden Generation or the Oxford Group. Alongside poets such as Stephen Spender, C. Day Lewis, and Louis MacNeice, Auden rejected the prevailing modernist aesthetics of the previous decade and sought to create poetry that was more accessible, politically engaged, and relevant to contemporary concerns. Auden's poetry in the 1930s reflected his evolving political and philosophical beliefs. Initially, he was drawn to left-wing ideologies and engaged with socialist and Marxist ideas. His collection "Poems" expressed concern for social justice and the struggles of the working class. In works like "Spain", Auden addressed the Spanish Civil War, expressing his support for the Republican cause and his disillusionment with totalitarianism.

However, as the decade progressed, Auden's political views transformed. He became disenchanted with the political left and turned towards a more conservative stance, embracing Christianity and exploring existential questions. This shift in his thinking is evident in his collection "Another Time", which showcases a more introspective and spiritual approach to poetry. Auden's poetry of the 1930s often combined personal and political themes, reflecting the turbulent times in which he lived. He employed a distinctive voice characterised by a conversational tone, a wide-ranging intellect, and a keen sense of irony. His poems grappled with issues of love, loss, societal decay, and the search for meaning in a world that seemed increasingly uncertain.

One of Auden's most famous poems from the 1930s is "September 1, 1939", written in response to the outbreak of World War II. The poem explores themes of fear, disillusionment, and the erosion of individual liberties in the face of political upheaval. It also reflects Auden's struggle with his role as a poet and the responsibility of art in times of crisis. Beyond his poetry, Auden's essays and critical writings also made a significant impact during this period. His essay "The Poet and the City" explored the relationship between poetry and politics, emphasising the poet's role as a critical observer and a conscience of society.

******

The 1936 Berlin Olympics were significant because they took place during a period of growing tension and political turmoil in Europe, leading up to World War II. Initially, there were debates within Britain about whether to participate in the Olympics hosted by Nazi Germany. Some individuals and groups called for a boycott due to Hitler's anti-Semitic policies and the persecution of Jews in Germany. However, the British Olympic Association ultimately decided to participate, believing that the Olympics could promote international understanding and sportsmanship. The British delegation consisted of 208 competitors in 17 sports. Britain won a total of 14 medals, including four gold, seven silver, and three bronze, the gold medals were won in athletics, yachting and rowing.

******

The 1930s witnessed a rise in nationalist movements and demands for independence across various British colonies. In India, the Indian National Congress, led by figures like Mahatma Gandhi, called for self-rule and independence. Similarly, nationalist movements emerged in African colonies, such as Nigeria and Kenya, demanding greater autonomy. In 1931, the British Parliament passed the Statute of Westminster, which granted self-government and full legal autonomy to the dominions of the British Empire, including Canada, Australia, New Zealand, and South Africa. This marked an important step in the process of granting greater independence to these dominions.

The threat of war and geopolitical tensions prompted the British Empire to prioritise defence and security. The Royal Navy continued to play a crucial role in safeguarding imperial interests, maintaining a global presence and protecting trade routes. The British Empire also relied on the strategic alliance with the Commonwealth countries to enhance its defence capabilities. In the 1930s, the British Empire saw some territorial changes. In 1935, Italy invaded Ethiopia (then Abyssinia), prompting international condemnation but limited action to protect Ethiopian sovereignty. In 1937, the British Raj in India saw the creation of the new provinces of Orissa and Sind, aimed at addressing regional demands for self-governance.

1940s
Rationing and Parliamentary Coalitions

The 1940s was a decade of immense significance for Britain as the nation faced the challenges and repercussions of World War II. The decade began with Britain already at war with Germany. The early years of the 1940s were marked by the Battle of Britain, a pivotal aerial conflict between the Royal Air Force (RAF) and the German Luftwaffe. The RAF's successful defence against German air attacks played a crucial role in preventing a German invasion and boosting British morale. The war effort became all-encompassing, affecting every aspect of British society. Rationing was introduced to ensure the fair distribution of scarce resources. Food, clothing, and other essential items were rationed, leading to a collective sense of sacrifice and solidarity among the population. Women played a vital role in the war effort, taking up jobs in industries previously dominated by men, such as munitions production and transportation. The Blitz, a sustained bombing campaign by the German Luftwaffe, devastated British cities, most notably London. The civilian population endured regular air raids, leading to widespread destruction and loss of life. However, amidst the chaos, the resilience and spirit of the British people shone through, as communities came together to support one another and rebuild their lives.

Politically, the war led to a coalition government, with Winston Churchill serving as Prime Minister. Churchill's leadership during the war was pivotal in galvanising the nation and inspiring determination in the face of adversity. The war also brought about a newfound sense of unity among political parties, as they worked together to ensure victory over the Axis powers. The social fabric of Britain underwent significant changes during the 1940s. The war provided opportunities for social mobility, as people from different backgrounds worked side by side for a common cause. The Women's Auxiliary Air Force (WAAF) and Women's Auxiliary Territorial Service (ATS) allowed women to serve in non-combat roles within the armed forces, contributing to the changing roles and status of women in society. The war also had a profound impact on cultural life in Britain. The entertainment industry played a crucial role in boosting morale, with films, music, and theatre providing an escape from the hardships of daily life. Popular entertainers such as Vera Lynn became symbols of hope and inspiration through their performances and songs. In 1945, the war finally came to an end, marking the beginning of a new era for Britain. The post-war years were characterised by the challenges of reconstruction and the establishment of a new world order. The Labour Party, led by Clement Attlee, won the general election of 1945 and implemented a series of social reforms. The National Health Service (NHS) was established in 1948, providing free healthcare for all, and measures were taken to address social inequality and create a welfare state.

Britain's international standing was transformed during the 1940s. The war led to the decline of the British Empire, as colonies in India, Africa, and the Caribbean sought independence. The partition of India in 1947 resulted in the creation of India and Pakistan as separate nations, while nationalist movements gained momentum in other parts of the empire. The 1940s in Britain was a decade of challenges, sacrifice, and resilience. The impact of World War II left an indelible mark on the nation, both physically and emotionally. The war effort brought about social changes and advancements, including the recognition of women's contributions and the establishment of a welfare state. The post-war period marked a new chapter in British history, with the nation rebuilding and redefining its role on the world stage.

******

Popular music in Britain in the 1940s was diverse and encompassed various genres and styles. The decade was marked by the impact of World War II, which influenced the themes and sentiments of many songs. Big band swing music was incredibly popular during this era with band leaders like Glenn Miller and Benny Goodman gaining popularity. They played energetic and rhythmic music that encouraged dancing and uplifted spirits during a challenging time. Given the wartime context, sentimental and patriotic songs resonated strongly with the British public. Vera Lynn, known as the "Forces' Sweetheart", became an iconic figure with songs like "We'll Meet Again" and "The White Cliffs of Dover". These songs conveyed messages of hope, unity, and longing for loved ones. Crooners and vocalists played a significant role in the popular music scene of the 1940s. Artists like Bing Crosby, Frank Sinatra, and Nat King Cole gained popularity in Britain as their smooth, romantic ballads provided an escape from the realities of war and evoked a sense of nostalgia and romance. Dance halls were also an essential part of British social life in the 1940s, providing a space for people to gather and enjoy live music. Dance bands like those led by Joe Loss, Harry Roy, and Geraldo provided the energetic and lively music necessary for dancing and entertainment. Traditional popular music, characterised by catchy melodies and easy-to-sing-along lyrics, remained popular in the 1940s. Artists like Gracie Fields, Anne Shelton, and George Formby entertained audiences with their cheerful and often humorous songs. While the popularity of music halls and vaudeville declined during this period, they still had a presence in the entertainment scene. These shows featured a variety of acts, including comedic skits, musical performances, and novelty acts.

******

At the outset of the decade, Britain was led by Prime Minister Neville Chamberlain, who was replaced by Winston Churchill in May 1940 as a coalition government was formed to unite political parties and harness the collective effort in the face of the global conflict. This coalition government played a critical role in steering the country through the war years and coordinating the war effort. The coalition included members from the Conservative Party, Labour Party, and Liberal Party, forming what was known as the "National Government". This cross-party collaboration was essential for maintaining national unity and pooling together the talents and expertise of politicians from different backgrounds. The government aimed to address the challenges posed by the war in a united and efficient manner. It allowed Churchill to draw on a broad range of knowledge and experience within the political spectrum. By including members from different parties, it demonstrated a commitment to national interests above partisan politics.

One of the notable figures within the coalition government was Clement Attlee, the leader of the Labour Party. Attlee served as the Deputy Prime Minister and played a significant role in coordinating domestic affairs and supporting Churchill's leadership during the war. Attlee later succeeded Churchill as the Prime Minister in 1945 when the Labour Party won the general elections held shortly after the end of the war. The coalition government focused on key areas such as military strategy, defence production, rationing, and civilian morale. Churchill's leadership was crucial in inspiring the nation and rallying support for the war effort. His speeches, such as the famous "We Shall Fight on the Beaches" address, became rallying cries for the British people and conveyed the spirit of resilience and determination. The government also worked closely with the military and established strong communication channels to ensure effective coordination between political leadership and the armed forces. This collaboration was essential for decision-making, strategic planning, and maintaining morale among the troops. What is more, the coalition government played a vital role in strengthening Britain's alliances with other nations, particularly the United States and the Soviet Union. Churchill worked closely with U.S. President Franklin D. Roosevelt and Soviet Premier Joseph Stalin to forge the Grand Alliance, which coordinated the efforts of the Allied powers in defeating Nazi Germany. The World War II coalition government in Britain demonstrated the power of unity and collective action in times of crisis. It showcased the ability to set aside political differences and work towards a common goal. This collaboration and shared sense of purpose were instrumental in navigating the challenges of the war and ultimately achieving victory.

******

During the war years in Britain regular football league competitions were suspended. Instead, alternative football leagues were established to provide entertainment and maintain morale among the public during the war. These alternative leagues were known as War Leagues. The Football League, which consisted of the top four tiers of English football, was suspended after the 1939-1940 season. It did not resume until the 1946-1947 season. During the war years, football clubs organised regional competitions to keep the sport alive. These regional competitions varied in structure and organisation, with teams often representing towns, cities, or regions. One of the main war competitions was the Football League War Cup, which was held annually between 1939 and 1945. This cup tournament involved clubs from the Football League and non-league teams. West Ham United, Portsmouth, Wolverhampton Wanderers, and Bolton Wanderers were among the successful clubs in the Football League War Cup. In addition to the Football League War Cup, various regional war leagues were established to provide competitive football. These leagues included the Football League North and South, the London League, the Midland League, the Southern League, and many others. The teams participating in these leagues were often made up of guest players, servicemen, and youth players, as many professional footballers had enlisted in the armed forces. It's worth noting that during this period, football stadiums were also used for other purposes related to the war effort.

******

George Formby, born George Hoy Booth, was a prominent entertainer in Britain during the 1940s. He was renowned for his unique comedic style, ukulele playing, and cheeky sense of humour. Formby's popularity reached its peak in the 1930s, but he continued to entertain audiences throughout the 1940s, making a significant impact on the music and comedy scene of the era. Formby's distinctive persona and repertoire were characterised by a blend of comedy, catchy songs, and his virtuosic ukulele playing. His songs often had humorous and double entendre laden lyrics, delivering lighthearted entertainment during a time of war and uncertainty. He was known for his cheeky charm and catchy tunes that resonated with the British public, providing them with much-needed laughter and enjoyment. During the 1940s, Formby's career faced challenges due to the war's impact on the entertainment industry. Many venues were closed or repurposed for wartime efforts, and the availability of resources for performers was limited. However, Formby adapted to these circumstances and found ways to continue entertaining his fans.

Formby's films, which had been highly successful in the 1930s, remained popular during the 1940s. His movies, such as "Let George Do It" and "Turned Out Nice Again", showcased his comedic talents and musical performances. These films provided escapism and laughter to audiences who sought relief from the realities of the war. Formby's music was also a source of comfort and entertainment. His catchy tunes, often accompanied by his trademark ukulele, offered an upbeat and cheerful respite. Some of his popular songs from the 1940s include "Bless 'Em All", "Leaning on a Lamp Post", and "It's Turned Out Nice Again". These songs captured the spirit of the times and allowed people to momentarily forget their worries. In addition to his films and music, Formby contributed to the war effort through his performances. He entertained troops and worked to boost morale through his comedic acts. He became an honorary sergeant in the Royal Air Force, and his performances for the armed forces were highly appreciated. Formby's presence on the entertainment front played a role in uplifting the spirits of both soldiers and civilians during the challenging war years. Despite the challenges of the wartime era, George Formby's popularity remained strong. His distinct style, combining comedy and music, offered a unique form of entertainment that appealed to a wide audience. His performances brought joy and laughter to the British public, providing a much-needed escape from the harsh realities of the time.

******

Cinema in Britain during the 1940s underwent significant changes and faced unique challenges due to the impact of World War II. The war affected all aspects of the film industry, from production to exhibition, and had a profound influence on the themes, styles, and content of British films. War films and propaganda played a prominent role in British cinema during the 1940s. With the outbreak of World War II in 1939, the British film industry became an essential tool for the government to boost morale, promote patriotism, and support the war effort. War films in the 1940s aimed to foster a sense of national unity and pride among the British people. They depicted heroic soldiers, brave civilians, and the collective strength of the nation. These films emphasised the importance of sacrifice and perseverance in the face of adversity. War films often portrayed the heroism and bravery of soldiers and their contribution to the war effort. They showcased the valour and determination of

British servicemen, highlighting their sacrifices and showcasing them as role models for the audience.

Many war films of the 1940s sought to depict the realities of war. They portrayed the harsh conditions faced by soldiers, the emotional toll of combat, and the devastating impact of the conflict on both individuals and communities. These films aimed to convey the seriousness and gravity of the situation. War films also portrayed the enemy forces, often depicting them as villainous or brutal. This portrayal served to demonise the enemy and reinforce the idea of British righteousness and the justness of the war. These films aimed to maintain public support and bolster the national spirit.

The government used cinema as a medium for propaganda and public information during the war years. Films were produced to disseminate important messages, such as rationing, air raid precautions, and other aspects of the home front. They aimed to educate and inform the public while maintaining morale and unity. These films provided firsthand accounts, coverage of battles, and insights into the experiences of soldiers and civilians. They contributed to the dissemination of information and created a sense of solidarity among the British population.

While war films primarily served propaganda purposes, there were also films produced for entertainment and escapism. These films offered audiences a break from the grim realities of war, providing lighter and more comedic narratives that offered temporary respite and distraction. Ealing Studios emerged as a significant production company during the 1940s, known for producing a variety of films, particularly comedies. The studio gained popularity with its lighthearted and often satirical films, providing much-needed laughter during a difficult period. Films like "Passport to Pimlico" and "Whisky Galore!" showcased the British sense of humour and offered a sense of escapism. The

1940s witnessed a shift towards realism and films that addressed social issues. Directors like David Lean and Carol Reed explored darker and more somber themes in their films. Lean's "Brief Encounter" portrayed an illicit love affair, while Reed's "The Fallen Idol" delved into the complex dynamics of childhood and deceit. The 1940s witnessed an increase in female filmmakers and a focus on female representation in British cinema. Directors like Muriel Box and Wendy Toye emerged during this period, challenging gender norms and offering different perspectives. Films like "The Seventh Veil", directed by Compton Bennett and featuring strong female characters, showcased a growing recognition of women's roles both behind and in front of the camera.

As the war ended, British cinema underwent a period of rejuvenation. The industry experienced a surge in creativity and a broader range of themes and styles. Directors like Michael Powell and Emeric Pressburger created innovative and critically acclaimed films such as "The Red Shoes" and "A Matter of Life and Death", showcasing the artistic possibilities of British cinema. It's important to note that the war had a significant impact on the film industry in terms of resources, censorship, and the ability to produce and distribute films. Rationing and shortages affected the availability of film stock, while censorship boards controlled the content to maintain national morale and security.

******

Glenn Miller, a renowned American bandleader and musician, had a significant impact on Britain during the 1940s. Miller and his orchestra became immensely popular, and their music played a crucial role in boosting morale and providing entertainment during the challenging years of World War II. In 1944, Miller brought his band to Britain as part of the U.S. military's efforts to entertain the troops stationed there. Their arrival created a wave of excitement, as Miller was already a well-known figure due to his successful career in the United States.

His big band sound, characterised by its smooth, melodic arrangements, captured the hearts of the British public. Miller's music, often referred to as "swing", was highly infectious and encouraged dancing and a sense of unity. Songs like "In the Mood", "Moonlight Serenade", and "Chattanooga Choo Choo" became instant hits in Britain, captivating audiences with their catchy melodies and lively rhythms. The orchestra's performances, both live and on the radio, provided a much-needed escape from the harsh realities of war and became an integral part of British culture at the time.

Miller's time in Britain was cut short, tragically, as he went missing in December 1944 when his plane disappeared over the English Channel. His untimely death only added to his legend, and he became a symbol of the wartime era and the impact of his music. Despite his short time in Britain, Glenn Miller left an indelible mark on the country's music scene. His music continued to be celebrated and played on the radio, providing comfort and entertainment to the British public throughout the 1940s. The Glenn Miller Orchestra, led by various musicians after Miller's death, carried on his legacy and kept his music alive. Miller's influence extended beyond the war years. His music played a significant role in shaping the post-war popular music scene, contributing to the development of new genres and styles. His fusion of big band swing with elements of jazz and pop paved the way for future artists and bands.

******

The Blitz was a strategic bombing offensive conducted by the German Luftwaffe between 7th September 1940 and 11th May 1941 primarily targeting major cities and industrial centres in England. The main objective was to weaken the British morale, destroy their war industry, and force the British government to surrender or seek a negotiated peace with Germany. London, being the capital city and a major hub, was a primary target, but other cities like Birmingham, Coventry, Liverpool, and Manchester also suffered heavy bombardment.

The impact of the Blitz on the population of Britain was profound. The constant threat of air raids created a state of fear and uncertainty among civilians, forcing them to make adjustments to their daily lives. Many people sought shelter in underground stations, basements, or purpose-built air raid shelters. The government distributed gas masks and implemented blackout measures to protect civilians from aerial attacks at night. These measures aimed to minimise casualties and maintain public morale. The bombings resulted in a significant loss of life and property. Tens of thousands of civilians were killed, and hundreds of thousands were injured. Entire neighbourhoods and historic landmarks were reduced to rubble. London, in particular, experienced heavy damage, however, despite the destruction, the British people demonstrated remarkable resilience and determination.

The shared experience of enduring the bombings created a sense of solidarity and camaraderie among the British people. Communities came together to support each other, and acts of bravery and heroism became commonplace. The image of the stoic Londoners enduring the bombings and carrying on with their lives became a symbol of British resilience and defiance. The Blitz did not achieve its intended objective of breaking

British morale or forcing the government to surrender. Instead, it strengthened the resolve of the British people and galvanised their determination to resist Nazi Germany. The spirit of resilience displayed during the Blitz became an enduring symbol of national identity and was instrumental in shaping the course of the war.

******

During World War II, the Labour Party in Britain played a significant role in implementing social reforms and shaping policies that aimed to address the social and economic challenges of the time. As part of the coalition government led by Prime Minister Winston Churchill, the Labour Party had an opportunity to influence and contribute to the war effort and the domestic policies implemented during the war. The Labour Party, under the leadership of Clement Attlee, focused on improving the welfare and well-being of the British people during the war. In 1942, the government introduced the Beveridge Report, which outlined a comprehensive plan for social security and welfare reforms. The report was largely influenced by the ideas of the Labour Party. It proposed a system of universal social insurance, protecting against various social risks, such as unemployment, sickness, and old age.

The Labour Party placed a strong emphasis on education during the war. The 1944 Education Act, often referred to as the "Butler Act" after Conservative politician R.A. Butler, was supported by the Labour Party. The act aimed to provide free and compulsory education for all children aged 5 to 15. It also sought to introduce a tripartite system of education, which included grammar schools, secondary modern schools, and technical schools. The Labour Party played a significant role in advancing the provision of healthcare services during World War

II. The Emergency Medical Service (EMS) was established in 1939, before the war, as a response to the threat of air raids. The EMS provided medical care and emergency services during the war and laid the groundwork for the post-war establishment of the National Health Service (NHS) in 1948. The Labour Party recognised the need for improved housing conditions, particularly for those affected by the bombings and the housing shortages caused by the war. The government introduced the Temporary Housing Programme to address the immediate housing needs. The Labour Party advocated for the construction of affordable and quality homes for the working class and aimed to tackle the issue of slum housing.

******

The 1946-47 Ashes series between Australia and England concluded with a resounding victory for the Australian cricket team. Led by the formidable Don Bradman, the Australians defeated England 3-0 in the five-match series, retaining the Ashes and inflicting England's worst defeat in a Test series since 1924-25. The English cricket team, under the captaincy of Wally Hammond, arrived in Australia for a "Goodwill Tour" aimed at re-establishing sporting relations after the Second World War. Despite their sound team composition, which was considered on par with Australia's, England faced significant challenges due to the aging nature of their side. With only Godfrey Evans under the age of 28, the team heavily relied on Alec Bedser and Doug Wright for their bowling prowess. Unfortunately, Bedser and Wright were overused and exhausted from shouldering the bowling responsibilities. The Australian selectors, on the other hand, opted for experienced cricketers who had made their names in the 1930s. Their selection strategy seemed inclined towards pleasing the English public, who were more familiar with the older players. Only a few newcomers, such as Alec Bedser, Godfrey Evans, and Norman Yardley, who had played little or no first-class cricket before the war, made it into the squad.

The first Test of the series took place in Brisbane from 29th November to 4th December 1946. Australia dominated the match, scoring a massive total of 645 runs in their first innings, led by Don Bradman's 187 and Lindsay Hassett's 128. England struggled to respond and were dismissed for 141 runs, with Ken Rutherford Miller taking seven wickets for 60 runs. Following on, England fared no better, managing only 176 runs. Australia won the match by an innings and 332 runs, setting the tone for the series to come.

The second Test, held in Sydney from 13th to 19th December 1946, saw England once again falter against Australia's strong performance. England scored 255 runs in their first innings, with Bill Edrich top-scoring with 79 runs. In response, Australia piled on a mammoth total of 659 for 8 declared, driven by double centuries from Sid Barnes 234 and Don Bradman also 234. Facing a deficit of 404 runs, England struggled and could only manage 371 runs. Australia won the match by an innings and 33 runs.

The third Test, held in Melbourne from 1st to 7th January 1947, saw a draw, which was a rarity in Tests played in Australia at the time. Australia scored 365 runs in their first innings, with Colin McCool remaining unbeaten on 104. England responded with 351 runs, led by Bill Edrich's 89. In their second innings, Australia posted a formidable total of 536 runs, with Arthur Morris 155 and Ray Lindwall 100 making significant contributions. England, in their chase, reached 310 for 7 before the match ended in a draw.

The fourth Test, held in Adelaide from 31st January to 6th February 1947, witnessed a competitive match between the two teams. England scored 460 runs in their first innings, with Denis Compton leading the charge with 147. In response, Australia posted 487 runs, courtesy of individual from Keith Miller who scored 141 not out and Arthur Morris' 122. England declared their second innings at 340 for 8, with Compton scoring 103 not out. Australia, requiring 201 runs for victory, reached 215 for 1 before the match ended in a draw.

The fifth and final Test, played at the Sydney Cricket Ground from 28th February to 5th March 1947, saw Australia secure a five-wicket victory. England scored 280 runs in their first innings, with Len Hutton remaining unbeaten on 122. Ray Lindwall's exceptional bowling performance of 7 for 63 restricted England's total. In response, Australia scored 253 runs, with Sid Barnes contributing 71. Chasing a target of 186 runs, Australia achieved victory with five wickets in hand. The 1946-47 Ashes series was a resounding success for the Australian cricket team, as they dominated England throughout the contest. The English side, burdened by the challenges of an aging team and overworked bowlers, struggled to match the performance of their Australian counterparts. Don Bradman's leadership and Australia's strong batting lineup proved to be the difference between the two teams. Despite the defeat, the English team upheld the spirit of goodwill on their tour, refraining from public complaints about what they perceived as incompetence on the part of the Australian umpires. The series highlighted the disparity between the two teams and left England with much to ponder as they sought to regain the Ashes in future encounters.

******

The war had a profound effect on the theatre industry, with many venues being repurposed or destroyed, resources being scarce, and restrictions on productions. Despite these obstacles, theatre continued to thrive and adapt, offering a range of performances that reflected the times and provided both escapism and commentary on the war and its aftermath. During the war, theatres played a crucial role in boosting morale and raising funds for the war effort. Numerous productions were geared towards supporting patriotic sentiments and encouraging unity. These included plays that highlighted British heroism, showcased the spirit of resistance, or offered comedic relief.

War-themed plays and musicals, such as "Flare Path" by Terence Rattigan, portrayed the challenges faced by servicemen and the resilience of the home front. Theatre also played a significant role in entertaining troops. Many actors and performers volunteered to travel and perform for servicemen stationed both at home and abroad. These performances were an important source of entertainment and offered a brief escape from the harsh realities of war. Organisations like the Entertainments National Service Association (ENSA) organised shows and concerts for the armed forces, featuring popular actors, comedians, and musicians of the time.

Theatre in the 1940s also served as a platform for political and social commentary. Playwrights such as George Bernard Shaw and J.B. Priestley used their work to explore social issues and question prevailing norms. Their plays often addressed topics such as class divisions, inequality, and the need for social change. Works like Priestley's "An Inspector Calls" and Shaw's "Heartbreak House" provided audiences with thought-provoking and critical examinations of society. The post-war years saw the emergence of new theatrical movements.

The Theatre Workshop, led by Joan Littlewood, pioneered a style of "documentary theatre", combining factual research, interviews, and performance to shed light on social issues. This innovative approach sought to engage audiences in a more participatory and socially conscious manner.

******

The Beveridge Report of 1942, officially titled "Social Insurance and Allied Services", was a significant document that laid the foundation for the development of the modern welfare state in Britain. The report was authored by Sir William Beveridge, a social economist, and it outlined a comprehensive plan for social security and welfare reforms. The British government recognised the need to address the social and economic challenges faced by the nation during and after the war, including issues such as poverty, unemployment and inadequate social support systems. The report aimed to provide a blueprint for a post-war society that would ensure economic security and social justice for all citizens. The key principles and proposals outlined in the Beveridge Report included:

The report proposed a system of universal social insurance that would cover all citizens, regardless of their income, employment status, or social background. The concept of universalism aimed to ensure that social welfare benefits and services were available to everyone as a matter of right, rather than being means-tested or limited to specific groups. The Beveridge Report argued that a universal social insurance system would be more effective and efficient than a selective or means-tested approach. By encompassing all citizens, regardless of their income or employment status, it aimed to avoid the stigma associated with means-tested benefits and create a sense of shared ownership and entitlement. According to the report, universal social insurance would be financed through contributions from both employers and employees, creating a sense of collective responsibility and shared investment in the welfare system.

The benefits provided under this system would include unemployment benefits, sickness benefits, maternity benefits, and retirement pensions. The concept of universalism in the Beveridge Report was influential in shaping subsequent social policy developments in Britain. It laid the foundation for the establishment of the welfare state and influenced the design of key social programs, such as the National Health Service (NHS) and the social security system. The Beveridge Report identified what it called the "five giant evils" that needed to be tackled in order to create a more equitable and prosperous society.

"WANT" referred to poverty and economic insecurity. The report emphasised the need to alleviate poverty and provide a minimum standard of living for all citizens. It recommended the establishment of a comprehensive social insurance system to provide financial support for those facing unemployment, sickness, and other forms of economic hardship.

"DISEASE" focused on the need to improve public health and healthcare services. The report called for the creation of a National Health Service (NHS) that would ensure access to healthcare for all, regardless of income or social status. This vision laid the foundation for the establishment of the NHS in 1948.

"IGNORANCE" referred to the lack of educational opportunities and inadequate access to knowledge and skills. The report highlighted the importance of education in creating equal opportunities and recommended the expansion of educational provisions, including free and compulsory education for all children up to the age of 15. This recommendation laid the groundwork for the Education Act of 1944.

"SQUALOR" referred to poor housing conditions, overcrowding, and inadequate living environments. The report emphasised the need for improved housing and urban planning. It called for the construction of quality homes and the elimination of slums, aiming to provide safe and decent housing for all citizens.

"IDLENESS" focused on unemployment and the need to promote full employment. The report recognised the importance of job creation and the active engagement of individuals in the labor market. It called for government intervention to stimulate employment opportunities and reduce unemployment rates.

The identification of these five giant evils reflected the recognition that social and economic problems were interconnected and needed to be addressed comprehensively. The Beveridge Report aimed to provide a blueprint for a post-war society that would tackle these challenges and create a more inclusive and equitable society.

The report suggested the introduction of family allowances to provide financial assistance to families with children. It aimed to alleviate child poverty and promote the well-being of families. It emphasised the importance of achieving full employment and called for the government to take an active role in creating job opportunities and reducing unemployment. The publication of the Beveridge Report sparked widespread public debate and generated significant public support for its proposals. The report's recommendations were highly influential and laid the groundwork for subsequent social welfare reforms in post-war Britain. Many of its ideas were eventually implemented through legislation, including the establishment of the National Health Service (NHS) in 1948 and the Social Security Act of 1946.

******

The 1948 Summer Olympics were held in London, England. The Games took place from 29th July to 14th August 1948 and marked the first Olympics held since the outbreak of World War II. The aftermath of the war presented numerous challenges, including a scarcity of resources, rationing, and the need for post-war reconstruction. Despite these difficulties, the organisers were determined to stage the Olympics as a symbol of international unity and peace. The London Olympics of 1948 were often referred to as the "Austerity Games" due to the economic constraints and modest preparations. The focus was on utilising existing facilities and improvising wherever possible. Many venues that were damaged during the war were repaired and brought back into use for the Games.

The British delegation consisted of 404 competitors in 21 sports. Britain won a total of 23 medals, including three gold, fourteen silver, and six bronze. the gold medals were won in yachting and rowing. The British athletes' achievements were particularly notable considering the limited resources and the fact that they were still recovering from the war's effects.

******

Literature in 1940s Britain was shaped by the tumultuous events of World War II and its aftermath. The war had a profound impact on the literary landscape, influencing the themes, styles, and perspectives of British writers during this period. The war loomed large in literature during the 1940s. Many writers focused on depicting the experiences of soldiers, civilians, and the impact of war on society. War novels, such as Evelyn

Waugh's "Sword of Honour" trilogy, Graham Greene's "The Ministry of Fear", and Elizabeth Bowen's "The Heat of the Day", explored the moral, psychological, and social consequences of war. The 1940s witnessed a rise in social realism and working-class literature, giving voice to previously marginalised communities. Novels began to depict the struggles and aspirations of working-class individuals, addressing issues such as poverty, inequality, and social injustice. As the war came to an end, literature began to reflect on the challenges of reconstruction, social change, and the rebuilding of society.

J.B. Priestley, an influential British playwright, novelist, and social commentator, had a significant impact on the cultural and political landscape of 1940s Britain. Priestley's works during this period reflected his concerns about social inequality, the impact of war, and the need for collective responsibility. Priestley was deeply concerned with social justice and equality. His plays often depicted the stark divisions between social classes and highlighted the need for a more compassionate and equitable society. Priestley believed that the war had exposed the flaws in the British class system and argued for a more inclusive and fair post-war society. Priestley's works, particularly "An Inspector Calls", resonated strongly with audiences during the 1940s. The play examined the hypocrisy and moral decay of the upper class, critiquing their lack of empathy and responsibility towards society. "An Inspector Calls" emphasised the interconnectedness of individuals and the importance of collective responsibility for the well-being of society. Priestley's writings in the 1940s also grappled with the effects of World War II on British society. His plays, such as "They Came to a City", explored themes of hope, disillusionment, and the need for a reimagining of society after the war. Priestley questioned the traditional values and systems that had led to the conflicts and sought to offer alternative visions for a more inclusive and progressive Britain. Priestley was a prominent social commentator, using his platform to critique societal norms and advocate for change. Through his plays, essays, and broadcasts, he challenged established power structures and advocated for a more egalitarian society. Priestley's radio broadcasts, particularly the "Postscripts" series, addressed issues such as unemployment, education, and social welfare, offering a vision for a better post-war Britain. Priestley's work during the 1940s was marked by a desire to engage with a wide audience. He aimed to bridge the gap between highbrow and popular culture, making his ideas accessible and relatable to a broad spectrum of society. His plays were often characterised by a blend of humour, drama, and social commentary, appealing to both intellectual and popular audiences.

******

George Orwell, one of the most influential British writers of the 20th century, made significant contributions to literature and political commentary in 1940s Britain. Orwell's experiences during World War II and his strong convictions about totalitarianism and social injustice shaped his writings during this period. During the 1940s, Orwell served as a war correspondent for the British Broadcasting Corporation (BBC) and wrote essays and articles about his experiences. He witnessed the horrors of war firsthand, including the Blitz on London and the impact of the conflict on ordinary people. These experiences informed his later works, highlighting the destructive nature of war and its effects on society.

Orwell's allegorical novella, "Animal Farm", published in 1945, is one of his most celebrated works. The book uses a farm and its animals to satirise the events leading to the Russian Revolution and the subsequent rise of totalitarianism under Joseph Stalin. Orwell's critique of authoritarianism and his exploration of power dynamics resonated with readers in 1940s Britain, offering a scathing indictment of political corruption and the abuse of power.

"Nineteen Eighty-Four", published in 1949, is considered a seminal work of literature. Set in a totalitarian society where Big Brother monitors every aspect of citizens' lives, the novel explores themes of government surveillance, propaganda, and the erosion of individual freedoms. Orwell's warnings about the dangers of totalitarianism struck a chord in the aftermath of World War II, reflecting the anxieties and concerns about the future of democracy and the potential for authoritarian rule. Orwell's writings during the 1940s were characterised by his sharp political and social commentary. Through his essays, articles, and novels, he critiqued the abuse of power, social inequality, and the erosion of civil liberties. Orwell's works urged readers to question authority, think critically, and remain vigilant against threats to individual freedom and democratic principles. Orwell's ideas and concepts, particularly those explored in "Nineteen Eighty-Four", have had a lasting impact on political discourse. Concepts such as "Big Brother", "thoughtcrime", and "Newspeak" have entered the cultural lexicon, becoming shorthand for the dangers of government surveillance and manipulation. Orwell's work has inspired discussions on the nature of truth, propaganda, and the importance of safeguarding democratic values.

******

In the post-war period of 1940s Britain, the Conservative Party was initially skeptical of extensive state intervention and had concerns about the potential impact of government control on individual freedoms and the economy. However, the Conservative Party did engage in post-war planning and played a role in shaping policies during that time. The Conservative Party advocated for a return to free-market principles and a reduction in government control over the economy. They were critical of the level of state intervention implemented during the war and expressed concerns about the potential negative effects on economic growth and individual liberties. The party emphasised the importance of private enterprise, reduced government spending, and the promotion of free trade. Also recognised was the need for post-war reconstruction and the improvement of housing conditions. They supported initiatives to address the housing shortage and aimed to encourage private investment in housing. The party promoted policies that facilitated the construction of new homes and the restoration of war-damaged areas. The Conservative Party recognised the importance of education and supported efforts to expand educational opportunities. They emphasised the need for a well-trained workforce and the provision of quality education for all. The party advocated for a more decentralised education system, with greater local control and autonomy for schools.

While the Conservative Party was initially cautious about the expansion of the welfare state, they did not advocate for its dismantling. Instead, they sought to modify and refine its implementation. The party focused on improving the efficiency and effectiveness of social welfare programs, reducing bureaucracy, and encouraging individual responsibility. They placed significant emphasis on maintaining Britain's global influence and its relationships with the Commonwealth and the United States. They supported the continuation of British imperial policies and the preservation of the Empire, although these positions would evolve over time. It is important to note that the Conservative Party's stance on post-war planning varied among its members, and there were differing opinions and approaches within the party. Over time, as the welfare state became more firmly established in Britain, the Conservative Party adapted its positions and sought to balance economic liberalism with social responsibility.

******

The 1945 general election was held on 5th July 1945 shortly after the end of World War II, and it resulted in a landslide victory for the Labour Party, led by Clement Attlee. The Labour Party campaigned on a platform of social reform, inspired by the principles outlined in the Beveridge Report. The party's emphasis on tackling the five giant evils, expanding social security, and establishing a comprehensive welfare state resonated with the public, who were looking for a vision of a fairer and more equitable society after the sacrifices made during the war. The Labour Party formed a majority government and wasted no time in implementing its policy agenda. The new government undertook a series of transformative reforms, including the establishment of the National Health Service (NHS) in 1948. The NHS provided universal healthcare access and represented a significant step towards ensuring equal access to healthcare for all citizens, regardless of their socioeconomic background.

The Labour government implemented a range of social welfare policies and programs, building upon the recommendations of the Beveridge Report. These included the expansion of social security systems, the introduction of family allowances, the improvement of housing conditions, and the promotion of education and employment opportunities for all. The welfare state aimed to provide a safety net for individuals and families, reduce poverty, and promote social equality. Alongside the development of the welfare state, the post-war era also saw the acceptance and consolidation of a mixed economy in Britain. While Labour's social reforms involved an expansion of the state's role in providing public services and social security, private enterprise and market mechanisms were still recognised as essential components of the economy. This mixed economy model aimed to strike a balance between government intervention and the free market, with the state playing a role in regulating and ensuring social protections. The developments of the 1940s set the foundation for subsequent social policy and shaped the political consensus around the importance of a welfare state in providing essential services and support to the population. The legacy of these reforms continues to influence British politics and debates on social welfare and economic equality.

******

The formation of the National Health Service (NHS) in Britain in 1948 was a monumental achievement that fundamentally transformed healthcare provision in the country. However, its establishment was not without challenges and controversies. Estimating the cost of implementing the NHS was a complex task. The Beveridge Report, which laid the foundation for the NHS, did not provide specific cost projections. As a result, there were uncertainties and debates over the financial implications of the proposed healthcare system. Various estimates were presented, and the government had to carefully assess and reconcile these projections. Determining how to finance the NHS was a crucial aspect of its establishment. The government had to devise a funding mechanism that would provide sustainable and adequate resources. It was decided that the NHS would be funded through a combination of national insurance contributions and general taxation. This approach aimed to distribute the financial burden broadly and ensure that the system remained affordable and accessible to all. A balance had to be struck between the level of services provided by the NHS and the available financial resources. It was essential to ensure that the healthcare system offered a comprehensive range of services while remaining financially viable. This involved making choices regarding the scope of services covered, the availability of medical technologies, and the allocation of resources across different areas of healthcare. The process of transitioning from the pre-NHS healthcare system to the new model incurred additional costs. There was a need to build new hospitals, expand existing facilities, and equip them with the necessary medical technologies. What is more, the recruitment and training of additional healthcare professionals, as well as the integration of previously separate services, required financial investment. Establishing effective budgetary control mechanisms was crucial to ensure responsible financial management within the NHS. The government had to develop systems for budget allocation, financial oversight, and cost control to prevent overspending and promote efficient resource utilisation. This required the establishment of administrative structures and financial reporting systems to monitor and manage NHS expenditure.

While not all medical professionals opposed the creation of the NHS, a significant number expressed concerns and voiced their opposition. One of the primary concerns raised by medical professionals was the fear of losing professional autonomy and control over their practices. The NHS proposed a centralised system of healthcare delivery, which some doctors viewed as a threat to their independence. They were apprehensive that government control and bureaucracy could interfere with their clinical decision-making and undermine their professional judgment. Some doctors and professional organisations held a philosophical objection to state intervention in healthcare. They believed that healthcare should primarily be a private matter, with minimal government interference. They were concerned that the creation of a government-run healthcare system would lead to a decline in the quality of care, increased bureaucracy, and limitations on their ability to practice medicine. Another factor that contributed to resistance was the fear among doctors that their income would be significantly reduced under the new system. The NHS aimed to provide healthcare services to all citizens, regardless of their ability to pay. This meant that doctors would no longer rely on private fees and would instead receive salaries from the government. Some doctors were concerned that the income caps and standardisation of salaries could lead to a decrease in their earnings.

The NHS sought to integrate various healthcare services, including hospitals, general practitioners, and other healthcare providers, into a unified system. This process of integration was complex and involved coordination and collaboration between different entities. The amalgamation of previously independent services and the establishment of regional health authorities presented organisational challenges and required significant coordination and planning. The creation required substantial investment in infrastructure and resources. Building new hospitals, expanding existing facilities, and ensuring an adequate supply of medical equipment and personnel posed logistical challenges. The government had to undertake a massive construction and recruitment program to meet the demands of the new healthcare system. The transition from the pre-NHS healthcare system to the new model was not without difficulties. The process of transferring services and personnel to the NHS was complex, and it took time for the new system to become fully operational. There were logistical challenges in terms of managing patient records, implementing new administrative structures, and ensuring a smooth transition without disruptions to patient care.

******

Fashion in Britain during the early years of the 1940s was greatly influenced by the prevailing events of World War II. The war had a significant impact on clothing styles, materials, and the overall aesthetics of fashion. Rationing and limited resources meant that practicality and utility became essential factors in clothing design, with an emphasis on conserving materials for the war effort. The British government introduced the Utility Scheme in 1941, which aimed to standardise clothing designs and conserve resources. Utility clothing was functional, simple, and made from economical materials. It often featured minimal embellishments and was designed to be versatile and long-lasting. The scarcity of fabrics and materials led to the implementation of austerity measures in fashion. Rationing was enforced, and individuals were allocated specific amounts of clothing coupons to purchase garments.

After V.E. Day, the immediate effect on fashion in Britain was marked by a sense of relief and liberation. The end of the war brought a shift in attitudes, leading to changes in clothing styles and a departure from the practical and austere fashions that characterised the wartime years. With the end of rationing and a newfound sense of freedom, there was a resurgence of glamour in fashion. Women embraced more feminine and luxurious clothing styles, characterised by flowing skirts, nipped-in waists, and elegant silhouettes. Fabrics such as silk and satin, which had been scarce during the war, became more readily available. During the war, clothing was often limited to muted and practical colours due to dye and fabric shortages. After V.E. Day, there was a return to vibrant colours and playful prints. Floral patterns, polka dots, and bold stripes became popular, reflecting the desire for joy and celebration. The iconic "New Look" introduced by Christian Dior in 1947 had a significant influence on post-war fashion. It featured full skirts that emphasised a tiny waist, creating an hourglass silhouette. This style brought a sense of femininity and elegance, in contrast to the boxy, utilitarian shapes of the war years. In addition to full skirts, tailored suits and pencil skirts were also in vogue. The tailored suits had padded shoulders, fitted jackets, and knee-length skirts, exuding sophistication and professionalism. Pencil skirts, which were narrow and tapered, became a staple for women's workwear. The end of the war saw an influx of American fashion into Britain. American servicemen stationed in the UK brought with them the latest styles from the United States, including sportswear, casual clothing, and denim. This influence contributed to a more relaxed and casual approach to fashion. Accessories played a crucial role in post-war fashion. Women adorned themselves with gloves, hats, and handbags, adding a finishing touch to their outfits. Pearl necklaces, brooches, and statement earrings were also popular accessories, adding a touch of elegance to ensembles. The end of the war provided an opportunity for the revival of the British fashion industry. Designers and manufacturers began to reclaim their pre-war prominence, showcasing British creativity and craftsmanship.

******

India was often referred to as the "crown jewel" of the British Empire due to its strategic importance, vast resources, and economic potential. As the largest colony in the empire, India played a crucial role in sustaining British economic interests and global dominance. However, the Indian independence movement, which gained momentum in the early 20th century, eventually led to the end of British colonial rule in 1947. The process of independence and the subsequent partition of India had significant historical and humanitarian consequences. The Indian independence movement emerged as a response to British colonial rule and the demand for self-rule and independence. Led by influential figures such as Mahatma Gandhi, Jawaharlal Nehru, and Subhas Chandra Bose, the movement encompassed various strategies, including nonviolent civil disobedience, boycotts, and protests. It galvanised the Indian population and ignited a strong desire for freedom and self-governance.

On 15th August 1947, India and Pakistan gained their independence from British rule. India became a secular democratic republic, while Pakistan was established as an Islamic state, comprising West Pakistan (present-day Pakistan) and East Pakistan (present-day Bangladesh, which later gained independence in 1971). The partition of India was a result of religious and political divisions within the country. The Indian National Congress, representing a predominantly Hindu population, and the All-India Muslim League, advocating for Muslim interests, held differing visions for the post-independence future. The British government, facing difficulties in reconciling these conflicting demands, eventually agreed to the partition of India along religious lines, creating two separate nations: India (with a Hindu majority) and Pakistan (with a Muslim majority). This partition resulted in one of the largest migrations in history and led to widespread violence, communal riots, and displacement. Millions of Hindus, Muslims, and Sikhs were uprooted from their homes, leading to immense suffering and loss of life.

India had long been an important source of raw materials for British industries. British colonial rule facilitated the extraction of resources such as cotton, jute, tea, and minerals, which were vital to Britain's manufacturing sector. With Indian independence, Britain lost direct control over these valuable resources, leading to disruptions in supply chains and economic adjustments. Furthermore, India was an essential market for British goods. As a colony, it provided a captive market for British manufactured products, including textiles, machinery, and consumer goods. The independence of India meant the loss of preferential trade arrangements, and British businesses faced increased competition in the Indian market from local industries. The shift in trade dynamics further strained Britain's economy. The independence of India coincided with the end of World War II, a period when Britain was grappling with post-war reconstruction efforts and financial strains. The war drained Britain's resources, and the cost of maintaining an empire became increasingly burdensome.

The loss of India further exacerbated Britain's economic woes and forced the country to reassess its global role and priorities. To mitigate the economic impact of Indian independence, Britain sought to forge new economic relationships with other Commonwealth countries and former colonies. The Commonwealth became a platform for economic cooperation, and Britain aimed to redirect trade and investment towards these nations. However, the economic benefits derived from these efforts were insufficient to fully compensate for the loss of India. Additionally, Britain faced the challenge of restructuring its industries and finding alternative sources of raw materials. The loss of Indian cotton, for example, led to a decline in the British textile industry, which struggled to adapt to new circumstances. Britain had to diversify its sources of supply and seek new trading partners to make up for the shortfall.

******

After World War II, sports in Britain played a crucial role in rebuilding communities, boosting morale, and providing a sense of normalcy. The resumption of sports activities was a significant step towards recovery and helped bring people together. Football was one of the first sports to resume in Britain after the war. The Football League, which had been suspended since 1939, recommenced in the 1946-1947 season. Football clubs returned to their pre-war divisions, and competitive league matches began again. Cup competitions, such as the FA Cup, also resumed. The FA Cup, the oldest football competition in the world, played an important role in revitalising the sport. The first post-war FA Cup final took place in 1946, with Derby County defeating Charlton Athletic 4-1.

Cricket also made a comeback in the post-war period. The County Championship, the premier domestic cricket competition in England, resumed in 1946. Many cricketers who had served in the armed forces returned to the sport, and matches were played across various county grounds. The Ashes series between England and Australia resumed in 1946-1947, with Australia touring England. The series was highly anticipated and helped reignite the passion for cricket. Australia won the series 3-0 with two matches drawn.

Various other sports gradually restarted after the war. Athletics, rugby, tennis, and boxing were among the sports that resumed their competitions. The Wimbledon Championships, one of the most prestigious tennis tournaments, resumed in 1946 after a six-year hiatus due to the war. Additionally, sports events and exhibitions were organised to raise funds for war relief and reconstruction efforts. These events, such as charity matches and exhibition games, brought communities together and demonstrated the resilience and unity of the nation. Sports played a vital role in the healing process and the rebuilding of Britain after the war. They provided a sense of normalcy, entertainment, and distraction from the hardships endured during the conflict. Sports also helped in fostering a renewed sense of community, bringing people together and providing a platform for shared experiences.

1950s
Youth Culture and a Special FA Cup Final

The 1950s marked a transformative era for Britain, characterised by a blend of post-war recovery, political shifts, and the rise of popular culture. The 1950s witnessed the rise of rock and roll, a genre that revolutionised popular music. British musicians like Tommy Steele and Cliff Richard embraced this new sound, heavily influenced by American artists such as Elvis Presley and Chuck Berry. The skiffle craze, characterised by homemade instruments and a mix of folk, blues, and jazz, gained popularity with acts like Lonnie Donegan. The emergence of the jukebox and radio broadcasts helped disseminate these new musical styles to a wider audience. Television became a dominant medium in British households during the 1950s. The BBC, which had launched the world's first regular television service in

1936 but was halted during World War II, resumed broadcasting in 1946 and expanded its programming in the 1950s. Popular shows such as "The Grove Family" and "Sunday Night at the London Palladium" entertained audiences, and the introduction of the commercial network ITV in 1955 added further diversity to television programming. The 1950s marked a golden era for British cinema, with the emergence of the "Kitchen Sink" dramas and the rise of the British New Wave. Films like "Room at the Top", "Saturday Night and Sunday Morning", and "Look Back in Anger" depicted the gritty reality of working-class life, challenging traditional cinematic conventions. British actors like Laurence Olivier, Alec Guinness, and Peter Sellers achieved international acclaim during this period. Fashion in the 1950s was influenced by various trends. Women's fashion saw a return to more feminine and elegant styles, with full skirts, nipped-in waists, and soft fabrics. Dior's "New Look" with its hourglass silhouette became a popular choice. Men's fashion favoured tailored suits, inspired by the classic English style. Teddy Boys, a subculture characterised by their Edwardian-inspired clothing and rebellious attitude, emerged as a significant youth movement.

In 1951, the Conservative Party, led by Winston Churchill, regained power. The government focused on stabilising the economy and rebuilding industries, such as manufacturing and housing. Countries like India, Pakistan, and Ceylon (now Sri Lanka) gained independence, marking the end of the British Empire. This process of decolonisation had a profound impact on Britain's political landscape and contributed to the reshaping of its global role. The Cold War tensions between the United States and the Soviet Union also affected Britain. The country aligned itself with the United States, becoming a founding member of NATO in 1949. The fear of communism led to political crackdowns, including the trial and imprisonment of

British spies such as the Cambridge Five. Britain saw the continued development of the welfare state, with the expansion of the National Health Service (NHS) and the implementation of social reforms. The NHS provided free healthcare to all citizens, symbolising the commitment to social equality and improving the lives of ordinary people.

The Football League and the FA Cup remained highly anticipated events. The 1953 FA Cup Final, known as the "Matthews Final", saw Blackpool's Stanley Matthews deliver a mesmerising performance that secured victory for his team. Test cricket remained a significant sporting event, with England competing against international teams. The Ashes series against Australia maintained its historic rivalry, with notable players like Denis Compton and Jim Laker achieving remarkable performances. The 1950s marked the birth of Formula One racing. The British Grand Prix held at Silverstone, became a staple event in the racing calendar. British drivers such as Stirling Moss and Mike Hawthorn achieved success and became national heroes. British athletes made their mark on the international stage during the 1950s. Roger Bannister famously broke the four-minute mile barrier in 1954, and Chris Chataway and Gordon Pirie were prominent long-distance runners.

******

The Festival of Britain was a major national exhibition held in 1951 to celebrate British arts, science, technology, and industry. It was organised to boost the morale of the British people after the devastation of World War II and showcase the nation's achievements in various fields. The idea for the Festival of Britain emerged in the late 1940s when the Labour government, led by Prime Minister Clement Attlee, sought to promote national unity, optimism, and a sense of progress. The festival aimed to highlight Britain's cultural and industrial heritage while presenting a vision for the country's future. The festival took place on the South Bank of the River Thames in London, primarily around the area that is now known as the Southbank Centre. The site was previously occupied by a mix of old buildings and bomb-damaged areas, which were cleared to make way for the festival structures.

The Festival of Britain officially opened on 3rd May 1951 and lasted for several months. It consisted of multiple exhibits, pavilions, and displays showcasing different aspects of British life and culture. The main venues included the Dome of Discovery, the Festival Hall, the Skylon (a distinctive steel structure), and the Telecinema (an early cinema featuring widescreen films). The festival showcased a wide range of exhibits and displays, covering topics such as architecture, design, science, industry, and the arts. It aimed to promote British achievements in fields such as engineering, manufacturing, textiles, and technology. The exhibits showcased innovative designs and products, including modern furniture, appliances, and artwork. The Festival of Britain also featured numerous cultural events, including concerts, plays, exhibitions, and outdoor performances. It brought together artists, musicians, and performers from different disciplines to celebrate British talent and creativity.

The festival attracted millions of visitors from around the country and had a significant impact on British society. It helped to boost national morale and provided a sense of hope and optimism in the post-war period. The Festival of Britain contributed to the wider cultural and social changes that took place in Britain during the 1950s, as the country transitioned from the austerity of the war years to a more prosperous and forward-looking era. While the physical structures of the festival were dismantled after its conclusion, its legacy endured.

******

The "Matthews Final" is one of the most iconic matches in the history of British football. It took place on 29th April 1953, at Wembley Stadium and pitted Blackpool against Bolton Wanderers in the final of the FA Cup. The match became legendary due to the remarkable performance of Blackpool's Stanley Matthews, who mesmerised the crowd with his exceptional skills and helped his team secure a memorable victory. Stanley Matthews, known as the "Wizard of the Dribble", was already a revered figure in British football. At the age of 38, he was playing in his third FA Cup final, having previously lost in 1948 and 1951. This final, however, would be his crowning glory.

The match started dramatically, with Bolton taking an early lead through Nat Lofthouse in the 3rd minute. The odds seemed stacked against Blackpool, but they showed resilience and fought back. In the 35th minute, Stan Mortensen scored for Blackpool before Willie Moir scored Boston's second, setting the stage for a thrilling second half. It was during the second half that Matthews truly showcased his exceptional skills. He effortlessly weaved through the Bolton defence, leaving defenders trailing in his wake. With his nimble footwork, precise passes, and lightning-fast dribbling, he posed a constant threat to Bolton's defence. Matthews mesmerised the crowd, who were in awe of his virtuosity on the pitch. Eric Bell scored again for Bolton before Stan Mortensen scored two more then Bill Perry scored Blackpool's winner in the 92nd minute.

Despite Bolton's efforts to find an equaliser, Blackpool held on to their slender lead, thanks in no small part to the heroics of Matthews. The final whistle blew, and Blackpool emerged victorious, securing a 4-3 win and their first-ever FA Cup title. Stanley Matthews' performance in the "Matthews Final" earned him widespread acclaim and adulation. He became the first footballer to be awarded the Football Writers' Association Footballer of the Year accolade in the same season as the FA Cup final. Matthews' display epitomised the beauty and artistry of the game, and he was hailed as a national hero. The "Matthews Final" remains etched in the annals of British football history as a testament to the indomitable spirit of Stanley Matthews and his impact on the sport. It serves as a reminder of the magic and joy that football can bring and continues to inspire generations of footballers and fans alike.

******

The Conservative Party, under the leadership of Winston Churchill and later Anthony Eden, held power for the majority of the decade. The Conservative Party won three general elections during the 1950s. In the 1951 general election, the party secured a narrow victory, leading to Churchill's return as Prime Minister. The party then won convincingly in the 1955 general election under Eden's leadership. In 1959, they won a third consecutive election, solidifying their hold on power. The Party advocated for a market-based approach to the economy, emphasising free trade, privatisation, and reduced government intervention. The government pursued policies aimed at promoting economic stability and growth, including maintaining a fixed exchange rate and encouraging foreign investment. The Conservative governments of the 1950s generally upheld traditional social values and policies. There was a focus on family values, patriotism, and respect for institutions such as the monarchy. Social conservatism was prevalent, and there was limited support for social reform or significant changes to societal norms. The Conservative Party placed great importance on maintaining Britain's global influence and maintaining a strong position in international affairs. This was particularly evident in the handling of the Suez Crisis in 1956, where the government, led by Eden, took military action against Egypt to protect British interests in the Suez Canal. The 1950s saw heightened tensions between the Western powers and the Soviet Union during the Cold War. The Conservative Party aligned itself with the United States and the NATO alliance, emphasising the need for a strong defence against the perceived threat of communism. This stance appealed to a public concerned about national security. There was a degree of political consensus during the 1950s, with both major parties, the Conservatives and the Labour Party, broadly supporting a mixed economy and the welfare state established after World War II. This consensus contributed to a sense of stability and continuity in British politics during the period.

******

Before rock 'n' roll fully took hold in Britain, there was a strong skiffle movement that served as a precursor. Skiffle, with its blend of folk, jazz, and blues, played a crucial role in introducing British audiences to American music and acting as a bridge to the rock 'n' roll sound. Skiffle artists like Lonnie Donegan, as mentioned earlier, gained popularity by performing skiffle versions of American rock 'n' roll hits. Artists like Elvis Presley, Chuck Berry, Little Richard, Buddy Holly, and Jerry Lee Lewis became idols and inspirations for British musicians. As the popularity of rock 'n' roll grew, British musicians started to create their own brand of rock 'n' roll music. They adapted the American sound to suit their local audiences and added their own unique twists. Some notable British rock 'n' roll artists of the 1950s include Cliff Richard and The Shadows, Billy Fury, Tommy Steele, Marty Wilde, and Johnny Kidd & The Pirates. Record labels played a crucial role in bringing rock 'n' roll to the

British public. Companies like Decca, EMI, and Pye Records signed British artists and released their rock 'n' roll recordings. Moreover, radio stations such as Radio Luxembourg and the BBC's "Saturday Club" helped popularise rock 'n' roll by playing it on the airwaves and reaching a wide audience.

Skiffle and rock 'n' roll clubs started to emerge in cities like London, Liverpool, and Manchester, providing platforms for young British musicians to perform and showcase their talent. These clubs, such as The 2i's Coffee Bar in London and The Cavern Club in Liverpool, became important hubs for the growth of the British rock 'n' roll scene. The 2i's Coffee Bar was an influential music venue in London during the 1950s. It played a significant role in the development of the emerging British rock 'n' roll scene and served as a gathering place for aspiring musicians. It was located at 59 Old Compton Street in London's Soho district and was a small, unassuming café that primarily catered to the local coffee-drinking crowd. The 2i's Coffee Bar became a popular meeting place for young musicians looking to break into the music industry. It provided an intimate and supportive environment for artists to showcase their talents. The café's owner, Freddie Mills, and his partner, Ray Hunter, would scout for talent among the performers and offer opportunities to those they believed had potential. Many aspiring musicians got their first break at the 2i's Coffee Bar. Several notable musicians and bands made their debut or gained early exposure at the 2i's. Some of the prominent artists associated with the venue include Tommy Steele, Cliff Richard, Adam Faith, Joe Brown, Terry Dene, and Vince Eager. The 2i's Coffee Bar played a pivotal role in shaping the British rock 'n' roll scene. It provided a platform for musicians to experiment with their sound, hone their skills, and gain recognition. Its influence extended beyond the 1950s, as many of the artists who started their careers there went on to become major figures in the subsequent British music scene.

While rock 'n' roll traditional pop music, characterised by smooth vocals and orchestral arrangements, remained popular in the 1950s. Artists like Frank Sinatra, Nat King Cole, and Doris Day were widely celebrated. Crooners, known for their smooth and romantic vocal styles, were also prominent during this period. Artists like Bing Crosby, Perry Como, and Dean Martin had significant success in the UK. The tradition of British dance bands continued into the 1950s. These bands, often featuring vocalists, performed swing and dance music. Popular groups of the era included Ted Heath and His Music, Ken Mackintosh, and Joe Loss and His Orchestra. The foundations of the British pop sound, which would explode in the 1960s, were laid in the 1950s. Artists like Cliff Richard, Adam Faith, and Billy Fury emerged as early British pop stars.

******

Molineux, the home stadium of Wolverhampton Wanderers, holds a significant place in the history of English football as one of the first grounds to install floodlights. The introduction of floodlights at Molineux was a pioneering move that revolutionised the game and opened up new opportunities for evening matches and televised football. The decision to install floodlights at Molineux came in the early 1950s. The club's chairman, Major Frank Buckley, recognised the potential benefits of floodlit matches, such as increased attendance, enhanced visibility for players and spectators, and the ability to play matches during the evening, which was more convenient for working fans.

Wolves became the first team in England to play competitive floodlit matches at their own ground. On 30th March 1953, Molineux hosted its first floodlit match, a friendly game against a South African XI. The event attracted a crowd of over 38,000 spectators, showcasing the tremendous interest in floodlit football. The success of the initial floodlit game encouraged Wolves to continue embracing this innovation. Other major club games at the time included victories over Borussia Dortmund and a 3–0 win over Real Madrid. Matches were played against sides such as Racing Club of Argentina and Spartak Moscow before Wolverhampton Wanderers versus Honvéd of Hungary became a landmark game for English football as it was televised live on the BBC.

Wolves' floodlit matches also played a significant role in their success during the 1950s. The team's attacking style of play and strong home record under the floodlights made Molineux a formidable fortress. The increased visibility provided by the floodlights allowed players like Jimmy Mullen and Roy Swinbourne to showcase their skills to full effect. The success of floodlit football at Molineux also had a broader impact on the game. Other clubs across England soon followed suit and started installing floodlights at their stadiums. Floodlit matches became increasingly popular, drawing larger crowds and creating a more vibrant atmosphere for evening games. Molineux's pioneering move to introduce floodlights reflected the club's ambition and forward-thinking approach. The floodlit matches at Molineux not only benefited Wolves but also contributed to the evolution of football in England. Floodlights became an integral part of the modern game, allowing matches to be played at any time of the day and making football more accessible to fans and viewers alike.

******

The Cambridge Five were spying for the Soviet Union while working in British intelligence and diplomatic circles during the Cold War. The group included Kim Philby, Guy Burgess, Donald

Maclean, Anthony Blunt, and John Cairncross. Among them, Burgess and Maclean were particularly notable figures. Guy Burgess was born on 16th April 1911, in Devonport, England. He attended Eton College and later studied at Trinity College, Cambridge, where he became involved in left-wing politics. Burgess was known for his charm, wit, and extravagant lifestyle. In the late 1930s, he joined the Foreign Office and later transferred to the intelligence agency MI6. Donald Maclean, born on 25th May 1913, in London, was also educated at Gresham's School and later attended Trinity College, Cambridge. Maclean was known for his intelligence, linguistic abilities, and diplomatic skills. Like Burgess, he joined the Foreign Office and subsequently worked for the intelligence agency MI6.

Both Burgess and Maclean were recruited by Soviet intelligence agents in the mid-1930s while they were still at Cambridge. They became Soviet spies and passed on classified information to the Soviet Union throughout their careers in British intelligence and diplomacy. Their espionage activities remained undetected until 1951 when suspicion began to arise within British intelligence circles. In 1951, Burgess and Maclean disappeared, fleeing to the Soviet Union. Their defection caused significant scandal and embarrassment for the British government and intelligence agencies. Burgess and Maclean lived in the Soviet Union for the rest of their lives, where they were celebrated as heroes by the Soviet regime. Burgess died in Moscow in 1963, while Maclean passed away in 1983. The actions of Burgess, Maclean, and the other members of the Cambridge Five had a profound impact on British intelligence and national security. Their betrayals raised serious questions about the effectiveness of British counterintelligence and led to significant reforms in the intelligence community.

******

The 1950s marked a period of recovery for the British film industry after the hardships of World War II. The government supported the industry through initiatives such as the Eady Levy, which provided financial assistance to British productions. The Eady Levy, also known as the Eady tax, was a government initiative introduced in 1948 in the United Kingdom to support and promote British film production. The levy was named after Sir Wilfred Eady, who chaired a government committee that recommended its implementation. The primary purpose of the Eady Levy was to provide financial support to British film productions and help the domestic film industry compete with the dominance of Hollywood films. It aimed to encourage the production, distribution, and exhibition of British films. The Levy was collected through a tax imposed on cinema ticket sales. A fixed percentage of the ticket revenue was levied, typically around 15%, which was then allocated to support British film production. The funds collected through the Eady Levy were distributed to British film producers based on the proportion of British content in their films. The more British content a film had, the larger share of the funds it would receive. This incentivised the production of British films and supported their distribution and exhibition.

Kitchen sink dramas were a prominent genre in 1950s British cinema, characterised by their realistic portrayals of working-class life and social issues. These films, often set in the industrial North of England, offered gritty and raw depictions of everyday people and their struggles. They emerged as a response to the prevailing trends in British cinema, which often featured polished and idealised portrayals of middle-class life. The kitchen sink dramas sought to bring social issues to the forefront and shed light on the realities of working-class existence. These films explored themes such as poverty, unemployment, class divisions, cramped living conditions, and limited opportunities. They presented characters dealing with challenging circumstances, often focusing on their frustrations, aspirations, and the clash between personal desires and societal expectations. Kitchen sink dramas were known for their realistic and naturalistic approach. They eschewed glamorous settings and emphasised gritty urban landscapes, cramped interiors, and everyday locations like small homes, pubs, and factories. The aim was to present an authentic portrayal of working-class life and the struggles faced by ordinary individuals. Significant emphasis was placed on character development. The protagonists were typically complex and multidimensional, grappling with personal dilemmas, relationships, and social constraints. These films explored the psychological and emotional depths of their characters, often with a focus on individual identity and self-discovery. Several notable directors made significant contributions to the kitchen sink drama movement. Filmmakers such as Tony Richardson, Karel Reisz, and Lindsay Anderson were associated with this genre. Key films from this period include "Look Back in Anger", "Saturday Night and Sunday Morning", and "A Taste of Honey".

The 1950s featured the rise of notable British stars and directors. Actors like Alec Guinness, Peter Sellers, Richard Burton, and Deborah Kerr gained international recognition. Directors such as David Lean, Carol Reed, and Michael Powell also made significant contributions to British cinema during this decade. Despite the growth of British cinema, Hollywood films continued to dominate the British box office. American movies had a strong presence in British theatres, and Hollywood stars and directors had a significant impact on the British film industry.

******

The 1953 Ashes series was a highly significant and memorable cricket contest between England and Australia. It is often referred to as the "Coronation Ashes" as it coincided with the coronation of Queen Elizabeth II. The series of 1953 consisted of five Test matches played between June and August. Australia, led by the legendary captain Lindsay Hassett, entered the series as the defending Ashes holders, having won the previous series in 1950-1951. England, under the captaincy of Len Hutton, was determined to reclaim the Ashes on home soil.

The first Test, held at Trent Bridge from 11th to 16th June 1953, saw Australia post a respectable total of 249 runs in their first innings. Arthur Morris 67 and Alan Hassett 115 were the standout performers, while Alec Bedser's impressive bowling figures of 7 for 55 restricted the Australian innings. In response, England could only manage 144 runs, with Len Hutton 43 leading the way. Ray Lindwall's bowling brilliance, with figures of 5 for 54, put Australia in a commanding position. However, rain affected the match, and it ended in a draw with Australia at 120 for 1 in their second innings.

The second Test, played at Lord's from 25th to 30th June 1953, showcased a closely contested battle between the two teams. Australia posted 346 runs in their first innings, with Arthur Morris 89, Keith Miller 109, and Neil Harvey 59 making significant contributions. Alec Bedser and Jim Laker claimed nine wickets between them for England. In reply, England responded strongly with 372 runs, thanks to a brilliant century from Len Hutton 145 and significant contributions from Tom Graveney 78 and Denis Compton 57. The Australian team fought back with their own strong batting display, led by Keith Miller's century 109 and Arthur Morris' 89. However, England's bowlers, particularly Fred Trueman with figures of 4 for 86, limited the

Australian lead, and the match ended in a draw with England at 282 for 7 in their second innings.

The third Test, held at Old Trafford from 9th to 14th July 1953, witnessed another draw. Australia posted 318 runs in their first innings, led by Neil Harvey's magnificent 122. Alec Bedser took five wickets for England. In reply, England scored 276 runs, with Len Hutton 66 and Denis Compton 45 leading the batting effort. The match took an intriguing turn when Australia collapsed to 35 for 8 in their second innings, with Johnny Wardle taking remarkable figures of 4 for 7. However, Ray Lindwall's resilience, along with the tailenders, helped Australia salvage a draw as they reached 167 for 9.

The fourth Test, played at Headingley from 23rd to 28th July 1953, witnessed another draw in the series. England struggled in their first innings, managing only 167 runs, with Tom Graveney's 55 as the lone bright spot. Ray Lindwall's impressive bowling performance of 5 for 54 kept Australia in control. In response, Australia scored 266 runs, with Neil Harvey 71 and Graeme Hole 53 leading the charge. Alec Bedser's bowling figures of 6 for 95 kept England in the game. In their second innings, England displayed better batting form, thanks to contributions from Bill Edrich 64, Denis Compton 61, and Jim Laker 48. The match ended in a draw with Australia at 147 for 4 in their second innings.

The fifth and final Test, held at The Oval from 15th to 19th August 1953, witnessed a memorable comeback by England, who clinched victory by eight wickets. Australia scored 275 runs in their first innings, with Ray Lindwall 62 and Alan Hassett 53 leading the charge. Fred Trueman and Alec Bedser were the pick of the English bowlers. In reply, England posted 306 runs, buoyed by strong performances from Len Hutton 82 and Trevor Bailey 64. Ray Lindwall's four-wicket haul kept the game finely balanced. In their second innings, Australia struggled, managing only 162 runs. Off-spinner Jim Laker with 4 for 75 and left-arm spinner Tony Lock with 5 for 45 spun England to victory. England chased down the required target of 132 runs with ease, thanks to an unbeaten half-century by Bill Edrich who finished the match on 55 not out. The 1953 Ashes series will be remembered as a captivating contest, with England displaying resilience and determination to secure victory. Australia showcased their batting prowess, but England's bowling attack, led by Alec Bedser and spinners Jim Laker and Tony Lock, proved instrumental in turning the tide. The series witnessed several individual performances of note, including Alan Hassett, Len Hutton, and Ray Lindwall. England's triumph in the final Test at The Oval ensured they reclaimed the Ashes after a long wait, sparking jubilation among cricket fans across the nation.

******

The Suez Crisis marked a significant turning point in British foreign policy and contributed to a reassessment of Britain's role in the post-colonial era. The Crisis arose from a complex set of factors, including the nationalisation of the Suez Canal by Egyptian President Gamal Abdel Nasser, Britain's declining colonial power, and the wider context of the Cold War. The Suez Canal was a vital waterway for international trade, and its nationalisation by Egypt threatened Western access and control.

The British government, led by Prime Minister Anthony Eden, saw the nationalisation as a direct challenge to Britain's interests and influence in the Middle East. Eden and his government, along with France and Israel, devised a plan to regain control of the canal by launching a military operation. In October 1956, British and French forces, with the support of Israel, launched an invasion of Egypt. The aim was to secure the canal and remove Nasser from power. However, the military operation faced international condemnation, particularly from the United States and the Soviet Union, who feared the escalation of the Cold War and opposed the use of force. The Suez Crisis exposed the declining influence of Britain as a colonial power and strained its relationship with its closest ally, the United States. The U.S., under President Dwight D. Eisenhower, opposed military action and exerted pressure on Britain, threatening economic consequences and a run on the British pound. This forced Britain to withdraw its forces and accept a UN peacekeeping mission in the region. The Crisis had a profound impact on British politics. Anthony Eden's handling of the crisis was heavily criticised, and his resignation followed soon after the withdrawal of British forces. The crisis also revealed Britain's diminished role on the world stage and exposed the cracks in the Empire. It marked a turning point in Britain's post-war foreign policy and accelerated the process of decolonisation. The Suez Crisis symbolised the end of an era of British dominance and the beginning of a new geopolitical landscape. It highlighted the limitations of military intervention and marked a shift towards diplomacy and multilateralism in international relations.

******

Ealing comedies and Hammer House of Horror were two distinct but influential film movements in 1950s Britain. The Ealing comedies were a series of British comedy films produced by Ealing Studios during the 1940s and 1950s. Although their peak popularity was in the late 1940s, some significant Ealing comedies continued to be made in the 1950s. The Ealing comedies were known for their distinct British humour, characterised by dry wit, eccentric characters, and satirical elements. Many Ealing comedies contained social commentary, often critiquing British society and institutions. They often poked fun at the class system, bureaucracy, and other aspects of British culture. They frequently featured ensemble casts of talented British actors, including Alec Guinness, Stanley Holloway, and Peter Sellers. Notable examples of Ealing comedies from the 1950s include "Kind Hearts and Coronets", "The Lavender Hill Mob", and "The Ladykillers". These films are still highly regarded for their sharp writing, performances, and enduring comedic appeal.

The 1950s marked the beginning of Hammer's venture into horror, and it laid the foundation for their success in the following decades. Hammer House of Horror became renowned for its distinctive take on gothic horror. Their films often featured atmospheric settings, lavish production designs, and a focus on classic horror creatures such as Dracula, Frankenstein's monster, and The Mummy. Their horror films were notable for their use of Technicolor, which enhanced the visual impact of the films. The vibrant colours added to the allure and atmosphere of their gothic settings. Hammer House of Horror featured iconic performances by actors like Christopher Lee and Peter Cushing. Lee's portrayal of Dracula and Cushing's role as Van Helsing in the Dracula series became particularly legendary. Hammer House of Horror gained international recognition and success, appealing to horror film enthusiasts worldwide. Their films brought a renewed interest in gothic horror and left a lasting impact on the genre.

******

In the 1950s, British drivers and team owners had a significant influence on Formula One motor racing. This was a pivotal period in the history of the sport, as it marked the establishment of the Formula One World Championship in 1950 and witnessed the rise of several British talents and teams. One of the most prominent British drivers of the era was Sir Stirling Moss. Moss achieved remarkable success during the 1950s and is widely regarded as one of the greatest drivers never to have won the World Championship. His skill, speed, and sportsmanship endeared him to fans around the world. Moss drove for various teams, including Vanwall, Maserati, and Mercedes-Benz, and his performances helped solidify the reputation of British drivers on the international stage. Another notable British driver of the time was Mike Hawthorn. Hawthorn became the first British driver to win the Formula One World Championship in 1958, driving for Ferrari. His triumph was a testament to the growing competitiveness of British drivers in the sport.

In addition to individual drivers, British team owners played a crucial role in shaping Formula One in the 1950s. One of the most influential teams was Vanwall, founded by Tony Vandervell. Vanwall became the first British team to win the Constructors' Championship in 1958, with Moss and Tony Brooks driving their cars. This victory marked a turning point in Formula One, as it demonstrated that British teams could challenge and outperform their international rivals. The Cooper Car Company was founded by Charles and John Cooper. The Coopers revolutionised the sport by introducing rear-engined cars, which provided a handling advantage over the traditional front-engined designs. Their innovative approach led to the Cooper Climax winning the Formula One World Championship in 1959, driven by Jack Brabham. The success of British drivers and teams in the 1950s contributed to the growth and popularity of Formula One in the United Kingdom. It also fostered a legacy of excellence that continued in subsequent decades.

******

Sir Stirling Moss, born on 17th September 1929, in London, England, was a British racing legend whose career spanned from the 1940s to the early 1960s. With his immense skill, daring driving style, and gentlemanly demeanour, Moss became one of the most beloved and respected figures in motorsport. His influence and impact on Formula One in the 1950s were nothing short of extraordinary.

Moss began his motorsport journey at a young age, nurtured by his father Alfred, a successful amateur racer. Stirling quickly developed a natural talent for driving, and his early success in minor events caught the attention of the racing world. In 1951, he made his Formula One debut, driving for the HWM team at the Swiss Grand Prix. Throughout the 1950s, Moss proved himself to be one of the finest drivers of his era, consistently challenging for victories and pushing the limits of the sport. Although he narrowly missed out on winning the World Championship, finishing as the runner-up on four occasions, his impact on the sport extended beyond mere statistics. Moss's partnership with Mercedes-Benz in the mid 1950s is widely regarded as a defining period of his career. In 1955, he joined the Mercedes-Benz team and quickly became an integral part of their success. He formed a formidable duo with the legendary Juan Manuel Fangio, often pushing each other to new heights. Moss's breakthrough victory came in the 1955 British Grand Prix at Aintree, where he showcased his exceptional driving skills in treacherous wet conditions.

Moss's prowess extended beyond Formula One, as he excelled in a wide range of racing disciplines. His victories in prestigious events such as the Mille Miglia and the Targa Florio cemented his status as a versatile and fearless driver. In 1955, he set a record time in the Mille Miglia, averaging over 97 miles per hour on public roads, a record that still stands today. Throughout his career, Moss developed a reputation for his remarkable consistency and his ability to extract the maximum performance from any car he drove. He possessed an innate understanding of racing lines, unmatched car control, and an intuitive feel for the limits of adhesion. Moss's ability to adapt to different tracks, conditions, and cars made him a force to be reckoned with in any race. Off the track, Moss was known for his sportsmanship, charm, and impeccable manners. He was a true ambassador for the sport, revered by fans and respected by fellow drivers. His dedication to his craft and his professionalism set a standard for future generations of racers. Despite never winning the World Championship, Moss's impact on Formula One in the 1950s cannot be overstated. His talent, personality, and sportsmanship helped popularise the sport and elevate it to new heights.

******

The 1950s were a transformative period for the Labour Party in Britain. The party, which had come to power in 1945 under the leadership of Clement Attlee, faced numerous challenges and opportunities during this decade. It had implemented significant social and economic reforms, experienced internal divisions, and navigated the shifting political landscape. One of the key figures within the Labour Party during this period was Aneurin Bevan, who served as the Minister of Health and played a significant role in the establishment of the NHS in the previous decade. Bevan's vision for a comprehensive and publicly funded healthcare system became one of the party's defining achievements. However, the implementation of these reforms faced challenges, including financial constraints and resistance from various interest groups which affected the Labour government in 1950 and 1951. Labour also faced foreign policy challenges during the 1950s, particularly in relation to the emerging Cold War. The party maintained a commitment to socialist principles and pursued a policy of disarmament and peaceful coexistence with the Soviet Union. However, tensions within the party emerged over issues such as Britain's nuclear weapons program, which some Labour members opposed. In 1951, the Labour Party lost the general election to the Conservative Party still led by Winston Churchill. This defeat marked the end of the party's first period in power and led to a period of reflection and reevaluation. The party faced internal debates over its future direction, with some members advocating for a return to more radical socialism while others sought a more moderate approach. The Labour Party underwent significant changes in leadership during the 1950s. Clement Attlee stepped down as party leader in 1955, and Hugh Gaitskell took over. Gaitskell represented a more centrist faction within the party and sought to modernise Labour's policies. He aimed to move the party away from its traditional socialist roots and advocated for greater economic flexibility and a pragmatic approach to foreign policy. The 1959 general election marked another defeat for the Labour Party, which further fuelled debates about the party's future direction. The defeats in the 1951 and 1959 general elections led to a period of introspection, with subsequent leaders attempting to position the party as more centrist and modern. These developments set the stage for the party's future evolution and its ongoing role in British politics.

******

Aneurin Bevan, born on 15th November 1897, in Tredegar, South Wales, was a prominent Welsh politician and one of the most influential figures in the British Labour Party. His commitment to social justice, fervent advocacy for the working class, and pivotal role in the creation of the National Health Service (NHS) have made him an enduring figure in British political history. Bevan grew up in a mining family and experienced firsthand the struggles and hardships faced by the working class. His experiences shaped his political beliefs and fuelled his determination to fight for a fairer society. After leaving school at the age of 13, he began working in the local coal mines but soon became involved in labor activism and trade unionism. Bevan rose through the ranks of the South Wales Miners' Federation, ultimately becoming its president in 1935.

Bevan's political career took off when he was elected as the Member of Parliament for Ebbw Vale in 1929. As a Member of Parliament, he quickly established himself as a fiery orator and a staunch advocate for socialist policies. Bevan aligned himself with the left-wing faction of the Labour Party and was a vocal critic of capitalism and inequality. One of Bevan's most significant achievements came during his tenure as the Minister of Health in the post-war Labour government led by Clement Attlee. In this role, he spearheaded the establishment of the NHS, which remains a pillar of British society to this day. Bevan passionately argued for the idea that healthcare should be free and accessible to all, regardless of their socioeconomic status. Despite facing opposition and skepticism, Bevan successfully navigated political hurdles to pass the National Health Service Act in 1946, leading to the creation of the NHS in 1948.

In addition to his work on healthcare, Bevan was also an influential figure in foreign affairs. He strongly opposed nuclear weapons and was a vocal critic of the United States and the Soviet Union during the Cold War. Bevan believed that disarmament was vital for global peace and advocated for nuclear disarmament at international forums. However, his stance on nuclear weapons created divisions within the Labour

Party and ultimately led to his resignation from the party's leadership in 1951, along with Harold Wilson, in what became known as the "Bevanite split". Despite this setback, Bevan remained an influential and respected figure within the Labour Party and continued to champion socialist principles throughout his career. He played a crucial role in shaping Labour's policies and was widely regarded as a man of integrity and conviction.

******

The Movement was a literary group that emerged in Britain in the 1950s, primarily associated with a circle of poets who sought to distance themselves from the prevailing trends of modernism and express a more traditional and accessible style of poetry. The key founding members of The Movement were Philip Larkin, Kingsley Amis, and Thom Gunn. They were joined by other poets like D.J. Enright, Donald Davie, and Elizabeth Jennings, who shared similar poetic sensibilities. The poets of The Movement emphasised a return to more traditional poetic forms and themes. They sought to write in a clear, direct, and conversational style, often focusing on everyday experiences, personal observations, and ordinary language. Their poetry often had a restrained and understated tone. The Movement can be seen as a reaction against the experimental and complex poetry of the modernist movement that dominated the early 20th century. The poets of The Movement rejected the dense symbolism and fragmented structures of modernist poetry in favour of more accessible and relatable verse. The Movement poets often explored themes of personal identity, love, loss, disillusionment, and the passage of time. They expressed a sense of nostalgia and reflected on the changing social and cultural landscape of post-war Britain. The poets associated with The Movement gained recognition through their publications, anthologies, and appearances in literary journals. Philip Larkin, in particular, became a prominent and influential figure in British poetry, known for his wit, keen observation, and introspective themes. It is important to note that The Movement was not a formal or organised literary group like the Bloomsbury Group. Rather, it represented a loose association of poets who shared common poetic principles and contributed to a significant shift in British poetry during the 1950s.

Realism and social critique were prominent features in literature in 1950s Britain. Many authors sought to provide realistic portrayals of society and engage in social commentary. The aftermath of World War II deeply influenced literature in the 1950s. Authors grappled with the social, economic, and psychological impacts of the war. They explored themes such as loss, disillusionment, and the struggle to rebuild society. A significant aspect of 1950s British literature was the exploration of working-class life. Authors delved into the realities, hardships, and aspirations of the working-class population, often shedding light on the inequalities and social divisions of the time. Many authors used their works to critique various aspects of society and its institutions. They examined the class system, the bureaucracy, the education system, and the changing values in post-war Britain. These critiques often highlighted the constraints and frustrations faced by individuals within these systems. Literature in the 1950s reflected the changing political and cultural landscape of Britain. Authors engaged in social and political commentary, addressing issues such as the rise of consumerism, the nuclear threat, the decline of empire, and the impact of American culture. Notable examples of literature from this period that embody realism and social critique include Kingsley Amis's "Lucky Jim", and John Braine's "Room at the Top".

John Wyndham was an influential British author who made significant contributions to science fiction literature in the 1950s. John Wyndham is best known for his post-apocalyptic and dystopian science fiction novels. His works often explore the consequences of scientific advancements and societal upheavals. "The Day of the Triffids" depicts a world struck by blindness after a meteor shower and the subsequent threat of aggressive, mobile plants known as triffids. It explores themes of survival, human nature, and the consequences of bioengineering. "The Kraken Wakes" explores the invasion of Earth by mysterious sea creatures and the gradual submersion of coastal regions due to rising sea levels. It addresses themes of environmental change, alien invasion, and human resilience. "The Chrysalids", set in a post-apocalyptic world, follows a group of telepathic children who must hide their abilities to survive in a society that fears and rejects "deviations". It touches upon themes of conformity, discrimination, and the dangers of fanaticism.

******

The quest to break the four-minute mile barrier captivated the world's attention for decades. Athletes, scientists, and sports enthusiasts were drawn to the seemingly insurmountable challenge. This incredible feat was first accomplished by Sir Roger Bannister in 1954, shattering the myth that a human could not run a mile in less than four minutes. For centuries, the four-minute mile was believed to be an unattainable goal. Many experts believed that the human body was simply incapable of achieving such a feat. However, in the early 20th century, as sports science and training methods advanced, athletes began to question this limitation. The pursuit of the four-minute mile became an obsession, driving athletes to test the boundaries of their physical capabilities.

On 6th May 1954, at Oxford University's Iffley Road track, Sir Roger Bannister etched his name into history. With fierce determination and impeccable preparation, Bannister ran a mile in 3:59.04s, becoming the first person to break the elusive four-minute barrier. Bannister's extraordinary achievement shattered the myth and inspired a generation of runners. Bannister's feat ignited a fierce rivalry between him and Australian runner John Landy. In 1954, just 46 days after Bannister's record-breaking run, the two competitors faced off in a highly anticipated showdown at the British Empire Games in Vancouver. In an iconic moment known as the "Miracle Mile", Landy led the race, but as he glanced over his shoulder to check on Bannister's position, Bannister seized the opportunity and passed him, winning the race.

Bannister's achievement opened the floodgates of possibility. In the years following his record-breaking run, the four-minute mile became a benchmark for middle-distance runners worldwide. The race to achieve this remarkable feat intensified, with numerous athletes pushing their limits to join the exclusive club. John Landy would go on to break Bannister's record, and the record has been lowered multiple times since then. The pursuit of the four-minute mile exemplifies the indomitable spirit of human ambition. Roger Bannister's historic achievement shattered long-held beliefs and inspired future generations to chase their own dreams. It remains a testament to the power of determination, perseverance, and the relentless pursuit of excellence in the face of seemingly insurmountable challenges.

******

In the 1950s, men's and women's fashion in Britain underwent significant changes influenced by post-war optimism and the rise of youth culture. Men typically wore suits as everyday attire, reflecting a sense of formality and sophistication. Suits were well-tailored with broad shoulders, fitted jackets, and high-waisted trousers. The popular colours for suits were dark shades such as charcoal gray, navy blue, and brown. Men's shirts were usually made of cotton or rayon and featured a narrow collar with a loop at the back. White shirts were the most common choice, but pastel shades and small patterns like checks and stripes gained popularity as well. Overcoats and trench coats were popular choices for outerwear during colder months. They were typically knee-length and made of wool or gabardine. Additionally, leather jackets, especially iconic motorcycle jackets, became popular among young men, inspired by rebellious youth subcultures. Classic leather Oxfords and brogues were commonly worn by men for both formal and casual occasions. Loafers were also favoured for a more relaxed style. Women's fashion in the 1950s emphasised feminine silhouettes. Full-skirted dresses with nipped-in waists were the epitome of style. These dresses often featured floral prints, polka dots, or solid colours. Necklines were modest, with high collars or boat necks, and sleeves were typically short or three-quarter length. Skirts were usually full and reached mid-calf or ankle length. Pencil skirts, which hugged the body and accentuated curves, were also popular for a more tailored look. Blouses were an essential part of a woman's wardrobe. They were often made of delicate fabrics like silk or cotton and featured feminine details such as ruffles, bows, or lace trims. Blouses were typically worn with skirts or undersuits for a more formal appearance. Coats and jackets in the 1950s were often fitted and emphasised the waistline. Fur-trimmed collars and cuffs were common, as were swing coats and tailored jackets. Trench coats were also a popular choice, particularly in neutral colours like beige or camel.

Overall, 1950s fashion in Britain represented a blend of elegance and conservatism, characterised by tailored looks for both men and women. These fashion trends played a significant role in defining the style of the era and continue to inspire contemporary fashion designers today.

The Teddy Boys were a prominent youth subculture in the 1950s. They were known for their distinctive style, which drew inspiration from Edwardian fashion. Teddy Boys wore long, drape-style jackets with velvet or satin collars, high-waisted trousers, and narrow ties. They also sported pompadour hairstyles, often greased and styled with precision. The rise of rock 'n' roll music had a profound impact on youth fashion in the 1950s. Inspired by rockabilly and early rock 'n' roll stars like Elvis Presley, young men and women adopted elements of their style. This included wearing tight-fitting jeans or trousers, leather jackets, collared shirts, and saddle shoes or loafers. Sweaters were a staple of youth fashion in the 1950s. Young men often wore crewneck or V-neck sweaters, sometimes layered with a collared shirt underneath. Cardigans, often worn buttoned up, were popular among both young men and women. Sweaters and cardigans were typically made of wool or cashmere and came in an array of colours.

******

Britain's post-war economic recovery in the 1950s was a crucial period of rebuilding and reconstruction after the devastation of World War II. The Marshall Plan, officially known as the European Recovery Program (ERP) provided significant financial aid to Britain, aiming to support its post-war economic recovery. Between 1948 and 1951, Britain received approximately $3.3 billion in economic assistance, which helped stabilise its economy and fostered economic growth. The funds were utilised in rebuilding Britain's infrastructure and industries. The aid contributed to the reconstruction of damaged infrastructure, including roads, bridges, and railways. It also supported the modernisation and revitalisation of industries such as manufacturing, steel, and coal mining. The aid from the Marshall Plan helped Britain enhance its trade and expand its exports. By investing in industrial reconstruction and modernisation, Britain was able to increase productivity and improve the quality of its goods. This, in turn, facilitated increased exports and helped earn foreign currency, strengthening the country's balance of payments. The Marshall Plan contributed to job creation and improved living standards in Britain. As industries recovered and expanded, employment opportunities increased, reducing unemployment and providing stability to the workforce. The economic growth supported by the aid led to rising wages and improved living conditions for many Britons.

Austerity measures were implemented in Britain during the 1950s as part of the post-war economic policies. Rationing of goods continued in the immediate aftermath of World War II due to shortages of essential commodities. Rationing, which had been in place since 1940, remained a key aspect of austerity measures during the 1950s. Items such as food, clothing, and fuel were subject to rationing, with individuals receiving specific allowances to ensure fair distribution. The government exercised control over prices and wages as part of its austerity policies. Price controls were imposed to prevent inflation and ensure affordability, especially for essential goods. Wages were also regulated to avoid excessive increases that could lead to inflationary pressures. The government focused on maintaining fiscal discipline and reducing public expenditure. This meant limiting government spending and prioritising essential services. Investment in infrastructure and social programs was constrained to manage the country's financial resources. Currency and exchange controls were put in place to manage foreign exchange reserves and stabilise the economy. These controls limited the ability of individuals and businesses to freely trade or transfer money abroad.

Austerity measures affected the public sector, including government departments, local authorities, and public services. Budgets were tightened, resulting in reduced funding for areas such as education, healthcare, and infrastructure development. Government austerity policies aimed to encourage savings and investments. The government introduced savings schemes, such as National Savings Certificates, to mobilise private savings and channel them towards investment in the country's economic recovery. The 1950s saw a focus on industrial reconstruction and modernisation. Efforts were made to rebuild and update factories, invest in new technologies, and increase productivity. Industries such as manufacturing, steel, and engineering received significant attention and support. The British government pursued export led growth as a means to earn foreign currency and rebuild the economy. Exports, particularly of manufactured goods, were actively promoted and supported through trade agreements and incentives.

In the late 1950s, Britain began exploring the possibility of joining the European Economic Community (EEC), a precursor to the European Union. Although Britain's initial application was vetoed by France in 1963, the discussions around European integration signalled a recognition of the importance of European markets for trade and economic development. The late 1950s witnessed a rise in consumerism, driven by increasing affluence and higher disposable incomes. This contributed to economic growth as demand for consumer goods and services increased, stimulating industries such as retail, entertainment, and leisure.

******

ITV was the first commercial broadcaster to launch in the country and has played a significant role in shaping British broadcasting since its inception. The birth of ITV can be traced back to the Television Act of 1954, which was introduced by the British government to establish commercial television alongside the existing public service broadcaster, the BBC. The act allowed for the creation of independent regional companies to provide programming and compete with the BBC. On 22nd September 1955, ITV made its debut with the launch of Associated-Rediffusion, the first company to begin broadcasting under the new commercial television framework. The initial transmission took place in the London region, and it marked a historic moment in British broadcasting history.

Following the success of Associated-Rediffusion, several other regional companies joined ITV in the subsequent years. These companies included Granada Television in the North of England, ATV in the Midlands, and Southern Television on the South Coast, among others. Each company operated independently and provided programming tailored to their specific regions.

One of the defining features of ITV was its commercial nature. Unlike the BBC, which was funded by a license fee paid by viewers, ITV relied on advertising revenue to finance its operations. This commercial model allowed ITV to attract significant investment and deliver a wide range of programming to its viewers.

******

The Cold War and foreign policy in Britain during the 1950s were deeply intertwined, as Britain found itself at the forefront of global politics during this period. The Cold War was a prolonged ideological, political, and military standoff between the Western bloc led by the United States and the Eastern Bloc led by the Soviet Union. Britain played a significant role in shaping the course of the Cold War and pursued a foreign policy that reflected its global interests and its position as a major power. The aftermath of World War II left Britain economically and militarily weakened, but it remained committed to maintaining its status as a world power.

One of the key pillars of Britain's foreign policy in the 1950s was its close alliance with the United States. The two countries shared a common interest in containing the spread of communism and countering the influence of the Soviet Union. This alliance was formalised through the creation of the North Atlantic Treaty Organisation (NATO) in 1949, with Britain playing a vital role in the defence of Western Europe. The UK stationed troops in Germany as part of NATO's military presence and developed its nuclear weapons capability, becoming the third country to test an atomic bomb on 3rd October 1952.

Another important aspect of Britain's foreign policy was its commitment to its colonial possessions. During the 1950s, numerous African and Asian colonies were seeking independence, and Britain faced pressure to decolonize. Despite the setbacks in Suez, Britain continued to pursue an active role in global affairs. It aimed to maintain its status as a bridge between the United States and Europe and actively participated in initiatives such as the European Coal and Steel Community, the precursor to the European Union. Additionally, Britain sought to maintain its global influence through the Commonwealth, an association of former British colonies and territories. The Commonwealth provided a platform for diplomatic engagement and cooperation, and Britain played a leading role in its activities.

******

Rugby union in 1950s Britain was a vibrant and transformative period for the sport. Despite the aftermath of World War II and the challenges faced by the country during post-war reconstruction, rugby union thrived and experienced notable developments during this decade.

The 1950s saw England, Scotland, Wales, France and Ireland continuing their annual battle for the Five Nations Championship. These nations played a significant role in shaping the sport and maintaining its popularity throughout the decade. The British and Irish Lions, a team comprised of players from England, Scotland, Wales, and Ireland, embarked on several successful tours during the 1950s. They traveled to New Zealand and Australia in 1950 and South Africa in 1955. These tours not only showcased the skills of British and Irish players but also helped foster relationships and camaraderie among the different nations.

The international matches of the 1950s were characterised by fierce competition and memorable moments. England won the Grand Slam in the 1957 Five Nations Championship, winning all their matches. Wales also had a successful decade, winning the Five Nations Championship in 1950, 1952 and 1956. Scotland and Ireland also had their share of victories and provided thrilling contests against their rivals.

The 1950s also witnessed the emergence of talented players who left an indelible mark on the sport. Players like Cliff Morgan, Phil Davies, Ken Jones, and Terry Davies showcased their skills and became icons of the era. These players not only represented their clubs and countries with distinction but also played crucial roles in raising the profile of rugby union.

1960s
British Invasion and The Kings Road

One of the defining features of the 1960s in Britain was the emergence of a vibrant youth culture. Young people rebelled against the conservative norms of the previous decades and sought to challenge established social conventions. The "Swinging Sixties" in London became a symbol of this cultural revolution, with Carnaby Street and the King's Road becoming hubs of fashion and music. Music played a crucial role in shaping the cultural landscape of the 1960s. The British music scene experienced a surge of creativity and innovation, with bands like The Beatles, The Rolling Stones, The Who, and The Kinks leading the "British Invasion" in the United States. The music of this era, particularly rock and roll and later psychedelic rock, reflected the spirit of rebellion and experimentation.

Fashion also underwent a radical transformation in the 1960s. The influence of designers like Mary Quant and the rise of "mod" culture brought about a shift in clothing styles. Miniskirts, bold patterns, and unconventional designs became popular, challenging traditional notions of propriety and femininity. The fashion industry embraced youth-oriented trends and catered to the changing tastes and desires of the younger generation.

Politically, the 1960s was a time of activism and protest. The civil rights movement in the United States had a significant impact on Britain, inspiring campaigns for racial equality and an end to racial discrimination. Groups like the Campaign Against Racial Discrimination (CARD) and the Anti-Apartheid Movement emerged to challenge institutionalised racism and advocate for social change.

Technological advancements also played a pivotal role in shaping the 1960s. The availability of television sets in most households brought about a media revolution, as people had access to news, entertainment, and cultural programming like never before. The coverage of significant events, such as the assassination of President John F. Kennedy and the moon landing, connected people to global happenings and fuelled discussions and debates.

The sexual revolution and changing attitudes towards sexuality were key features of the 1960s. The introduction of the contraceptive pill in 1961 gave women greater control over their reproductive rights and played a crucial role in the sexual liberation movement. Discussions around sexual freedom, reproductive rights, and gender equality became increasingly prominent. The emergence of feminist movements, such as the Women's Liberation Movement, challenged societal norms and advocated for gender equality. Issues like equal pay, reproductive rights, and the role of women in society were brought to the forefront of public discourse. Feminist literature, such as Betty Friedan's "The Feminine Mystique", ignited conversations and paved the way for future advancements in women's rights.

The 1960s also saw the decline of the British Empire, as former colonies gained independence. The process of decolonisation was accompanied by debates about national identity, immigration, and the changing demographics of Britain. Waves of immigrants from the Caribbean, India, and other parts of the former empire arrived in Britain, enriching the cultural fabric of the nation.

******

The 1960s marked a significant period of cultural and musical revolution in Britain. It was a time of immense creativity, social change, and the emergence of various influential music genres. From the energetic and rebellious sounds of rock 'n' roll to the introspective folk movement and the explosion of British pop bands, the music of the 1960s shaped a generation and left a lasting impact on the world. One of the defining moments of the decade was the British invasion, spearheaded by bands like The Beatles, The Rolling Stones, The Who, and The Kinks. These iconic bands took the United States by storm, with their catchy melodies, innovative songwriting, and charismatic performances. They brought a fresh and exciting sound that captured the hearts of millions of fans, establishing British rock as a dominant force in the global music scene.

The Beatles, in particular, revolutionised popular music during this era. With their undeniable talent, groundbreaking studio techniques, and thought-provoking lyrics, they became a cultural phenomenon. Hits like "She Loves You", "A Hard Day's Night", and "Hey Jude" became anthems of the era, showcasing the band's versatility and ability to connect with listeners on a profound level. While rock 'n' roll dominated the airwaves, the 1960s also saw the rise of folk music, inspired by the American folk revival. Artists like Bob Dylan and Donovan gained popularity with their introspective and socially conscious lyrics. They addressed themes of love, protest, and cultural change, influencing a new generation of singer-songwriters.

The likes of The Dave Clark Five, The Hollies, The Animals, and The Small Faces crafted infectious melodies and catchy hooks, often infused with a dose of youthful exuberance. These bands brought a sense of joy and escapism to the charts, becoming idols for a generation of fans. The music of the 1960s was not solely defined by bands and artists. The era also saw the rise of the influential counterculture movement, fuelled by the hippie movement and psychedelic music. Bands like Pink Floyd, The Jimi Hendrix Experience, and Cream pushed musical boundaries with their experimental sounds, mind-altering lyrics, and intricate instrumentations.

The psychedelic movement was characterised by its distinctive blend of rock, folk, and elements of Eastern music, creating a sonic landscape that reflected the changing social and cultural landscape of the time. The 1960s also witnessed the birth of iconic music festivals that would shape the future of live music events. The Isle of Wight Festival, Glastonbury Festival, and the legendary Monterey Pop Festival became platforms for artists to showcase their talents and connect with fans on a larger scale. These festivals embodied the spirit of the era, fostering a sense of community, creativity, and social experimentation. The music of the 1960s in Britain was a reflection of the cultural and social changes taking place. It provided a voice for the youth, challenging conventions, and expressing a desire for freedom and self-expression. From the infectious pop tunes to the thought-provoking lyrics and innovative sounds, the music of this era continues to inspire and influence generations of musicians and remains a cherished part of music history.

******

The introduction of the contraceptive pill in Britain in the 1960s was a transformative moment in reproductive healthcare and social attitudes towards contraception. The Pill provided women with a highly effective and convenient method of contraception, granting them greater control over their reproductive choices and expanding opportunities for family planning. The contraceptive pill was developed in the 1950s, and its availability and acceptance grew steadily throughout the 1960s. In 1961, the British Family Planning Association (FPA) played a crucial role in advocating for the pill's availability and accessibility. They campaigned for the pill to be prescribed to married women, primarily for contraceptive purposes, and emphasised its potential to reduce the number of unintended pregnancies and improve women's reproductive health.

In 1961, the National Health Service (NHS) made the pill available to married women through its family planning clinics. Initially, the pill was prescribed only to married women for medical reasons, such as menstrual irregularities, but it soon became clear that it was widely used for contraception. However, it wasn't until the 1967 Abortion Act that the pill was made available to all women, regardless of marital status. The act legalised abortion in certain circumstances and also facilitated access to the contraceptive pill. This change represented a significant step towards acknowledging and respecting women's reproductive autonomy and their right to make informed choices about their bodies and fertility. The introduction of the contraceptive pill had profound social and cultural implications. It played a pivotal role in the sexual revolution of the 1960s, challenging traditional attitudes towards sexuality and enabling more open discussions about contraception. The pill allowed women to separate sexual activity from reproduction and empowered them to pursue education, careers, and personal goals with greater freedom. The availability of the pill also had demographic implications. It contributed to a decline in birth rates and a shift in family planning practices. Women and couples had more control over the timing and spacing of their children, leading to smaller family sizes and changes in societal expectations around motherhood and family dynamics.

Despite its revolutionary impact, the introduction of the contraceptive pill in the 1960s was not without controversy. It sparked debates about moral values, sexual liberation, and the potential risks and side effects of the pill. Some religious and conservative groups expressed concerns about the pill's impact on traditional family structures and moral values.

******

The Grand National in the 1960s was an exciting and eventful decade for the iconic horse race held at Aintree Racecourse. In 1960 the race was won by 13/2 favourite Merryman II, ridden by jockey Gerry Scott and trained by Neville Crump. The 1963 race is particularly remembered for the dramatic last fence fall of the leading horse, Carrickbeg, who was well ahead of the pack. 66/1 outsider Ayala, ridden by jockey Pat Buckley, emerged victorious. In 1965 the legendary American bred racehorse Jay Trump started at odds of 100/6. jockey Tommy Smith claimed victory. Jay Trump became the first American bred horse to win the race, adding to the excitement and significance of the victory.

The Grand National in 1967 is remembered as one of the most unpredictable and chaotic races in the history of the prestigious steeplechase event held annually at Aintree Racecourse near Liverpool, England. On 8th April 1967, the Grand National took place with a field of 44 horses competing over the challenging four-and-a-half-mile course, which included daunting fences such as Becher's Brook and The Chair. Heavy rain before the race had left the ground soft, making the course even more treacherous. Foinavon, a little-known 100/1 outsider ridden by jockey John Buckingham, was considered an underdog and was largely ignored by the betting public. The horse tended to jump erratically and had previously fallen in races. The chaos unfolded at the 23rd fence, now known as the "Foinavon Fence". A loose horse named Popham Down unseated its rider, leading to a pile-up of several horses and creating a significant gap between the remaining runners and those involved in the melee. Foinavon was far behind the leading pack at this point. As the remaining horses approached the fence, most jockeys had difficulty navigating around the fallen horses and refused the jump. However, Buckingham and Foinavon, being so far behind, had a clear path to jump over the fence without obstruction. Foinavon and Buckingham capitalised on this extraordinary stroke of luck and cleared the fence effortlessly, quickly gaining a considerable lead over the other horses. The duo continued to race unchallenged, and Foinavon crossed the finish line, securing a remarkable victory by 15 lengths. The Foinavon Grand National victory of 1967 is often regarded as a true underdog story and has become one of the most famous moments in the race's history. The unexpected outcome and the horse's unlikely triumph have made Foinavon and the Foinavon Fence synonymous with unpredictability and the spirit of the Grand National.

******

The 1960s in Britain were a transformative period for the visual arts, witnessing the emergence of various artistic movements and the rise of influential artists who challenged traditional norms and pushed the boundaries of creativity. It was a time of experimentation, social change, and the exploration of new artistic mediums. One of the most prominent artistic movements of the era was Pop Art, which found its roots in both the United States and Britain. British artists like Richard Hamilton, Peter Blake, and David Hockney played significant roles in defining the Pop Art movement and bringing it to the forefront of the art world. Pop Art celebrated popular culture, consumerism, and mass media, incorporating imagery from advertisements, comic books, and everyday objects into their artworks. The movement rejected elitism and embraced a more democratic approach to art, blurring the lines between high and low culture. In addition to Pop Art, the 1960s saw the emergence of other artistic movements such as Op Art and Kinetic Art. Op Art, championed by artists like Bridget Riley, focused on creating optical illusions through geometric patterns and repetitive forms, stimulating the viewer's perception. Kinetic Art, represented by artists like David Medalla and Liliane Lijn, incorporated movement and technological elements into their artworks, challenging static notions of traditional art forms. Sculpture also underwent significant developments in the 1960s. The traditional notions of sculpture were challenged by artists like Henry Moore and Barbara Hepworth, who embraced abstraction and introduced organic forms and the exploration of negative space. Their works, characterised by smooth curves and the use of materials like bronze and stone, created a sense of harmony between the artwork and its surroundings. The 1960s were also a time of social and political upheaval, with artists responding to the cultural climate through their work. Artists like Peter Kennard and Richard Long used their art as a means of protest and activism, addressing issues such as war, consumerism, and environmental concerns. Their works aimed to provoke thought and spark conversations about pressing social issues.

******

David Hockney is a renowned British artist known for his vibrant and distinctive style, innovative use of technology, and his exploration of various artistic mediums. Born on 9th July 1937, in Bradford, West Yorkshire, Hockney has become one of the most influential figures in contemporary art. Hockney's artistic journey began at an early age when he showed a talent for drawing and painting. He studied at the Bradford College of Art before moving on to the Royal College of Art in London in 1959. It was during his time at the Royal College of Art that Hockney began to develop his unique style, influenced by the works of artists like Pablo Picasso and Henri Matisse.

In the 1960s, Hockney emerged as a prominent figure in the British art scene, particularly associated with the Pop Art movement. His paintings of swimming pools, landscapes, and portraits were characterised by their vibrant colours, flat compositions, and bold graphic style. Hockney's subject matter often depicted scenes from his personal life, reflecting his experiences as a gay man in an era when homosexuality was still heavily stigmatised. Throughout his career, Hockney continually pushed the boundaries of artistic expression, exploring new mediums and techniques. In the 1970s, he became interested in photography and experimented with creating photo collages, often known as "joiners". These works, composed of multiple photographs arranged in a grid-like pattern, offered a fragmented and multi-perspective view of a subject, challenging the traditional notions of representation.

Hockney's contributions to the art world extend beyond his paintings and digital creations. He has also delved into set design, stage production, and printmaking. His collaboration with the Metropolitan Opera in New York City resulted in the creation of visually stunning stage sets for productions like "The Rake's Progress" and "Turandot". Over the years, Hockney's talent and innovation have been widely recognised and celebrated. He has received numerous awards and honours, including being appointed a Companion of Honour by Queen Elizabeth II in 1997 and receiving the Order of Merit in 2012. His artwork has been exhibited in major galleries and museums around the world, cementing his status as one of the most influential artists of his generation.

******

The Profumo affair was a political scandal that unfolded in Britain in the early 1960s, leading to the resignation of Secretary of State for War John Profumo and ultimately contributing to the fall of the Conservative government. The affair came to light in 1963 when it was revealed that John Profumo, a prominent Conservative politician, had engaged in a sexual relationship with Christine Keeler, a young model and showgirl.

Keeler's early life was marked by personal challenges and difficulties. Born on 22nd February 1942 in Uxbridge, Middlesex she grew up in a working-class family and experienced a troubled childhood. After leaving school at the age of 15, she worked a variety of jobs, including as a model and showgirl. In 1961, Keeler became involved in the social and political circles of London. It was during this time that she became romantically involved with John Profumo, who was then the Secretary of State for War in the Conservative government. Simultaneously, Keeler was also having an affair with Yevgeny Ivanov, a Soviet naval attaché, which raised concerns about potential national security risks. The revelation of Keeler's involvement with both Profumo and Ivanov led to a major scandal in 1963. The affair captured the public's attention and exposed the social and political tensions of the era. The scandal highlighted issues of class divisions, sexual morality, and national security.

Keeler's role in the Profumo affair made her a media sensation. Her image, often portrayed as a glamorous and provocative young woman, became an enduring symbol of the sexual revolution and social changes happening in Britain during the 1960s. In the aftermath of the scandal, Keeler faced legal repercussions. She was charged with perjury and conspiracy in unrelated cases and served time in prison. After her release, she struggled with various personal challenges, including financial difficulties and ongoing media scrutiny.

The Profumo affair became a major political scandal that undermined public trust in the government and raised questions about the integrity and judgment of those in power. Profumo initially denied any impropriety in the House of Commons, but later admitted to the affair, leading to his resignation on 5th June 1963. The scandal had broader implications beyond Profumo's conduct. It exposed issues of class divisions and social inequalities, with Christine Keeler being seen as a symbol of the "swinging sixties" and the sexual liberation of the era. It also highlighted concerns about corruption, moral values, and the abuse of power within the political establishment.

The fallout from the Profumo affair severely damaged the reputation of the Conservative government, led by Prime Minister Harold Macmillan. The scandal further eroded public confidence in the government's ability to govern effectively and led to a sense of disillusionment among the British public. While the Profumo affair itself did not directly cause the fall of the Conservative government, it contributed to an atmosphere of political instability and played a role in the Conservative Party's defeat in the 1964 general election.

******

The Beeching report, officially titled "The Reshaping of British Railways", was a significant report published in 1963 that outlined a plan for the restructuring and modernisation of the national railway system in Britain. The report was commissioned by the Conservative government under the leadership of Prime Minister Harold Macmillan and led by Dr. Richard Beeching, the Chairman of the British Railways Board. The Beeching report aimed to address the financial challenges faced by the British Railways system, which was suffering from declining passenger numbers and significant financial losses. Beeching was tasked with identifying measures to improve efficiency, reduce costs, and make the railways more financially viable.

The report recommended a series of drastic measures, including the closure of around a third of Britain's railway network and the removal of thousands of miles of track, stations, and services. Beeching argued that these cuts were necessary to eliminate unprofitable lines and focus resources on the most economically viable routes. The closures proposed in the Beeching report were met with widespread public opposition and generated significant controversy. Many affected communities argued that the closures would lead to isolation, job losses, and a decline in local economies. The closures also sparked debates about the government's commitment to public transport and the impact on rural areas and small towns. Between 1963 and 1970, approximately 5,000 miles of track were closed, and over 2,000 stations were shut down as a result of the implementation of the Beeching report's recommendations. The closures were accompanied by a shift towards a more centralised and streamlined railway system, with a greater focus on intercity services and the reduction of branch lines. While the Beeching report was intended to make the railway system more financially sustainable, its long-term impact on the network and communities has been a subject of ongoing debate. Critics argue that the report's emphasis on cost-cutting and profitability overlooked the broader social and economic benefits of a comprehensive rail network, particularly for rural and remote areas.

******

Tennis in Britain during the 1960s witnessed significant achievements, transformative changes, and the rise of iconic players who left a lasting impact on the sport. From notable successes in Grand Slam tournaments to the introduction of Open tennis and the emergence of legendary British players, the decade was a pivotal period in British tennis history. In terms of Grand Slam success, the 1960s were notable for British players. Angela Mortimer won the Women's Singles title at Wimbledon in 1961, solidifying her status as one of the top female players of the time. Another British player who achieved remarkable success in the 1960s was Ann Jones. She won the French Championships in 1961 and 1966 reached the Wimbledon final in 1967 losing to Billie Jean King and emerged victorious in 1969 this time beating Billie Jean King. Jones's consistent performances and her triumph at Wimbledon elevated her to the forefront of British tennis. The 1960s also marked a significant milestone in tennis history with the introduction of Open tennis. Previously, amateur and professional players competed separately. However, in 1968, the sport transitioned to an open era, allowing professionals to compete alongside amateurs in major tournaments. This change had a profound impact on the sport globally, fostering increased competition and attracting more top players to major events. The British grass-court season, highlighted by the prestigious Wimbledon Championships, remained a pinnacle of the tennis calendar. Wimbledon continued to be a symbol of British tennis excellence, attracting players from around the world.

The 1960s also saw the development of tennis infrastructure in Britain. The All England Lawn Tennis and Croquet Club, the home of Wimbledon, underwent significant renovations during this period to accommodate growing crowds and enhance the spectator experience. Off the court, British tennis experienced significant advancements in coaching and development programs. The Lawn Tennis Association (LTA) focused on nurturing young talent, improving facilities, and promoting tennis at the grassroots level. These initiatives aimed to cultivate a new generation of British tennis stars and ensure the sport's future growth in the country.

******

The decade witnessed the rise of the British New Wave, also known as the "Kitchen Sink" movement, which challenged the traditional conventions of British cinema and explored social realism and personal narratives. One of the key films that symbolised the British New Wave was "Saturday Night and Sunday Morning", directed by Karel Reisz and based on the novel by Alan Sillitoe. The film starred Albert Finney and depicted the life of a rebellious young factory worker who struggles with the constraints of his working-class existence. It was a gritty and honest portrayal of post-war Britain and marked a departure from the polished and class-conscious films of the previous era. Another influential film of the 1960s was "A Taste of Honey", directed by Tony Richardson. Adapted from the play by Shelagh Delaney, the film tackled themes of race, gender, and class, revolving around the unconventional relationship between a young working-class girl and a black sailor. It was a pioneering work that challenged social norms and gave voice to marginalised characters.

The James Bond franchise also came to prominence in the 1960s, with the release of "Dr. No", starring Sean Connery as the iconic British spy. The Bond films became international sensations and showcased the glamour, action, and espionage that captivated audiences around the world. They became synonymous with British cinema and contributed to the global popularity of the spy genre. The 1960s also saw the emergence of a new wave of British directors who pushed the boundaries of filmmaking. Directors like Lindsay Anderson, John Schlesinger, and Ken Loach became key figures in the British film industry, exploring social issues, class divisions, and political commentary through their works. Anderson's "If..."., Schlesinger's "Darling", and Loach's "Kes" are examples of films that challenged the status quo and reflected the changing social landscape of the era. In addition to the British New Wave, the 1960s witnessed the rise of surreal and avant-garde cinema in Britain. Filmmakers like Stanley Kubrick, who was based in Britain at the time, pushed the boundaries of cinematic storytelling with films like "A Clockwork Orange" and "2001: A Space Odyssey". These films explored existential themes, technological advancements, and the human condition in a visually striking and thought-provoking manner. British cinema in the 1960s also experienced a resurgence in historical epics and literary adaptations. Films like "Lawrence of Arabia", "The Lion in Winter", and "Oliver!"

achieved critical acclaim and commercial success, showcasing the diversity and range of British filmmaking.

******

The birth of the Carry On film franchise is attributed to the collaboration between producer Peter Rogers and director Gerald Thomas. The first Carry On film, titled "Carry On Sergeant", was released in 1958, but it was in the 1960s that the franchise truly took off and became synonymous with British comedy. "Carry On Sergeant" set the template for the series by featuring a mix of slapstick humour, innuendos, and a cast of recurring actors who would become the familiar faces of the Carry On films. The film followed the misadventures of a group of National Service recruits and was a box office success, prompting Rogers and Thomas to continue exploring this comedic formula.

In the 1960s, the Carry On films became an annual event, with a new instalment released almost every year. The success of the franchise was attributed to its ability to tap into the British sense of humour, combining witty wordplay, visual gags, and risqué humour that often relied on double entendres. The Carry On films featured a repertory company of actors who became beloved figures in British comedy. The core ensemble included actors such as Sid James, Kenneth Williams, Joan Sims, Charles Hawtrey, Hattie Jacques, and Barbara Windsor, among others. These actors brought their unique comedic talents to each film, playing various roles and contributing to the series' enduring popularity.

The Carry On films covered a wide range of themes and settings, often parodying specific genres or historical periods. Some of the most memorable entries in the franchise include "Carry On Cleo", a parody of ancient Roman epics, and "Carry

On Camping", which humorously explored the pitfalls of holiday camping. What set the Carry On films apart was their ability to tap into the changing social attitudes of the time. The series played with innuendo, flirtation, and sexual humour, pushing the boundaries of what was considered acceptable comedy in the 1960s. While the films were not overly explicit, they found a balance between titillation and cheeky humour that resonated with audiences.

The popularity of the Carry On franchise led to numerous sequels, including "Carry On Nurse", "Carry On Teacher", "Carry On Regardless", and "Carry On Up the Khyber", among many others. The films became staples of British cinema, creating a recognisable brand and generating a dedicated fan base. The Carry On films continued to be made well into the 1970s and early 1980s, with the final instalment, "Carry On Columbus", released in 1992. Although the later films received mixed reviews, the franchise remains a significant part of British comedy history, with its distinct style and memorable characters.

******

The 1966 FIFA World Cup was a historic moment for England and its national football team. It was the eighth edition of the tournament and the first time that England had hosted the event. The tournament took place from 11th July to 30th July 1966, and it culminated in England's victory, which remains their only World Cup triumph to date. Led by manager Alf Ramsey, the English team entered the tournament with a squad filled with talented players, including legendary figures such as Bobby Moore, Bobby Charlton, Geoff Hurst, and Gordon Banks. England were placed in Group 1 alongside Uruguay, Mexico, and France for the group stage. In the group stage, England won two out of their three matches. They started with a 0-0 draw against Uruguay but followed it up with a convincing 2-0 victory over Mexico, courtesy of goals from Bobby Charlton and Roger Hunt. In their final group match, England faced France and emerged victorious with a 2-0 win, thanks to two goals from Roger Hunt. Having finished first in their group, England advanced to the knockout stage and in the quarter-finals, they faced Argentina. After a highly contentious match that saw Argentine captain Antonio Rattin controversially sent off and the England manager refusing to allow his team to swap shirts at the end of the game, England secured a 1-0 victory courtesy of a goal from Geoff Hurst. The semi-final clash against Portugal proved to be a memorable encounter. In a hard-fought match at Wembley Stadium, England emerged triumphant with a 2-1 victory. Bobby Charlton scored the goals that sent England to their first-ever World Cup final.

The final, held on 30th July 1966, at Wembley Stadium, was a historic moment for English football. England faced West Germany in a thrilling match that ended in a 4-2 win after extra time. Geoff Hurst scored a hat-trick, becoming the first and only player to achieve this feat in a World Cup final. His crucial goals in the 101st and 120th minutes sealed a victory for England, securing their place in football history. England's World Cup win in 1966 was a watershed moment for the nation. It brought immense pride and joy to the country, solidifying football's position as the national sport.

******

The Labour Party's victory in the 1964 general election ended 13 years of Conservative rule under the leadership of Harold Macmillan and later Alec Douglas-Home. Wilson campaigned on the promise of modernisation and a "white heat of technology" to revitalise the British economy and society. One of the key priorities of the Wilson government was to address economic challenges and promote economic growth. The government introduced various measures to stimulate the economy, including increased public spending, investment in technology and infrastructure, and the establishment of the National Economic Development Council to coordinate economic planning.

During its tenure, the Wilson government faced several significant events and challenges. In 1967, the devaluation of the British pound occurred, reducing its value against other currencies. The devaluation was a response to economic difficulties, including a balance of payments crisis. It aimed to make British exports more competitive and boost the economy. The government also implemented social reforms and policies aimed at improving the lives of ordinary people. These included the introduction of comprehensive education, which aimed to provide equal opportunities for all children regardless of their background. The Wilson government also passed legislation to liberalise divorce laws and decriminalise homosexuality.

Foreign policy was another important area for the Wilson government. Britain's relationship with the European Economic Community (EEC) was a key focus. The government submitted an application for British membership in 1967, but it faced resistance and was initially vetoed by French President Charles de Gaulle. Despite this setback, the Wilson government continued to pursue closer ties with Europe. The Wilson government also faced challenges in terms of industrial relations. There were frequent strikes and labor disputes during this period, which impacted the economy and led to disruptions in various industries.

In 1970, the Wilson government narrowly lost the general election to the Conservatives under the leadership of Edward Heath. This marked the end of the Labour government's tenure, but Wilson remained an influential figure in British politics and later served as Prime Minister for a second time from 1974 to 1976.

******

The "white heat of technology" was a phrase famously coined by British Prime Minister Harold Wilson during a speech in 1963. It became synonymous with the vision and ambition of the Wilson government in the 1960s to harness science and technology to drive economic growth and social progress in Britain. Harold Wilson, who had a background in science and technology, believed that Britain needed to embrace technological advancements to stay competitive in a rapidly changing world. He saw science and technology as crucial tools for modernisation and economic development, and he used the phrase "white heat of technology" to convey his commitment to harnessing these forces for the country's benefit.

The concept of the "white heat of technology" encapsulated Wilson's vision of a future Britain driven by innovation, scientific research, and technological advancements. He believed that through investments in research and development, the country could create new industries, increase productivity, and improve the standard of living for its citizens. To support this vision, the Wilson government introduced several policies and initiatives aimed at promoting technological progress. It established the Ministry of Technology in 1964, which had the mandate to coordinate and support scientific research and technological development. The government also increased funding for scientific research and invested in projects related to space exploration, nuclear power, and electronics.

The Wilson government's focus on technological advancement was not limited to the industrial sector. It also sought to modernise public services and improve efficiency through the use of technology. This included initiatives to computerise government operations and introduce new technologies in areas such as transportation and telecommunications. However, despite the ambitious rhetoric and efforts to promote technological advancement, the Wilson government faced challenges and encountered mixed results. Economic difficulties, including balance of payments issues and currency devaluation, hindered the government's ability to fully implement its vision. Industrial unrest and labour disputes also posed challenges to economic stability and productivity.

Nonetheless, the concept of the "white heat of technology" and the Wilson government's emphasis on science and technology left a lasting legacy. It contributed to a broader cultural and societal shift, popularising the idea that science, innovation, and technological progress were crucial for national development and competitiveness.

******

The 1960s saw the emergence of various influential styles, from the early 1960s conservative fashion to the revolutionary counterculture of the late 1960s. In the early part of the decade, fashion was still influenced by the 1950s, with women's clothing focusing on a feminine and polished look. The silhouette was defined by fitted dresses, pencil skirts, and tailored suits, often paired with accessories like gloves, pillbox hats, and pearls. This early 1960s fashion, popularised by icons like Jacqueline Kennedy, represented elegance and sophistication. However, as the decade progressed, there was a seismic shift in fashion that mirrored the cultural revolution happening in society. The influence of youth culture, music, and the British "Swinging London" scene became prominent. One of the most significant developments was the rise of the Mod subculture, with its distinctive and stylish fashion. Mod fashion embraced a minimalist and modern aesthetic, characterised by clean lines, bold geometric patterns, and slim-fitting garments. Women's fashion in the mid 1960s featured mini-skirts, shift dresses, and bold colour combinations. The iconic designer Mary Quant was at the forefront of this movement, popularising the mini-skirt and creating designs that were youthful, fun, and rebellious.

In contrast to the Mod style, the latter half of the 1960s witnessed the emergence of hippie or bohemian fashion. This countercultural movement rejected the conventional norms of dress and embraced a free-spirited and nonconformist style. It was influenced by global cultures, psychedelic art, and a focus on natural fabrics and relaxed silhouettes. Hippie fashion embraced flowing maxi dresses, tie dye patterns, bell-bottom trousers, fringed vests, and embroidered details. Accessories such as headbands, round sunglasses, and beaded jewellery were also popular. The bohemian style represented a rejection of the mainstream and a celebration of individualism and peace.

The influence of music and pop culture was instrumental in shaping 1960s fashion. The Beatles, for instance, had a massive impact on the fashion choices of young people. Their distinctive collarless suits and shaggy hairstyles inspired a new wave of style. In terms of hair and beauty, the 1960s were a time of experimentation. Women's hairstyles ranged from the sleek and polished bouffant popularised by Jackie Kennedy to the iconic pixie cut made famous by Twiggy. The beehive, the mod bob, and long, flowing locks were also popular styles. Makeup became bolder, with trends like dramatic winged eyeliner and pale lips gaining popularity.

******

British football clubs had a significant impact on European competitions in the 1960s, leaving a lasting impression on the continent. English and Scottish clubs showcased their talent, winning major European trophies and establishing themselves as forces to be reckoned with. The pinnacle of British success in European football during the 1960s came in 1968 when Manchester United became the first English club to win the prestigious European Cup. Under the management of Sir Matt Busby, United defeated Benfica 4-1 in extra time at Wembley Stadium. This victory symbolised the resurrection of a club that had overcome the tragic Munich air disaster in 1958, which claimed the lives of several players. Key players in Manchester United's triumph included Bobby Charlton, George Best, and Denis Law. Another English club that made its mark in Europe during the 1960s was Tottenham Hotspur. They became the first British club to win a major European trophy when they lifted the European Cup Winners' Cup in 1963. Managed by Bill Nicholson, Tottenham defeated Atletico Madrid 5-1 in the final, with Jimmy Greaves scoring twice. Two years later West Ham United won the European Cup Winners' Cup beating German side 1860 Munich 2-0 in the final with Alan Sealey scoring both goals. Scottish clubs also enjoyed success on the European stage. Glasgow Celtic, managed by Jock Stein, achieved historic glory by winning the European Cup in 1967. They became the first British club to win the competition, defeating Inter Milan 2-1 in the final held at the Estádio Nacional in Lisbon, Portugal. The "Lisbon Lions", as they were famously known, showcased exceptional talent and teamwork.

******

The Sexual Offences Act of 1967 was a landmark piece of legislation in the United Kingdom that partially decriminalised homosexuality. Before the Act, male homosexuality was illegal and considered a criminal offence, leading to widespread discrimination, persecution, and social stigma against the gay community. The Act was introduced as a private member's bill by Leo Abse, a Welsh Labour Member of Parliament, and received support from a group of progressive politicians who aimed to challenge the discriminatory laws surrounding homosexuality. The Act primarily focused on England and Wales but had significant implications for the broader LGBT rights movement in the UK. The Sexual Offences Act of 1967 legalised consensual sexual acts between two men over the age of 21 in private settings. It effectively decriminalised homosexuality between adults, although some restrictions remained in place, such as the prohibition of same-sex relations in the armed forces and the age of consent being set higher than for heterosexual acts. The Act marked a significant shift in societal attitudes towards homosexuality, challenging prevailing prejudices and acknowledging the rights of gay individuals. It was a pivotal moment for the gay rights movement in the UK, providing hope and legal recognition for same-sex relationships.

However, it is important to note that the Act did not fully grant equality and rights to the gay community. Discrimination, prejudice, and societal stigma persisted, and further advancements in gay rights would be needed in the years that followed. Subsequent revisions and amendments to the law gradually improved the rights and protections for individuals. The age of consent for same-sex relationships was equalised with heterosexual relationships in 2000, and further legislation, such as the Equality Act 2010, provided greater protection against discrimination based on sexual orientation.

******

Mary Quant, born on 11th February 1934, in London, is a British fashion designer and one of the most influential figures in 1960s fashion. Quant attended Goldsmiths, University of London, where she studied illustration and pursued her passion for design. In 1955, she opened her first boutique, called Bazaar, on the King's Road in Chelsea, London. This marked the beginning of her groundbreaking career and her significant impact on fashion. Quant's designs were characterised by their youthful and playful nature. She rejected the traditional notions of high fashion and instead focused on creating accessible and affordable clothing for young women. Her designs reflected the changing attitudes of the time, embracing the spirit of the 1960s and the emerging youth culture. One of Quant's most significant contributions to fashion was the introduction of the mini-skirt. In the mid 1960s, she started experimenting with shorter hemlines, inspired by the miniskirts worn by young women in London's Chelsea neighbourhood. Quant saw the potential of this daring style and created her version of the mini-skirt, which quickly became a sensation.

The mini-skirt revolutionised women's fashion, challenging the traditional ideas of modesty and femininity. It became a symbol of freedom, self-expression, and the changing roles of women in society. Quant's mini-skirt designs, often paired with bold tights or stockings, captured the spirit of the Swinging London scene and were embraced by young women around the world. Her designs featured bright colours, playful prints, and innovative materials, reflecting the dynamic and forward-thinking spirit of the '60s. Quant's impact on fashion was recognised with numerous awards and accolades throughout her career. In 1966, she was awarded the prestigious Order of the British Empire (OBE) for her contributions to the fashion industry. She also received the Hall of Fame Lifetime Achievement Award from the British Fashion Council in 1990.

******

Formula One in Britain during the 1960s was a vibrant and influential period that saw the country play a significant role in the development and success of the sport. With iconic circuits, legendary drivers, and groundbreaking technological advancements, Britain emerged as a dominant force in the world of Formula 1. The decade began with British teams and drivers making their mark on the sport. Teams like Lotus, BRM, and Cooper became powerhouses, revolutionising car design and engineering. Lotus, led by the visionary Colin Chapman, introduced innovative concepts such as the monocoque chassis, rear-engine layout, and aerodynamic advancements. These breakthroughs not only improved performance but also set new standards for safety and handling.

British drivers like Graham Hill, Jim Clark, and Jackie Stewart rose to prominence during this period, achieving remarkable success and becoming household names. Graham Hill, known as "Mr. Monaco" for his unmatched record at the prestigious Monaco Grand Prix, won two Formula One World Championships in the 1960s. His skill, versatility, and affable personality made him a beloved figure among fans and a true ambassador for British motorsport. Jim Clark, the talented Scotsman, emerged as one of the greatest drivers of his era. With his smooth and precise driving style, Clark secured two World Championships driving for the Lotus team. Jackie Stewart, another Scottish driver, burst onto the scene in the mid 1960s and went on to win three World Championships. Stewart's technical brilliance, tenacity, and advocacy for driver safety brought about significant changes in the sport, elevating him to the status of a true legend.

The British Grand Prix, held at the iconic Silverstone Circuit, was a highlight of the Formula One calendar in the 1960s. The race attracted a large and enthusiastic crowd, showcasing the nation's passion for motorsport. Silverstone's fast and demanding track layout provided a thrilling spectacle for both drivers and spectators, making it a favourite among the Formula One community. The 1960s also witnessed the rise of British engine manufacturers. Coventry Climax and BRM produced powerful and reliable engines that were sought after by numerous teams. These British engines played a pivotal role in the success of teams and drivers during this era.

Moreover, British engineers and designers contributed significantly to the technological advancements in Formula 1. The renowned British motorsport engineer, Harry Weslake, developed innovative engine designs, while Frank Costin and Keith Duckworth made significant contributions to chassis and engine development, respectively.

******

Graham Hill, known as "Mr. Monaco" for his immense success on the challenging Monaco circuit, was a British racing driver who left an indelible mark on the world of motorsport. Born on 15th February 1929, in Hampstead, London, Hill's passion for racing ignited at a young age, and he would go on to become one of the most celebrated and versatile drivers in Formula 1 history. Hill's early racing career saw him compete in various disciplines, including sports car racing and Formula 2. His determination and talent caught the attention of the British Racing Motors

(BRM) team, who signed him as a works driver for the 1960 Formula 1 season. Hill's debut in Formula 1 marked the beginning of an extraordinary journey.

In 1962, Hill clinched his first Formula 1 World Championship. Driving the BRM P57, he showcased remarkable consistency and skill, winning three races that season. His triumph in the championship solidified his place among the elite drivers of his time. Hill's success continued in subsequent years, as he secured numerous podium finishes and established himself as a force to be reckoned with. However, it was in the 1960s that Hill truly flourished and etched his name in Formula 1 history. In 1963, he joined the legendary Lotus team led by Colin Chapman, a partnership that would propel him to even greater heights. It was with Lotus that Hill became synonymous with the prestigious Monaco Grand Prix, earning him the moniker "Mr. Monaco". Hill's triumph at the 1963 Monaco Grand Prix was the first of five victories he would achieve on the narrow, twisting streets of Monte Carlo. The following year, in 1964, he achieved his best season performance to date, finishing as the championship runner-up behind John Surtees. Hill's driving style, characterised by precision and tenacity, earned him immense respect from his peers and fans alike.

In 1968, Hill once again tasted glory as he secured his second Formula 1 World Championship. Driving the Lotus 33, he won six races, becoming the first driver to win the championship with a Ford-powered car. Hill's dominance, coupled with his impeccable sportsmanship, endeared him to the motorsport community and elevated him to legendary status. Beyond his success on the track, Graham Hill possessed a captivating personality. Known for his affable nature, he had a charismatic charm that endeared him to the public. Hill's warm smile and engaging manner made him a favourite among fans, who admired not only his driving skills but also his down-to-earth demeanour.

******

The "Rivers of Blood" speech, delivered by Enoch Powell on 20th April 1968, remains one of the most controversial and divisive speeches in British political history. Powell, a Conservative Member of Parliament, used the speech to express his strong opposition to mass immigration and the Race Relations Bill, which aimed to address racial discrimination in Britain. In the speech, Powell warned of dire consequences if immigration continued at its current rate, stating that he foresaw "the River Tiber foaming with much blood" as a metaphorical depiction of potential racial conflict and social unrest. He expressed concerns about the impact of immigration on social cohesion, the preservation of cultural identity, and the strain on public services and housing.

The "Rivers of Blood" speech provoked immediate outrage and condemnation from many quarters, including within Powell's own Conservative Party and from anti-racist campaigners. Critics accused him of using inflammatory and racially charged language, promoting discrimination, and stoking xenophobia and racial tension. Powell was subsequently dismissed from his position as Shadow Defence Secretary by Conservative Party leader Edward Heath due to the controversy surrounding his speech. Despite this, Powell continued to garner support from some segments of the population who shared his concerns about immigration and its perceived impact on British society. The speech ignited a heated national debate about immigration, race relations, and the limits of free speech. It raised questions about the responsibility of political leaders to promote tolerance and inclusivity and the potential consequences of divisive rhetoric. While the "Rivers of Blood" speech had a significant impact on public discourse and political debate, it did not result in significant policy changes. The Race Relations Act was passed later in 1968, despite Powell's opposition and subsequent legislation has further aimed to address racial discrimination and promote equality in Britain.

******

Jim Clark, widely regarded as one of the greatest racing drivers in the history of Formula 1, was born on 4th March 1936, in Kilmany, Scotland. With his unparalleled skill, unmatched talent, and humble demeanour, Clark rose to become a true legend of the sport, leaving an enduring legacy that continues to inspire generations of drivers. From a young age, Clark exhibited a natural affinity for speed. His passion for motorsport led him to pursue a career in racing, and his journey towards greatness began in the early 1960s. In 1960, Clark made his Formula 1 debut driving for the Lotus team at the Dutch Grand Prix. While it took some time for him to find his footing, it was clear that he possessed a rare talent that would soon set him apart from his peers. In 1963, Clark's exceptional driving skills reached new heights. It was a breakout year for the Scottish driver as he clinched his first Formula 1 World Championship. Behind the wheel of the Lotus 25, Clark won an impressive seven out of the ten races that season, setting a new record for the highest number of wins in a single season at the time. His smooth and precise driving style, coupled with a keen understanding of the mechanics of his car, allowed him to dominate the competition. In the 1965 season, Clark reached the pinnacle of his career by securing his second Formula 1 World Championship. Driving the Lotus 33, he won six races that season, including victories at the prestigious Monaco Grand Prix and the British Grand Prix. Clark's driving was characterised by finesse, precision, and an uncanny ability to extract maximum performance from his car.

His technical brilliance, combined with his calm and focused demeanour, made him virtually unbeatable.

However, tragedy struck on 7th April 1968, when Jim Clark's life was cut short during a Formula 2 race at Hockenheim, Germany. Clark's Lotus veered off the track and collided with trees, resulting in his untimely death at the age of 32. The motorsport world mourned the loss of a true icon, whose extraordinary talent and remarkable sportsmanship had captivated fans around the globe. In the realm of motorsport, Jim Clark will always be remembered as the maestro of speed, a driver whose remarkable skill, technical brilliance, and unwavering dedication continue to inspire generations of racing enthusiasts. His name will forever be etched in the annals of Formula 1 as one of the

******

In the 1960s, European integration and Britain's relationship with the European Economic Community (EEC) were significant topics of discussion and debate. The EEC, established by the Treaty of Rome in 1957, aimed to promote economic cooperation and political integration among its member states. In 1961, the Conservative government, under the leadership of Prime Minister Harold Macmillan, submitted an application for British membership in the EEC. However, the application was vetoed by French President Charles de Gaulle, who had concerns about Britain's commitment to European integration.

The rejection by de Gaulle did not deter the British government's desire for EEC membership. In 1967, under Prime Minister Harold Wilson and the Labour Party, a second application was submitted. This time, negotiations were successful, and in January 1973, Britain officially became a member of the EEC alongside Denmark and Ireland. The decision to join the EEC had both economic and political implications for Britain. Economically, membership in the EEC provided access to a larger market and facilitated trade and economic cooperation with other member states. It offered opportunities for British businesses to expand their markets and benefit from the removal of trade barriers and the establishment of a common external tariff.

Politically, joining the EEC signalled a commitment to European integration and closer cooperation with other European nations. It was seen as a way to strengthen Britain's influence and voice in shaping European policies and decisions. However, there were also concerns about the potential loss of sovereignty and the impact on national decision-making. The debate surrounding European integration and Britain's membership in the EEC was often polarised. Supporters of European integration argued that it would bring economic benefits, enhance cooperation, and foster peace and stability in Europe. Critics, on the other hand, raised concerns about the loss of national sovereignty, the impact on domestic industries, and the erosion of British identity.

******

John Surtees, born on 11th February 1934, in Tatsfield, Surrey, was a British racing driver who achieved unparalleled success in both motorcycle racing and Formula 1. His unique and extraordinary career earned him a place in the annals of motorsport history, as the only person to have won World Championships on both two wheels and four. Surtees began his racing journey in the world of motorcycles. In the 1950s, he quickly established himself as a formidable force, showcasing exceptional talent and determination. In 1956, at the age of 22, Surtees won his first 500cc Motorcycle World Championship riding for the MV Agusta team. This victory marked the beginning of an illustrious career that saw him win a total of seven World Championships in the 350cc and 500cc categories between 1956 and 1960. After conquering the world of motorcycle racing, Surtees set his sights on a new challenge, Formula 1. In 1964, driving for the Ferrari team, Surtees achieved his most significant milestone in Formula 1 by clinching the World Championship. The season proved to be a hard-fought battle, with Surtees consistently delivering exceptional performances. He secured two victories and finished on the podium in six out of ten races, showcasing his adaptability and versatility as a driver. Surtees' World Championship triumph was not only a personal milestone but also a historical moment in the sport. He became the first and, to this day, the only person to have won World Championships on both two wheels and four. This achievement solidified his status as a true motorsport legend, transcending the boundaries of different disciplines.

Following his championship success, Surtees continued to compete in Formula 1, representing various teams throughout his career, including Honda, BRM, and his own Surtees Racing organisation. While he did not secure another World Championship, he achieved numerous podium finishes and remained a respected and admired figure in the paddock. After retiring from Formula 1 in 1972, Surtees continued to make significant contributions to the motorsport world. He established the Surtees Racing organisation, which competed in various racing series, including Formula 2 and Formula 5000. Additionally, he nurtured young talent and mentored promising drivers, sharing his vast knowledge and experience with the next generation.

1970s
High Inflation and the Three Day Week

The 1970s began with a series of economic challenges for Britain. The country faced inflation, rising unemployment, and a decline in industrial productivity. The oil crisis of 1973, triggered by political tensions in the Middle East, led to a significant increase in oil prices and exacerbated economic difficulties. This period became known as the "Winter of Discontent", marked by strikes and labor disputes that further disrupted the economy. Politically, the 1970s witnessed a shift in power, as the Conservative Party, under the leadership of Edward Heath, was succeeded by the Labour Party, led by Harold Wilson. Wilson's government implemented policies aimed at addressing the economic crisis, including attempts to control inflation and stimulate economic growth. However, these measures faced significant challenges and did not fully resolve the underlying issues. The Troubles in Northern Ireland, a conflict between paramilitary groups seeking to determine the status of Northern Ireland, intensified during this period. The violence and political divisions had a profound impact on British society and shaped the political landscape for years to come. Social movements also emerged, seeking to challenge established norms and promote social change. The women's liberation movement gained momentum, advocating for equal rights and opportunities for women. Issues such as reproductive rights, workplace equality, and domestic violence were at the forefront of the movement's agenda. Another significant social movement of the 1970s was the gay rights movement. Activists fought for the decriminalisation of homosexuality. The Sexual Offences Act of 1967 decriminalised homosexual acts between consenting adults in private, but discrimination and prejudice remained prevalent. Culturally, the 1970s witnessed a diverse range of artistic expressions. The music scene reflected the changing times, with genres such as glam rock, punk rock, and disco gaining popularity. Artists like David Bowie, Queen, the Sex Pistols, and ABBA made significant contributions to the musical landscape of the decade. The fashion of the 1970s was characterised by a mix of retro influences, glam aesthetics, and bold, flamboyant styles.

Television and film played a significant role in shaping popular culture during the 1970s. Shows like "Monty Python's Flying Circus" and "Fawlty Towers" pushed the boundaries of humour and satire, while dramas like "Upstairs, Downstairs" and "The Sweeney" reflected the changing social dynamics of the era. Films like "A Clockwork Orange" and "The Rocky Horror Picture Show" challenged traditional storytelling conventions and explored themes of rebellion and societal breakdown. The 1970s were also marked by significant global events that had an impact on Britain. The United Kingdom joined the European Economic Community (EEC) in 1973, marking a major step towards European integration. However, divisions over Europe would continue to shape British politics for decades to come.

In 1979, Margaret Thatcher became the first female Prime Minister of Britain and initiated a period of conservative governance that would define the following decade. Thatcher's policies focused on free-market economics, privatisation, and reducing the influence of trade unions. These policies had far-reaching consequences for the British economy and society, reshaping the political landscape and leading to a period of economic growth and restructuring.

******

Liverpool FC's dominance in European football during the 1970s was a remarkable period in the club's history. Under the management of Bill Shankly and later Bob Paisley, Liverpool established themselves as a formidable force, winning numerous domestic and European titles. The decade started with Liverpool's first taste of European success when they won the UEFA Cup in the 1972-73 season. They defeated German side Borussia Mönchengladbach 3-2 on aggregate in the final to claim their first major European trophy. This victory laid the foundation for their future European triumphs.

Liverpool's European dominance truly took off in the mid-1970s when they clinched four European Cup titles in seven years. The first of these victories came in the 1976-77 season, with Bob Paisley at the helm. Liverpool faced German powerhouse Borussia Mönchengladbach in the final once again and emerged as 3-1 winners to claim their maiden European Cup. This triumph not only marked their ascendancy on the European stage but also secured their qualification for the

European Super Cup, where they defeated European Cup Winners' Cup holders Hamburger SV 7-1 on aggregate.

In the 1977-78 season, Liverpool reached the European Cup final for the second time, this time facing FC Bruges at Wembley. In a thrilling encounter, Liverpool emerged as 1-0 winners once again, with Kenny Dalglish scoring the decisive goal. This victory made them the first English club to win the European Cup two times, solidifying their reputation as a European powerhouse. Liverpool's third European Cup triumph came in the 1980-81 season, which falls within the 1970s era of dominance. They faced Spanish giants Real Madrid in the final. After a tightly contested match, Liverpool emerged as 1-0 winners, with Alan Kennedy scoring the winning goal in the 82nd minute. This victory marked their third European Cup win in five seasons and showcased their continued supremacy in European football.

In addition to their European success, Liverpool enjoyed domestic dominance during the 1970s. They clinched six English First Division titles from 1976 to 1983. This period of sustained success in both domestic and European competitions cemented Liverpool's status as one of the most successful clubs of the era. The key to Liverpool's success in Europe during the 1970s can be attributed to their cohesive team structure, strong defensive organisation, and a core group of talented players. The team featured notable figures such as Kenny Dalglish, Kevin Keegan, Ray Clemence, Alan Hansen, Phil Neal, and Graeme Souness, among others. These players formed the backbone of Liverpool's success, showcasing exceptional skill, teamwork, and tactical discipline. Liverpool's dominance in Europe during the 1970s established the club as a European powerhouse and set the stage for their continued success in subsequent decades. Their achievements on the continental stage brought immense pride to the city of Liverpool and established a rich legacy that continues to be celebrated by fans to this day.

******

Music in 1970s Britain was a diverse and vibrant period that saw the emergence of various genres, the rise of iconic bands and artists, and significant cultural shifts. The decade witnessed the continuation of some '60s music styles while introducing new sounds that would shape the future of popular music. One of the defining genres of 1970s British music was progressive rock. Bands like Pink Floyd, Genesis, Yes, and King Crimson pushed the boundaries of rock music by incorporating complex musical arrangements, extended song structures, and philosophical lyrics. Their albums, such as Pink Floyd's "The Dark Side of the Moon" and Genesis' "Selling England by the Pound", became timeless classics. Glam rock was characterised by its theatricality, flamboyant fashion, and catchy pop hooks. Artists like David Bowie, T. Rex, and Roxy Music embraced glam rock's androgynous style and created memorable hits that blended rock, pop, and artistry. Bowie's alter ego Ziggy Stardust became an iconic symbol of the era.

The punk rock movement in Britain during the 1970s was a revolutionary cultural phenomenon that challenged the established music industry and societal norms. Emerging as a response to the perceived complacency and commercialisation of mainstream rock music, punk rock brought a raw, rebellious, and do-it-yourself (DIY) ethos to the forefront. The roots of punk rock can be traced back to the mid 1970s in London, particularly at the iconic music venue, the 100 Club. It was in this underground scene that bands like the Sex Pistols, The Clash, and The Damned began to make their mark. These bands, along with others, would become the figureheads of the punk movement. Punk rock music was characterised by its fast, aggressive, and stripped-down sound. The music was raw, often featuring three-chord structures, simple melodies, and confrontational lyrics. The lyrics were often politically charged, expressing frustration, disillusionment, and a desire for change. Punk songs tackled social issues, unemployment, urban decay, and the general dissatisfaction with the status quo.

The influence of punk rock extended beyond the music itself. It had a profound impact on fashion, art, film, and even politics. Punk's rebellious spirit and its challenge to authority and the status quo resonated with many disillusioned youths, who saw it as a way to express their dissatisfaction and voice their concerns. While the initial wave of punk began to subside by the late 1970s, its impact continued to be felt in subsequent decades. Punk's DIY ethos and its emphasis on individualism and counterculture have influenced countless musicians and subcultures that followed. punk rock remains an enduring symbol of youth rebellion and a testament to the power of music as a catalyst for change.

******

One of the defining characteristics of the Conservative government in the early 1970s was its focus on economic management. Upon coming to power in the 1970 General Election with a 30 seat majority, Prime Minister Edward Heath inherited a troubled economy characterised by high inflation, rising unemployment, and industrial unrest. To address these challenges, the government pursued a policy known as "Stop-Go" economics, aiming to balance economic growth with the control of inflation. This involved measures such as tightening credit and controlling public spending during periods of economic expansion. What is more, the Conservative government sought to reduce the power of trade unions, which were seen as major contributors to the industrial unrest of the time. In 1971, the government introduced the Industrial Relations Act, which aimed to bring about greater regulation of trade unions and limit their ability to take strike action.

However, the Act faced strong opposition from unions and was ultimately repealed by the Labour government that came into power in 1974. In terms of foreign policy, the Conservative government faced significant challenges. One notable event was the United Kingdom's entry into the European Economic Community (EEC) in 1973, marking a pivotal moment in British history. The government's decision to join the EEC, which later became the European Union (EU), had far-reaching consequences for the country's relationship with Europe and its future integration into the European project.

Another significant issue the Conservative government grappled with was the Troubles in Northern Ireland. The early 1970s saw a surge in violence and sectarian conflict, with escalating tensions between the Catholic and Protestant communities. The government implemented measures to restore law and order, including the deployment of British troops to Northern Ireland. However, these efforts were met with mixed results, as the conflict continued for many years, with profound implications for the region's stability and the relationship between Britain and Ireland. Socially, the Conservative government of the early 1970s faced challenges related to social change and cultural shifts. The period witnessed an evolving society marked by changing attitudes towards traditional institutions and values. Issues such as women's rights, environmentalism, and multiculturalism gained prominence, challenging the government to respond to shifting public expectations. Moreover, the Conservative government introduced various social and welfare policies during this time.

Notably, the Family Income Supplement (FIS) was established to provide additional financial support to low-income families. Additionally, the government made efforts to tackle homelessness through the introduction of the Housing Finance Act 1972, which aimed to improve the availability and affordability of housing.

******

The British and Irish Lions clinched a historic series victory against New Zealand in their 1971 tour. The Lions, who had suffered a whitewash defeat in their previous visit to the country, displayed resilience and determination to overcome the mighty All Blacks. Led by a Welsh coach and captain, and fuelled by the success of Wales' Grand Slam in the Five Nations Championship, the Lions proved their mettle on New Zealand soil. The tour kicked off with an intense battle at Carisbrook, Dunedin, where the Lions triumphed 9-3 in the first Test. The match showcased the Lions' defensive prowess, limiting the All Blacks to a single penalty goal. On the offensive front, two penalties from John and a try by Ian McLauchlan secured a hard-fought victory for the Lions. However, complacency crept in during the second Test in Christchurch, leading to a resounding 22-12 defeat for the Lions. The All Blacks roared back with five tries, while the Lions could only manage two through Davies. It was a wake-up call for the Lions, who realised the challenges that lay ahead. The pivotal third Test, held at Athletic Park in Wellington, witnessed a resolute Lions side. Learning from their mistakes, the Lions exhibited discipline and determination, emerging triumphant with a 13-3 scoreline. Two converted tries and a drop goal showcased the Lions' attacking prowess, while the All Blacks could only manage a solitary try. With a 2-1 series lead after the third Test, the Lions faced a high-stakes showdown at Eden Park in Auckland. A win for the All Blacks would have secured a drawn series, while a draw or Lions victory would grant the Lions an unprecedented series win. The tension was palpable as both teams battled fiercely. At halftime, the scores were level at 8-8, with a try, conversion, and penalty apiece. The second half unfolded as a seesaw battle, with the Lions landing a crucial penalty goal and the All Blacks responding with a try. With the scores tied at 11-11, Lions fullback JPR Williams seized the moment. From 45 meters out, he executed a remarkable drop goal, propelling the Lions ahead 14-11. Williams' successful drop goal, the only one he would ever land in his Test career, proved to be the decisive moment. Despite the All Blacks managing a late penalty to draw the game 14-14, the result secured the series for the Lions. It was a remarkable achievement, given their previous struggles on New Zealand soil. The Lions' victory in the 1971 series against New Zealand will go down in history as a testament to their character, resilience, and unity. The Welsh influence, both in terms of players and leadership, played a crucial role in shaping this triumph. The Lions defied expectations, and their success will undoubtedly inspire future generations of British and Irish rugby players.

******

The Three-Day Week was introduced in January 1974, by Edward Heath's Conservative government, as a means to conserve energy and prevent a complete shutdown of essential services. It involved restrictions on the use of electricity, with businesses and households limited to a maximum of three consecutive days of normal working hours per week. The energy crisis of 1973 was triggered by a global oil embargo imposed by the Organisation of Arab Petroleum Exporting Countries (OAPEC). This led to a significant increase in oil prices and disrupted oil supplies to many countries, including the UK. As a result, the government had to grapple with a shortage of oil and rising fuel costs, which had severe implications for the country's energy supply. Additionally, the coal mining industry in the UK was facing a series of strikes by the National Union of Mineworkers (NUM). The strikes were prompted by disputes over pay and working conditions. The miners' industrial action led to reduced coal production, further exacerbating the energy crisis. To cope with the limited electricity supply, the government introduced the Three-Day Week as an emergency measure. During this period, businesses and industries were required to operate for only three consecutive days a week, with restricted working hours. Street lighting was reduced, and television programming was limited. Non-essential services and industries, such as commercial television, were forced to shut down temporarily. The Three-Day Week had a significant impact on the economy and daily life in Britain. Many businesses and factories had to alter their operations and adjust working schedules, leading to disruptions and reduced productivity. The limited availability of electricity affected public services, transportation, and manufacturing processes.

The measures taken during the Three-Day Week were controversial and met with mixed responses. Some argued that the restrictions were necessary to manage the energy crisis and prevent a complete breakdown of essential services. However, others criticised the government's handling of the crisis and argued that alternative strategies should have been pursued to address the underlying issues. The energy crisis and the Three-Day Week had political ramifications as well. The Conservative government of Edward Heath called a general election to take place on 28th February 1974, which resulted in a hung parliament. The subsequent minority Labour government, led by Harold Wilson, ultimately repealed the Three-Day Week and took steps to address the industrial disputes and energy shortages.

******

Several notable developments took place during this time, shaping the direction of West End theatre. One significant shift in the 1970s was the increasing popularity of musicals. Musicals became a prominent and lucrative genre in the West End, attracting large audiences and creating a sense of spectacle. Shows such as "Jesus Christ Superstar", "Grease", and "Evita" captivated audiences with their memorable songs, dynamic choreography, and stunning production values. These productions played a crucial role in bringing commercial success to the West End and expanding its global reputation.

Alongside the rise of musicals, the 1970s also witnessed a continued commitment to classic and contemporary plays. Established playwrights such as Harold Pinter, Tom Stoppard, and Alan Ayckbourn presented thought-provoking and critically acclaimed works that explored social, political, and psychological themes. Productions like Pinter's "The Homecoming" and Stoppard's "Travesties" showcased the depth and diversity of theatrical storytelling in the West End.

The decade also saw the emergence of groundbreaking and unconventional productions that challenged traditional theatrical conventions. Experimental plays and avant-garde works found a home in theatres like the Royal Court, which showcased the works of playwrights pushing the boundaries of form and content. These productions tackled provocative and controversial topics, reflecting the changing social and political climate of the era. In addition to established theatres, new venues and spaces began to play a role in the West End theatre scene. Smaller theatres and studio spaces provided a platform for emerging talents and experimental works. These venues, including the Royal Court's Upstairs Theatre and the Donmar Warehouse, allowed for more intimate and immersive experiences, attracting audiences seeking alternative theatrical experiences.

During the 1970s, the Edinburgh Festival Fringe continued to grow in size and popularity, attracting artists, performers, and theatre companies from around the world. The festival provided a unique opportunity for artists to showcase their work in an open-access environment, where anyone with a show and a venue could participate. This open-door policy allowed for a diverse range of performances, ensuring that the Fringe offered something for everyone. The 1970s Fringe saw a surge in experimental and avant-garde theatre. Artists and theatre companies pushed the boundaries of traditional theatre, exploring new forms, and challenging conventional storytelling techniques. The Fringe became a hub for innovative works that blurred the lines between different art forms, incorporating elements of dance, music, multimedia, and visual arts into theatrical performances.

One notable aspect of the 1970s Fringe was its role in providing a platform for politically engaged theatre. With the backdrop of social and political changes happening in the world, artists used the festival as a space to explore and comment on pressing issues. Plays addressing themes of feminism, civil rights and anti-war sentiments became prevalent. The Fringe became a site for provocative and thought-provoking performances that sought to challenge the status quo and spark conversations. The spirit of experimentation and risk-taking permeated the Fringe in the 1970s. Many emerging artists and theatre companies used the festival as a launching pad for their careers, with some going on to achieve significant success in the industry. The 1970s Fringe also witnessed an expansion of venues and an increase in the number of shows on offer. The festival spread beyond traditional theatres and spilled into unconventional spaces such as pubs, church halls, and even the streets of Edinburgh. This allowed for a more immersive and accessible experience for both performers and audiences, breaking down the barriers between art and everyday life.

******

British Formula One in the 1970s witnessed a mix of success, tragedy, and significant developments. The decade saw British drivers and teams make their mark on the sport, with notable achievements and memorable moments. One of the standout figures of British Formula One in the 1970s was Sir Jackie Stewart. Stewart is known for his exceptional driving skills and commitment to driver safety. Another notable British driver of the 1970s was James Hunt. Known for his flamboyant and charismatic personality, Hunt captured the hearts of fans around the world. British teams also made their presence felt during the 1970s. McLaren, founded by New Zealander Bruce McLaren, was based in the UK and became a force to be reckoned with. The team achieved multiple victories and established itself as a top contender in Formula One. Lotus, a British team with a rich history, continued to be a prominent force in the 1970s. Led by Colin Chapman, Lotus produced innovative and competitive cars. The team achieved success with drivers such as Emerson Fittipaldi, who won the World Championship in 1972.

However, the 1970s also witnessed tragedy in British Formula One. In 1970, Bruce McLaren, the founder of McLaren, tragically died while testing a car at the Goodwood Circuit. In 1973, Roger Williamson, a promising British driver, lost his life in a fiery crash at the Dutch Grand Prix. These incidents served as stark reminders of the dangers faced by drivers and reinforced the need for improved safety measures. In terms of technological advancements, the 1970s saw the introduction of ground-effect aerodynamics, pioneered by British engineer and designer Colin Chapman. Ground-effect technology, which utilised the underside of the car to generate downforce, revolutionised Formula One and significantly enhanced the performance of the cars.

******

Jackie Stewart, born on 11th June 1939, in Milton, Scotland, is a legendary figure in the world of motorsport. With his exceptional talent, unwavering determination, and tireless advocacy for driver safety, Stewart became one of the most successful and influential drivers in the history of Formula 1. Stewart's racing journey began in the early 1960s when he started competing in various racing categories, including Formula 3 and sports car racing. His undeniable skill and passion for the sport caught the attention of Ken Tyrrell, who would later become his mentor and team owner. In 1965, Stewart made his Formula 1 debut with the BRM team at the South African Grand Prix, marking the start of an illustrious career. It was in the late 1960s and early 1970s that Stewart's talent truly blossomed. In 1969, driving for Matra-Ford, he clinched his first Formula 1 World Championship. Stewart's meticulous approach to racing, coupled with his ability to extract maximum performance from his car, set him apart from his competitors. He secured six victories that season, including wins at the Dutch, French, and Italian Grands Prix, solidifying his place among the elite drivers of his time. Stewart won further formula one titles in 1971 and 1973 driving for Ken Tyrrell.

Beyond his on-track success, Stewart became an outspoken advocate for driver safety. During an era marked by high accident rates and inadequate safety measures, Stewart worked tirelessly to bring attention to the need for improved safety standards in motorsport. His tireless efforts to protect drivers led to significant advancements in safety equipment, track design, and medical facilities, ultimately saving countless lives. Stewart's impact extended beyond his achievements. He played a pivotal role in transforming Formula 1 into a safer sport, setting a new standard for driver welfare. His outspoken nature and determination to bring about change earned him both praise and criticism, but he remained resolute in his mission to protect the lives of his fellow drivers.

******

After the hung Parliament of the February 1974 election the second General Election of 1974 was held on 10th October. Having triumphed this time with only a 3 seat majority the Labour government was confronted with an array of pressing issues. These included ongoing industrial disputes, economic instability, and the need to address social inequalities. One of the government's primary goals was to manage the fallout from the energy crisis and address the economic challenges facing the country. To tackle the economic difficulties, the government introduced measures such as wage restraint policies and increased government intervention in the economy. The Social Contract, a policy agreement between the government, trade unions, and employers, aimed to moderate wage demands in order to control inflation. However, the policy faced resistance from some trade unions, leading to further industrial disputes and strikes. The Labour government also pursued a more interventionist economic approach, advocating for nationalisation and increased state control over key industries. Notable examples include the nationalisation of the aircraft and shipbuilding industries, as well as the establishment of the

National Enterprise Board to oversee the government's role in industry and job creation. In terms of foreign policy, the Labour government focused on strengthening relations with Europe. On 5th June 1975 they held a referendum on the United Kingdom's membership in the European Economic Community (EEC), which later became the European Union (EU). The majority of voters supported continued membership, solidifying the UK's ties with Europe. The government also took steps to address social issues and inequality. The Equal Pay and Sex Discrimination Acts of 1975 were introduced to ensure equal pay for men and women performing similar work. The Sex Discrimination Act of 1975 prohibited discrimination based on sex in various areas, including employment, education, and housing. These legislative changes aimed to promote greater gender equality and address longstanding disparities.

Harold Wilson handed over the reins of leadership to James Callaghan in April 1976. Wilson's decision to step down came as a surprise to many, as he had won two general elections during his tenure. Wilson's decision to resign was driven by various factors. Firstly, there were growing concerns about his health. He had been experiencing symptoms of exhaustion and was facing increased pressure from his political opponents. Additionally, the Labour Party was facing challenges on multiple fronts, including a struggling economy, high inflation rates, and ongoing industrial disputes. James Callaghan, who had served as Chancellor of the Exchequer under Wilson, was elected as the new leader of the Labour Party and became the Prime Minister. Callaghan's premiership was marked by a continuation of the economic and social challenges faced by the country. He adopted a pragmatic approach to governance and sought to address the issues through negotiation and consensus-building. One of the significant events during Callaghan's premiership was the Winter of Discontent in 1978-1979. This period saw a series of widespread strikes and industrial action by trade unions, resulting in disruptions to essential services such as transportation, healthcare, and waste disposal. The strikes eroded public confidence in the government's ability to manage the economy and maintain social order. Callaghan's government ultimately lost a vote of no confidence in Parliament in 1979, triggering a general election. The Conservative Party, led by Margaret Thatcher, won the election, bringing an end to the Labour government's tenure.

******

British television saw the rise of innovative dramas, groundbreaking comedies, thought-provoking documentaries, and iconic children's programming. One of the most significant contributions of the 1970s was the emergence of gritty and socially relevant dramas. Series like "The Sweeney", "Upstairs, Downstairs", and "The Professionals" showcased a more realistic and edgier approach to storytelling, exploring the complexities of urban life, class dynamics, and crime.

In addition to drama, the 1970s witnessed the development of ground-breaking comedy shows that pushed the boundaries of humour and challenged societal norms. Series like "Monty Python's Flying Circus" brought absurdist and irreverent comedy to the forefront, while "Fawlty Towers" became a cult classic with its razor-sharp wit and unforgettable characters. These shows continue to be celebrated as comedic masterpieces and have had a lasting influence on the genre.

Documentaries also flourished during this era, tackling important social and political issues. Programs like "World in Action" and "The World at War" provided insightful and comprehensive coverage of global events, shedding light on topics such as war, politics, and social injustices. These documentaries not only informed audiences but also influenced public opinion and shaped the way television approached serious journalism. Children's programming also experienced a golden age in the 1970s. Shows like "Bagpuss", "The Magic Roundabout", and "The Wombles" captured the imagination of young viewers with their whimsical storytelling and memorable characters. These programs embraced a gentler and more imaginative approach to children's entertainment, fostering creativity and sparking a sense of wonder.

Furthermore, the 1970s marked a period of innovation in television production and technology. Advancements in colour broadcasting became more widespread, enhancing the visual experience for viewers. This decade also saw the introduction of new formats, such as the groundbreaking sketch show "The Goodies", which utilised innovative editing techniques and storytelling styles. The impact of British television in the 1970s was not limited to the domestic audience. Many of these shows gained international acclaim and garnered a global following. British programming showcased the country's creativity, talent, and ability to produce compelling stories that resonated with diverse audiences.

******

The Equal Pay Act and the Sex Discrimination Act of 1975, introduced by the Labour Government, were two landmark pieces of legislation introduced in Britain that aimed to address gender inequality and promote equal rights for women in the workplace and society. These acts were crucial steps in the ongoing struggle for gender equality and had a significant impact on the rights and opportunities available to women in Britain. The Equal Pay Act of 1975 was designed to ensure that men and women receive equal pay for equal work. It made it illegal to discriminate between men and women in terms of their contractual or employment terms, including pay and benefits. The Act required employers to provide equal pay to male and female employees who perform work of equal value, skill, effort, or responsibility. It also established mechanisms for individuals to take legal action to enforce their right to equal pay. The Equal Pay Act had a profound impact on narrowing the gender pay gap and promoting greater wage equality in Britain. It empowered women to challenge unequal pay practices and seek fair compensation for their work. The legislation highlighted the principle that gender should not be a factor in determining pay rates, fostering a more equitable and fairer working environment.

The Sex Discrimination Act of 1975 complemented the Equal Pay Act by addressing discrimination against women in a broader context. This Act prohibited discrimination based on sex in various areas, including employment, education, housing, and the provision of goods, facilities, and services. It aimed to eradicate discriminatory practices that hindered women's opportunities and limited their participation in various aspects of society. The Sex Discrimination Act made it illegal to treat individuals less favourably because of their gender, and it promoted equal opportunities for both men and women. It also established the Equal Opportunities Commission (EOC), which later became the Equality and Human Rights Commission (EHRC), to enforce and promote compliance with the legislation. The Act marked a significant step forward in tackling gender-based discrimination and creating a more inclusive and equal society.

These acts played a crucial role in challenging gender stereotypes and promoting gender equality in British society. They paved the way for increased opportunities for women in the workplace, as well as advancements in areas such as education, healthcare, and housing. The legislation not only empowered women to assert their rights and challenge discriminatory practices but also brought about a broader cultural shift, challenging societal norms and expectations.

******

James Hunt's victory in the 1976 Formula One World Championship was a remarkable and dramatic achievement that captured the hearts of motorsport fans around the world. The season unfolded as one of the most memorable and closely contested battles in Formula One history, pitting Hunt against his fierce rival, Niki Lauda. The 1976 season started with Lauda dominating the early races, driving for the Ferrari team. The Austrian driver displayed remarkable consistency and skill, winning five out of the first nine races. However, tragedy struck at the German Grand Prix at the Nürburgring when Lauda suffered a horrific crash, which left him with severe burns and injuries. In the absence of Lauda, Hunt, driving for McLaren, saw an opportunity to close the gap in the championship standings. The Englishman capitalised on his rival's absence and produced some outstanding performances. He showcased his speed and determination, securing victories at the Dutch, Canadian and USA Grands Prix. Lauda's remarkable recovery and determination to return to racing added further intensity to the championship battle. Just six weeks after his accident, Lauda made a courageous comeback at the Italian Grand Prix, finishing fourth. His return demonstrated his incredible resilience and set the stage for a thrilling showdown with Hunt.

The final race of the season took place in torrential rain at the Fuji Speedway in Japan. Lauda, still dealing with the physical and emotional aftermath of his accident, made the difficult decision to retire from the race due to the dangerous conditions.

Meanwhile, Hunt faced a daunting challenge as he needed to finish at least third to secure the championship. In an epic display of skill and bravery, Hunt battled his way through the treacherous conditions, overcoming multiple setbacks along the way. Despite a punctured tire and a pit stop to replace it, he managed to climb back up the field and finish third, securing enough points to become the 1976 World Champion.

The Hunt Lauda rivalry and the thrilling climax of the 1976 season remain legendary in the annals of Formula One. It was a battle that transcended the sport, captivating the imagination of fans and bringing a new level of excitement to Formula One racing. James Hunt's championship win in 1976 left an indelible mark on his career and cemented his place in Formula One history. His achievement, coupled with his colourful personality, made him an iconic figure in the sport.

******

The fashion of the 1970s was characterised by a sense of freedom, experimentation, and self-expression. It was a decade that saw the influence of various subcultures, the rise of disco, glam rock and punk and the continued evolution of women's liberation and gender norms. One of the prominent fashion trends of the 1970s was the bohemian or hippie style. Inspired by the counterculture movement of the 1960s, this style embraced natural fabrics, loose-fitting clothing, and a bohemian aesthetic. Maxi dresses, peasant blouses, bell-bottom pants, and fringed vests became popular staples of the bohemian look. The fashion was characterised by bold prints, earthy colours, and a free-spirited, relaxed vibe. In contrast to the bohemian style, the disco era brought a glamorous and flamboyant fashion trend to the forefront. With the popularity of disco music and dance clubs, people embraced flashy and glitzy clothing. Women's fashion featured shiny and metallic fabrics, sequins, and body-hugging silhouettes. Men's fashion saw the rise of wide-lapel suits, platform shoes, and open-collar shirts. Disco fashion was all about making a statement and standing out on the dance floor.

Glam rock also left its mark on fashion in the 1970s. Inspired by the androgynous and theatrical styles of artists like David Bowie and Marc Bolan, glam rock fashion featured bold makeup, platform boots, glittery outfits, and flamboyant accessories. It blurred traditional gender boundaries and celebrated self-expression through fashion. Denim became a fashion staple during the '70s, with denim jeans, jackets, and overalls being worn by people of all ages and backgrounds. The popularity of denim reflected the casual and relaxed attitude of the decade. Distressed and embroidered denim became fashionable, as did patchwork denim, which was often associated with the hippie movement.

Women's fashion in the 1970s saw a continued evolution from the previous decade, with a focus on feminism and gender equality. Women embraced pantsuits, blazers, and wide-legged trousers as a symbol of empowerment and liberation. The feminist movement influenced fashion choices, encouraging women to express themselves through clothing and challenge traditional gender roles. In terms of accessories, platform shoes were a defining trend of the 1970s. Both men and women wore high-heeled platform shoes, which added height and a sense of boldness to any outfit. Other popular accessories included large, round sunglasses, floppy hats, and wide-brimmed hats, as well as statement jewellery such as oversized earrings and long pendant necklaces.

******

In 1977 Virginia Wade achieved a momentous success in her tennis career by winning the Wimbledon Championships. This victory was not only a personal triumph for Wade but also a historic moment for British tennis, as she became the first British woman to win the prestigious title since Ann Jones in 1969. Wimbledon 1977 was a significant year for British celebrations, as it coincided with the Silver Jubilee of Queen Elizabeth II. The entire nation was captivated by the tournament, and Wade's remarkable run added to the patriotic fervour surrounding the event. Throughout the tournament, Wade displayed exceptional skill, determination, and mental fortitude. As an experienced player, she entered Wimbledon with a solid foundation and a reputation as a strong competitor. However, she faced formidable opponents along the way, and her path to the championship was no easy feat. Wade's journey to the final was marked by impressive victories. In the quarterfinals, she faced American Rosie Casals and emerged as the victor winning in 2 sets 7-5 6-2. This win set the stage for a highly anticipated semifinal clash against the reigning champion and World Number 1, Chris Evert. In the semifinals, Wade faced an uphill battle against the formidable Evert. The match was fiercely competitive, with both players showcasing their skills and tactical acumen. In a thrilling three-set encounter, Wade emerged as the winner, defeating Evert 6-2 4-6 6-1 and securing her place in the final. The final of the women's singles at Wimbledon 1977 was an iconic match that captivated the world. Wade faced another formidable opponent, Betty Stöve of the Netherlands. The match was played on the Centre Court of the All England Club, in front of a passionate crowd and millions of viewers around the globe. Wade's composed and powerful play, coupled with her ability to rise to the occasion, proved to be decisive.

She defeated Stöve in three sets, with a score of 4-6, 6-3, 6-1. Wade's victory in the final not only showcased her talent and skill but also demonstrated her mental strength and ability to perform under immense pressure. Wade's accomplishment brought joy and inspiration to tennis fans across the country. Wade's success in 1977 catapulted her to international stardom and established her as one of the leading figures in women's tennis. Her Wimbledon victory remains a remarkable moment in British tennis history and solidifies her place among the greats of the sport. While Wade's Wimbledon win was a significant highlight, she also achieved success in other tournaments. She reached won the Australian Open in 1972 and the US Open in 1968. Wade's consistent performances and her Wimbledon victory established her as one of the leading British female players of the era.

Sue Barker was another prominent British player of the 1970s. She won the French Open singles title in 1976 beating Renáta Tomanová of Czechoslovakia 2-6 6-2 6-1. Barker's success at Roland Garros showcased her skill on clay courts and established her as a respected competitor. Sue Baker also reached the semi-finals at Wimbledon in 1977 losing to Betty Stöve denying Britain an all English Wimbledon Final in Jubilee year. While these achievements highlighted the individual successes of British players, the country faced challenges in regaining the dominance seen in previous decades. The emergence of strong international players from other countries, particularly the United States, Australia, and Sweden, posed stiff competition for British players on the global stage. Additionally, the infrastructure and development of tennis in Britain faced some difficulties during the 1970s. The country struggled to produce a consistent pipeline of talent, and there was a lack of widespread participation and investment in the sport. This contributed to a decline in British tennis prominence during this period.

******

The Sex Pistols were a highly influential and controversial punk rock band that emerged in 1975, in London. They are credited as one of the pioneering bands of the punk rock movement and had a significant impact on the music and cultural landscape of the time. The band was formed by guitarist Steve Jones, drummer Paul Cook, bassist Glen Matlock, and lead singer Johnny Rotten (whose real name is John Lydon). Matlock was later replaced by Sid Vicious as the bassist. The Sex Pistols brought a raw, aggressive, and rebellious sound that resonated with disaffected youth and challenged the established norms of the music industry. Their confrontational and provocative image, combined with their controversial lyrics and energetic performances, garnered them both fame and notoriety. The band's debut single, "Anarchy in the U.K.", became an anthem for the punk movement, expressing the frustration and disillusionment of a generation. It was followed by other iconic songs such as "God Save the Queen" and "Pretty Vacant". The Sex Pistols' impact extended beyond their music. They were known for their chaotic live performances and their confrontational interactions with the media. The band's appearance on a television talk show in 1976 famously resulted in an expletive-laden interview that shocked viewers and led to their subsequent banning from many venues and media outlets. In 1977, the Sex Pistols released their only studio album, "Never Mind the Bollocks, Here's the Sex Pistols". The album is considered a classic of punk rock and is hailed as one of the most influential and groundbreaking albums in the genre. Its rebellious and confrontational lyrics, combined with the band's raw energy, solidified its place in punk rock history.

However, the Sex Pistols' career was short lived. Internal conflicts, including the dismissal of Sid Vicious and the departure of Johnny Rotten, led to the band's breakup in 1978. Despite their relatively brief existence, the Sex Pistols left an indelible mark on the music industry and paved the way for the punk movement's enduring legacy.

******

Over the winter of 1978 during the Winter of Discontent, various trade unions representing different sectors of the economy engaged in strikes and industrial action, demanding higher wages, improved working conditions, and stronger job security. The strikes affected a wide range of industries, including transportation, healthcare, education, and public services. The strikes led to severe disruptions in essential services, such as rubbish collection, hospital operations, and transportation networks. Rubbish piled up on the streets, hospitals faced difficulties in providing patient care, and public transportation was severely affected. These disruptions caused public frustration and a sense of social unrest. The strikes and labour disputes were driven by a combination of factors. Economic conditions at the time were challenging, with high inflation rates, rising unemployment, and wage stagnation. Many workers felt that their wages did not keep up with the increasing cost of living. Additionally, the political climate and the growing influence of trade unions played a role in the scale and intensity of the industrial action. The Winter of Discontent had significant political ramifications. The strikes and the perceived inability of the Labour government, led by Prime Minister James Callaghan, to effectively handle the situation eroded public confidence in the government's ability to manage the economy and maintain social order.

******

The Scotland Act 1978 was introduced by the Labour government in response to the growing demand for Scottish self-government and the desire for greater Scottish autonomy within the United Kingdom. The act proposed the establishment of a Scottish Assembly, which would have the power to make decisions on matters such as health, education, and housing. The SNP, as the primary proponent of Scottish independence and self-government, played a significant role in the discussions surrounding the Scotland Act. While the SNP initially supported the act, they believed it did not go far enough in granting full independence to Scotland. They argued for a stronger Scottish Parliament with greater legislative powers.

However, the passage of the Scotland Act faced challenges. The act required a referendum to be held in Scotland to determine public support for the establishment of a Scottish Assembly. The referendum, which took place on 1st March 1979, required a majority of the total electorate to vote in favour, not just a majority of those who participated in the referendum. This high threshold made it difficult for the act to be implemented. In the referendum, although the majority of voters supported the creation of a Scottish Assembly, the threshold of the total electorate was not met. As a result, the Scotland Act was not implemented, and the Scottish Assembly was not established.

The failure of the Scotland Act 1978 to bring about Scottish devolution had significant political implications. It led to a vote of no confidence in the Labour government, as the SNP and other opposition parties were critical of the government's handling of the devolution issue. The government subsequently lost the vote of no confidence in the House of Commons, triggering a general election.

******

At the heart of punk fashion was a sense of anti-establishment and anti-conformity. Punk style embraced a DIY approach, with individuals creating their unique looks from affordable and easily accessible materials. Torn clothing, safety pins, and badges became iconic symbols of punk fashion, representing a deliberate disregard for conventional notions of beauty and fashion. One of the key elements of punk fashion was the punk hairstyle. Punk rockers sported unconventional and attention-grabbing hairstyles that defied traditional norms. Iconic styles included brightly coloured or disheveled haircuts, shaved heads, and spiked or mohawk hairstyles. These hairstyles were often achieved through unconventional methods, such as using household products like gel or hairspray to create extreme volume and hold.

Punk fashion was characterised by its use of provocative and politically charged clothing. Punk clothing was often torn, ripped, and customised to reflect individuality and a sense of rebellion. Band t-shirts, leather jackets adorned with spikes or studs, and ripped jeans were popular staples of the punk wardrobe. Plaid shirts, fishnet stockings, and bondage-inspired clothing also made their way into punk fashion. Accessories played a crucial role in punk fashion. Safety pins became a signature punk accessory, used to hold clothing together or as decorative elements. Other accessories included heavy metal chains, dog collars, and leather wristbands. Punk fashion also embraced DIY jewellery, with individuals creating their own pieces from unconventional materials like bottle caps or rubber bands.

The punk fashion aesthetic extended to makeup and body modifications. Punk rockers often embraced a bold and unconventional approach to makeup, with heavy eyeliner, vibrant eyeshadows, and brightly coloured lipstick. Facial piercings, such as nose rings or lip rings, were also common, further enhancing the punk image. Punk fashion was not solely about making a fashion statement but was also a form of self-expression and rebellion against mainstream society. It was a way for individuals to challenge societal norms, express their frustrations, and reject consumerism and conformity.

******

Margaret Thatcher's rise to the leadership of the Conservative Party in the 1970s was a significant development in British politics. At the time, the Conservative Party was in opposition, having lost the general election to the Labour Party in 1974. The party was seeking a new leader who could revitalise its fortunes and provide a clear alternative to the prevailing political climate. In 1975, Thatcher emerged as a strong contender for the leadership of the Conservative Party. She ran against Edward Heath, the former Prime Minister, in the party's leadership election. Thatcher campaigned on a platform of free-market principles, smaller government, and a more assertive and resolute approach to governance. Thatcher's vision and leadership style resonated with a significant portion of the Conservative Party membership. She was seen as a staunch conservative and a champion of individual liberty and free enterprise. Thatcher's message struck a chord with those who believed in reducing the influence of the state and promoting entrepreneurialism.

In a surprising turn of events, Thatcher won the leadership contest with 52.9% of the vote after Edward Heath withdrew from a second ballot after it became clear he could not win. She became the first woman to lead a major political party in the United Kingdom and her victory represented a break from the party's traditional leadership and signalled a shift towards a more conservative and market-oriented direction. Thatcher's leadership of the Conservative Party marked a period of significant transformation within the party itself. She reshaped its ideological stance, infusing it with free-market principles and a commitment to reducing government intervention in the economy. Thatcher's leadership galvanised a new generation of conservatives and attracted widespread attention within the political sphere. Her rise to the leadership of the Conservative Party, her leadership style, determination, and ability to articulate a clear vision for the future of the country resonated with the British public and set the stage for her eventual election as Prime Minister on 3rd May 1979.

1980s
Deregulation and Privatisation of Industries

Margaret Thatcher's Conservative government dominated British politics throughout the 1980s. Thatcher, who became Prime Minister in 1979, pursued a vision of free-market economics, deregulation, privatisation, and reducing the power of trade unions. Known as Thatcherism, her policies aimed to reshape the British economy and society. Economically, the 1980s saw a restructuring of industries and the rise of neoliberalism. Thatcher's government implemented market-oriented reforms, privatising nationalised industries such as British Telecom, British Gas, and British Airways. This led to a shift towards a service-based economy, while traditional manufacturing industries experienced decline and job losses. The economic policies of the Thatcher government were characterised by a focus on individualism, entrepreneurship, and wealth creation. The deregulation of financial markets, known as the "Big Bang", transformed the City of London into a global financial hub. However, these policies also contributed to increasing income inequality and social divisions, as some regions and communities struggled to adapt to the changes.

Socially, the 1980s witnessed significant divisions and conflicts. The miners' strike of 1984-1985, a confrontation between the National Union of Mineworkers and the government, became a symbol of the broader struggles between the working class and Thatcher's government. The strike resulted in the closure of many coal mines and the decline of the mining industry, which had a profound impact on mining communities. The 1980s also saw the rise of youth subcultures and countercultural movements. The emergence of alternative music scenes challenged mainstream culture and expressed discontent with political and social conditions. Bands like The Clash and The Smiths were known for their politically charged lyrics and rebellious attitudes. Cultural developments in the 1980s were also reflected in the fashion and art of the era. The influence of designers like Vivienne Westwood and music icons like Madonna led to the popularity of punk-inspired fashion, bold colours, and exaggerated styles. British art experienced a surge of creativity, with the emergence of the Young British Artists (YBAs) such as Damien Hirst and Tracey Emin.

Global events had a significant impact on Britain in the 1980s. The Cold War tensions between the United States and the Soviet Union, which had been ongoing for decades, were particularly palpable during this period. The presence of American military installations, such as Greenham Common, and the debate over nuclear disarmament were central issues of political and social discourse. The Falklands War of 1982 between Britain and Argentina also had a profound impact on the nation. The conflict, which resulted in a British victory, sparked a sense of national pride and bolstered the popularity of the Conservative government.

The 1980s also witnessed advancements in technology and the rise of the digital age. Personal computers became more accessible, and the development of the World Wide Web in 1989 revolutionised communication and information sharing. These technological developments laid the foundation for the digital revolution that would follow in the subsequent decades.

******

The 1980s was a decade of creative exploration, commercial success and cultural influence. The British pop scene saw a resurgence, with artists like Culture Club, Wham! and George Michael achieving massive commercial success, they blended pop sensibilities with soul, funk, and disco influences, producing chart-topping hits that became anthems of the era. The music of this period was characterised by vibrant production, catchy hooks, and flamboyant performances.

In parallel, the 1980s also witnessed the rise of electronic and synth pop music, with bands like The Human League, Orchestral Manoeuvres in the Dark (OMD), Depeche Mode and Soft Cell pushing the boundaries of sound and technology. They embraced synthesisers, drum machines, and futuristic production techniques, creating a sound that would define the decade. The electronic beats and catchy melodies of tracks like "Don't You Want Me" by The Human League and "Tainted Love" by Soft Cell became iconic. Gothic rock and post-punk also had a significant presence in the 1980s British music scene. Bands like The Cure, Siouxsie and the Banshees, and Joy Division (later known as New Order) crafted dark and atmospheric soundscapes, exploring themes of introspection, melancholy, and social alienation. Their distinctive sounds and introspective lyrics resonated with a dedicated fanbase and influenced subsequent alternative and indie rock movements.

Another notable genre that emerged in the 1980s was the New Romantic movement, characterised by extravagant fashion, androgynous aesthetics, and synthesiser driven music. Bands such as Visage, Spandau Ballet and Duran Duran embraced a theatrical and flamboyant style, blending elements of glam rock, new wave, and electronic music. Their visually striking performances and anthems like "True" by Spandau Ballet epitomised the spirit of the era.

Beyond the mainstream, the 1980s also witnessed the emergence of independent and alternative music scenes. Bands like The Smiths, The Jesus and Mary Chain, and The Stone Roses garnered critical acclaim and developed dedicated cult followings. These acts drew from a range of influences, including indie rock, post-punk, and jangle pop, and helped shape the alternative music landscape for years to come.

******

Margaret Thatcher served as the Prime Minister from 1979 to 1990 and was the first female Prime Minister in British history. Thatcher's leadership was characterised by a commitment to conservative principles and a drive to implement her vision of a more free-market-oriented and less state-controlled society. Her policies, commonly known as Thatcherism, had a profound impact on various aspects of British life.

Economically, Thatcher implemented a range of reforms aimed at liberalising markets and reducing the influence of the state. She pursued a policy of privatisation, selling off state-owned industries such as British Telecom, British Gas, and British Airways. The goal was to enhance efficiency, increase competition, and reduce the burden on the public sector. Thatcher also championed deregulation, aiming to remove barriers to business growth and entrepreneurship. She implemented measures to curb the power of trade unions, including laws that restricted union activities and curtailed their influence in industrial disputes. These changes aimed to increase flexibility in the labor market and reduce the disruptive impact of strikes.

Thatcher's economic policies were influenced by monetarist principles, emphasising the control of inflation and the role of monetary policy in managing the economy. This approach focused on controlling the money supply and reducing government spending to curb inflation and maintain stable economic conditions. Thatcher's foreign policy was characterised by a strong stance against communism and an assertive approach to international affairs. She was a close ally of the United States and worked closely with US President Ronald Reagan to promote their shared values of free markets and limited government intervention. Thatcher's tenure was marked by a series of significant reforms and contentious policies. Her government faced opposition from various quarters, particularly during periods of social unrest, such as the miners' strike of 1984-1985. Critics argued that her policies exacerbated social inequalities and contributed to the decline of traditional industries in certain regions. However, Thatcher also enjoyed strong support from many who believed in her vision of a more competitive and entrepreneurial Britain. Supporters credited her with reviving the economy, reducing inflation, and restoring national pride and confidence.

Thatcher's impact on British society and politics remains highly debated. While she is widely admired by some for her conviction, leadership, and economic reforms, others criticise the social consequences of her policies and the impact on marginalised communities. Regardless of one's stance on Thatcher's policies, there is no denying the significant influence she and her Conservative government had on shaping British politics, the economy, and the role of the state during the 1980s and beyond.

******

The Ashes series of 1981, often referred to as "Botham's Ashes", was a remarkable chapter in English cricket history and a defining moment for Ian Botham. The series, contested between England and Australia, showcased Botham's exceptional all-round skills and saw a stunning turnaround in England's fortunes. Despite both teams being ranked below the dominant West Indies team of that era, the Ashes contest captured the imagination of cricket fans worldwide with its dramatic twists and turns.

England emerged triumphant, winning the series 3-1, despite facing an uphill battle after being 1-0 down following the first two Tests. The turning point came in the legendary third Test at Headingley, where the inspirational Mike Brearley was reinstated as England captain, replacing Ian Botham, whose captaincy had been unsuccessful and whose form with bat and ball had dipped. The match at Headingley witnessed an extraordinary performance from Botham, who took 6 wickets for 95 runs in Australia's first innings and scored 50 runs in England's innings. However, Australia posted a formidable total of 401 for 9 declared in their first innings, with John Dyson scoring 102. England was then bowled out for 174, and they were forced to follow-on, trailing by 227 runs. Geoff Boycott's resilient 46 was not enough to salvage the situation for England. However, in the second innings, Botham produced a remarkable innings of 149 not out. He formed crucial partnerships of 117 with Graham Dilley for the eighth wicket, 67 with Chris Old for the ninth, and 37 with Bob Willis for the tenth. England set Australia a target of 130 runs. Australia seemed well on their way to victory at 56 for 1, but a tactical bowling change by Brearley brought Willis into the attack from the favoured end. Willis delivered a magnificent spell, taking 8 wickets for 43 runs, dismissing Australia for 111. England secured a historic victory, becoming only the second team in Test history to win a match after being forced to follow-on.

The fourth Test at Edgbaston was another remarkable comeback for England. They conceded a 69 run first innings deficit but set Australia a target of just 151 runs in the fourth innings. Australia seemed poised for victory at 105 for 4, but Botham unleashed a devastating spell, taking 5 wickets for 11 runs, including a remarkable sequence of five wickets for just one run. Australia was bowled out for 121, and England secured a 29 run victory.

England continued their winning streak in the fifth Test at Old Trafford, clinching the series and retaining the Ashes. Botham once again played a pivotal role, scoring a breathtaking 118 from just 102 balls. He formed a contrasting partnership with Chris Tavaré, who played a blocking innings of 78 from 289 balls. Despite centuries from Allan Border and Graham Yallop in Australia's second innings, England emerged victorious.

The sixth and final Test at The Oval ended in a draw, with Dennis Lillee taking 11 wickets in the match and Botham claiming 10. It was a fitting end to a series filled with extraordinary performances and high drama. The 1981 Ashes series will be remembered as a testament to the fighting spirit and resilience of the English team. Botham's remarkable all-round performances, coupled with Brearley's astute captaincy, played a significant role in England's triumph. The series captured the hearts of cricket fans with its roller-coaster nature, making it a truly unforgettable chapter in Ashes history.

******

2 Tone Records was a record label founded in 1979 by Jerry Dammers, the keyboardist and main songwriter of the ska band The Specials. The label played a significant role in the early 1980s in popularising ska music and introducing it to a wider audience. 2 Tone Records was influenced by the music and cultural movements of the late 1970s. At the time of its formation, the British music scene was experiencing a surge in punk and new wave, and the label sought to combine these influences with the Jamaican ska and reggae sounds that had inspired Dammers and his bandmates. 2 Tone Records aimed to create a unique blend of punk energy, social commentary, and catchy ska rhythms.

The 2 Tone movement emerged as a response to the racial tensions and economic hardships faced by working-class youth in the late 1970s. The movement sought to promote racial unity and multiculturalism, using music as a means of breaking down barriers and fostering understanding. 2 Tone Records embraced this ethos and became synonymous with the 2 Tone movement. The record label signed and released music from a diverse roster of artists who became the faces of the label and the 2 Tone movement. The Specials, the label's flagship band, blended ska, punk, and reggae to create a distinct sound that addressed social and political issues. Their hit singles like "A Message to You, Rudy" and "Ghost Town" became anthems of the era. Other notable artists on the 2 Tone Records roster included Madness and The Beat, who both had their first single released by 2 Tone, The Selecter and The Bodysnatchers. Each band brought its unique style and sound to the label, contributing to the vibrant and energetic ska revival that swept through Britain. 2 Tone Records also played a pivotal role in the revival of Jamaican ska and reggae in the UK. The label rerecorded classic ska tracks from the 1960s, introducing a new generation to the music of artists like Desmond Dekker and Toots and the Maytals. The label's visual identity was equally distinctive, with the iconic 2 Tone Records logo featuring a black and white checkerboard pattern symbolising racial harmony and unity. This logo became synonymous with the label and its artists, appearing on album covers, promotional material, and merchandise. Although 2 Tone Records had a relatively short existence, lasting from 1979 to 1986, its impact on British music and cultural history is enduring. The label's fusion of ska, punk, and reggae paved the way for subsequent ska and ska-punk bands, and its messages of multiculturalism and social commentary remain relevant today. 2 Tone Records and its artists not only left a lasting musical legacy but also championed inclusivity and unity during a time of social and political turbulence.

******

The SDP was formed by a group of prominent politicians, known as the "Gang of Four", who were dissatisfied with the leftward shift of the Labour Party under the leadership of Michael Foot. The Gang of Four consisted of Roy Jenkins, David Owen, Shirley Williams, and Bill Rodgers. They believed that the Labour Party had become too dominated by leftist elements and had moved away from the centre ground, which they believed was necessary for electoral success. They aimed to create a new political party that would occupy the centre left space in British politics and provide an alternative to both Labour and the Conservative Party. The catalyst for the formation of the SDP was the Labour Party's 1980 conference, where a series of policy shifts, including the adoption of unilateral nuclear disarmament and withdrawal from the European Economic Community (EEC), were endorsed. This further disillusioned the Gang of Four and led them to conclude that their political objectives could no longer be achieved within the Labour Party. On 26th March 1981, the Gang of Four officially announced the formation of the SDP. They advocated for a moderate, centrist platform, promoting social justice, economic liberalism, and a pro-European stance. The SDP quickly gained attention and support, attracting disenchanted Labour Party members, intellectuals, and centrist voters who were dissatisfied with both Labour and the Conservative Party. The formation of the SDP had a significant impact on British politics. It challenged the traditional two-party system and introduced a new force that appealed to voters seeking a more centrist alternative. The SDP's electoral success was evident in the 1983 general election when it formed an electoral alliance with the Liberal Party, known as the SDP-Liberal Alliance. Although the alliance failed to make significant gains in terms of seats, it received a considerable share of the popular vote. However, internal divisions and strategic challenges plagued the SDP-Liberal Alliance, preventing it from achieving its full potential. Despite attracting a significant level of public support, the electoral system, which heavily favours the two major parties, hindered the SDP-Liberal Alliance's ability to convert votes into seats.

In 1988, the SDP and the Liberal Party merged to form the Social and Liberal Democrats (later renamed the Liberal Democrats). This merger aimed to consolidate the centrist vote and create a more united force to challenge the dominance of the Labour and Conservative parties. The formation of the SDP and its subsequent merger with the Liberal Party highlighted the desire for a centrist alternative to the two major parties and reshaped the political landscape by introducing a viable third force. The legacy of the SDP can still be seen today in the presence and influence of the Liberal Democrats.

******

Sebastian Coe and Steve Ovett were two legendary British middle-distance runners who captivated the world of athletics during the 1980s. Their fierce rivalry and exceptional performances made them household names and brought glory to British athletics on the global stage. Sebastian Coe, born on 29th September 1956, was known for his exceptional speed, tactical intelligence, and smooth running style. He specialised in middle-distance events, particularly the 800m and the 1500m. Coe's breakthrough came in the 1979 European Cup, where he won gold in the 800m, during the same year he broke the world 800m record three times in 41 days. Steve Ovett, born on 9th October 1955, possessed a unique combination of strength, versatility, and raw talent. He excelled in a range of distances, from the 800m to the 5000m. Ovett burst onto the scene in the late 1970s and early 1980s, achieving notable victories and setting records in various events. The rivalry between Coe and Ovett reached its peak during the 1980 Moscow Olympics, where they both competed in the 800m and the 1500m. In the 800m, Coe and Ovett faced each other in a highly anticipated showdown. In a thrilling race, Ovett emerged as the unexpected victor securing the gold medal in a time of 1:45.40. Coe won silver. However, the tables turned in the 1500m, where Coe showcased his brilliance and claimed the gold medal, while Ovett had to settle for bronze. This exchange of victories intensified the rivalry between the two athletes and fuelled speculation about their contrasting styles and competitive approaches. The rivalry continued to unfold in subsequent years, with both athletes setting world records and engaging in thrilling battles on the track. Coe was known for his precision, efficient running style, and ability to accelerate in the final stages of a race. Ovett, on the other hand, relied on his strength and endurance, often adopting a front-running approach to dictate the pace of a race.

At the 1984 Los Angeles Olympics they once again both competed in the 800m and the 1500m. In the 1500m Coe claimed his second Olympic gold while in the 800m he took silver. In the 800m Steve Ovett only managed eighth place in the final and in the 1500m while running in fourth place he dropped out of the race, he later collapsed with breathing difficulties and was taken away on a stretcher. Their contrasting styles and fierce competition captivated audiences and inspired a generation of athletes. Coe and Ovett's performances elevated British middle-distance running to unprecedented heights and left a lasting legacy in the world of athletics.

******

One notable aspect of British cinema in the 1980s was the rise of independent filmmaking and the development of a distinct British independent film movement. Filmmakers like Derek Jarman, Sally Potter, and Peter Greenaway challenged traditional storytelling conventions, experimenting with form, narrative, and visual aesthetics. Their films tackled provocative and controversial subjects, pushing the boundaries of cinema and challenging audience expectations.

The social realism genre also continued to thrive in the 1980s, with filmmakers like Ken Loach continuing to explore working-class struggles and social issues. Additionally, the 1980s marked a period of success for British period dramas. Films like "Chariots of Fire", directed by Hugh Hudson and produced by David Puttnam, showcased the talent of British actors and celebrated the nation's sporting achievements. The British comedy genre also thrived in the 1980s, with films like "A Fish Called Wanda", directed by Charles Crichton, and "Withnail & I", directed by Bruce Robinson, becoming cult classics. These films blended humour with sharp wit, memorable characters, and clever storytelling, showcasing the comedic talent of British actors and writers. Films like "Time Bandits", directed by Terry Gilliam, combined fantasy elements with satire and imagination, capturing the imaginations of audiences. The British film industry also experienced success in international co-productions during the 1980s. Films such as "The Killing Fields", directed by Roland Joffé, and "A Room with a View", directed by James Ivory, garnered critical acclaim and achieved commercial success, showcasing British talent on the global stage. In terms of notable British actors and actresses, the 1980s saw the rise of talented performers who would go on to achieve great success in the industry. Actors like Daniel Day-Lewis, Gary Oldman, and Helena Bonham Carter emerged during this period, showcasing their versatility and talent in a wide range of films.

******

The 1980 Winter Olympics held in Lake Placid, USA, marked a significant moment for British winter sports. Robin Cousins, a figure skater, claimed the gold medal in the men's singles event. His elegant and flawless performance captivated audiences and earned him the highest honours. Cousins' victory remains one of the most celebrated British achievements in Winter Olympics history. In the same Olympics, ice dancers Jayne Torvill and Christopher Dean made their Olympic debut, although they didn't secure a medal. At the 1984 Winter Olympics in Sarajevo, Yugoslavia, Great Britain had further successes. Torvill and

Dean's exceptional talent shone as they earned the highest honour by winning the gold medal in ice dancing. Their mesmerising routine to the music of Ravel's "Bolero" received unanimous perfect scores, solidifying their place in figure skating history. The 1988 Winter Olympics in Calgary, Canada, saw the British team secure another notable achievement. Michael Edwards, better known as "Eddie the Eagle", competed in ski jumping and became a popular figure worldwide. Although he didn't win a medal, Edwards' determination and underdog spirit resonated with audiences and made him a beloved symbol of the Olympics.

******

Jayne Torvill and Christopher Dean's performance at the 1984 Winter Olympics in Sarajevo, Yugoslavia, is one of the most memorable and iconic moments in figure skating history. Their stunning routine to Maurice Ravel's "Boléro" captivated audiences around the world and earned them a well-deserved gold medal. Torvill and Dean had already established themselves as a remarkable ice dancing pair before the 1984 Olympics. They were known for their innovative choreography, technical excellence, and an unmatched ability to bring emotion and storytelling to their performances. Their decision to skate to Ravel's "Boléro" was a bold and ambitious choice.

The music itself is powerful and evocative, building in intensity as it progresses. Torvill and Dean's interpretation of the music, combined with their exceptional skating skills, elevated their performance to new heights. On 14th February 1984, in front of a captivated audience at the Zetra Ice Hall, Torvill and Dean took to the ice for their free dance routine. Dressed in costumes that perfectly complemented the dramatic nature of the music, they began their mesmerising performance. Right from the start, it was clear that something extraordinary was unfolding on the ice. Their intricate footwork, seamless lifts, and graceful spins showcased their technical mastery. But it was their ability to convey emotion and tell a story through their movements that set them apart.

As the routine progressed, Torvill and Dean's chemistry and connection with each other and the music were palpable. They effortlessly captured the passion and intensity of the music, expressing it through their fluid movements and captivating expressions. Every nuance of the music was interpreted with precision and artistry. The judges and the audience were spellbound by Torvill and Dean's performance. The routine received unanimous perfect scores for artistic impression from all the judges, a rare achievement in figure skating. The crowd rose to their feet in a standing ovation, recognising the brilliance unfolding before them.

Torvill and Dean's gold medal-winning performance in Sarajevo was a historic moment. It was the first time in Olympic history that ice dancers had achieved perfect scores for artistic impression. Their achievement cemented their place in figure skating folklore and left an indelible mark on the sport. Following the Olympics, Torvill and Dean turned professional and continued to captivate audiences with their mesmerising routines. They went on to create numerous innovative and groundbreaking ice dance performances, thrilling fans around the world.

******

Carla Lane was an exceptional talent in the world of British sitcoms, leaving an indelible mark with her iconic creations. With a unique blend of wit, warmth, and social commentary, Lane crafted three beloved sitcoms that captivated audiences across the nation. From "The Liver Birds" to "Butterflies" and "Bread", Lane's sitcoms reflected the changing times and provided a delightful escape into the lives of memorable characters. Let us delve into the magic of these timeless shows. "The Liver Birds", which premiered on 14 April 1969, became an instant hit. Set in the vibrant city of Liverpool, the sitcom revolved around the lives of two young women, Sandra (Nerys Hughes) and Beryl (Polly James). Lane's clever writing brought to life the dreams, aspirations, and misadventures of these spirited friends as they navigated the challenges of work, romance, and friendship. The show struck a chord with viewers, capturing the essence of the swinging '60s and '70s, while also tackling issues of independence and women's liberation. It ran for a remarkable ten years, concluding on 31 December 1978, and remains a timeless classic in the annals of British television. Lane's second triumph came in the form of "Butterflies", which took flight on 10 November 1978. This poignant comedy-drama delved into the life of Ria Parkinson (Wendy Craig), a middle-aged housewife longing for something more. Ria's internal conflict between her responsibilities as a wife and mother and her desire for personal fulfillment resonated with audiences, bringing forth universal themes of self-discovery and the pursuit of happiness. Alongside her husband Ben (Geoffrey Palmer) and two sons, Russell (Andrew Hall) and Adam (Nicholas Lyndhurst), Ria embarked on a journey of self-reflection and transformation. The series concluded on 24 December 1983, leaving an enduring legacy of heartfelt storytelling.

In 1986, Lane created "Bread", a sitcom set in Liverpool's Boswell family, which premiered on 1 May 1986. With its working-class backdrop, the show offered a hilarious and sometimes bittersweet portrayal of the Boswell clan's trials and tribulations. Led by the formidable matriarch Nellie Boswell (Jean Boht), the eccentric family members navigated their way through financial challenges with their unique blend of resourcefulness, charm, and occasional mischief. "Bread" became an instant hit, blending comedy with astute social commentary on class and economic struggles. The series concluded on 3 November 1991, leaving an enduring legacy of laughter and warmth.

Carla Lane's sitcoms were not merely vehicles for laughter but also touched on important social issues of their time. Lane's genius lay in her ability to blend comedy with poignant storytelling, providing audiences with relatable characters and narratives that mirrored real life experiences. Her shows became a reflection of the changing social fabric, capturing the spirit of their respective eras while addressing deeper themes of female empowerment, self-discovery, and the complexities of family life.

Carla Lane's remarkable contributions to British television earned her a place among the greats of the genre. Her sitcoms, "The Liver Birds", "Butterflies" and "Bread" will forever be celebrated for their timeless appeal and their ability to entertain and engage audiences across generations. Lane's legacy endures, reminding us of the power of laughter, compassion, and insightful storytelling in bringing people together.

******

The decade saw the rise of snooker as a mainstream televised sport, with its dedicated tournaments, charismatic players, and nail-biting matches that kept viewers glued to their screens. One of the pivotal factors contributing to the popularity of snooker on television was the emergence of a group of talented and charismatic players, including Steve Davis, Alex Higgins, and Jimmy White. These players had distinctive personalities and playing styles that captured the public's imagination and brought a new level of excitement to the game.

The BBC played a significant role in promoting snooker on television. The broadcaster recognised the growing interest in the sport and began providing extensive coverage of major tournaments. The most prestigious event, the World Snooker Championship, held at the Crucible Theatre in Sheffield, received comprehensive live coverage, making it a must-watch event for snooker enthusiasts. The coverage of snooker tournaments on television was not limited to the World Championship. Other notable tournaments, such as the UK Championship and the Masters, also received substantial airtime. The BBC's coverage of these events was enhanced with expert commentary and analysis from renowned commentators, such as Ted Lowe and Clive Everton. Their expertise and insightful commentary added to the overall viewing experience.

The production quality of snooker broadcasts also improved significantly during the 1980s. Multiple camera angles, slow-motion replays, and close-ups of crucial shots allowed viewers to appreciate the skill and precision involved in the game. The use of graphics to display scores, break-building progress, and player statistics further enhanced the viewing experience, making snooker more accessible and engaging to a wider audience. The timing of snooker broadcasts also played a role in its popularity. Matches were often scheduled during the evenings and weekends, allowing fans to tune in and enjoy the sport without conflicting with their work or daily routines. This convenient scheduling contributed to the growing fan base and viewership numbers. The dramatic and intense nature of snooker matches also added to their appeal. The tension-filled atmosphere, particularly during crucial frames and close matches, kept viewers on the edge of their seats. The psychological battles between players, strategic shot-making, and pressure-cooker situations created captivating narratives that drew viewers in and made snooker a thrilling spectator sport. Notable moments and rivalries from the 1980s, such as the intense clashes between Steve Davis and Dennis Taylor in the 1985 World Championship final and the flamboyant style of Alex Higgins, further fuelled the public's fascination with snooker. These captivating storylines, combined with the skill and drama on display, made snooker a staple of television viewing in the 1980s.

******

British television in the 1980s was a vibrant and diverse landscape, with a wide range of programming that captivated audiences across the country. From sitcoms and dramas to game shows and children's programs. The 1980s saw the emergence of popular sitcoms such as "Only Fools and Horses", "Blackadder", "Yes Minister", and "To the Manor Born". These shows offered humour, memorable characters, and clever writing, becoming long-lasting favourites.

British game shows experienced a resurgence in popularity during the 1980s. Shows like "Blankety Blank", "Bullseye", and "Family Fortunes" entertained audiences with their blend of humour, competition, and prizes. The tradition of variety shows continued in the 1980s with shows like "The Two Ronnies", "The Kenny Everett Video Show", and "The Generation Game". These shows featured a mix of comedy sketches, music performances, and celebrity guests. Iconic dramas of the 1980s included "Brideshead Revisited", "The Jewel in the Crown", "Edge of Darkness", "Tinker Tailor Soldier Spy", "The Singing Detective", and "Boys from the Blackstuff". These gripping series tackled a variety of themes, from social issues to historical events, and featured stellar performances from talented actors.

These compelling dramas attracted critical acclaim and showcased the talents of talented writers and actors. The 1980s produced beloved children's programs that still hold a special place in the hearts of many. "Blue Peter", "Grange Hill", "Rainbow", and "Thomas the Tank Engine" captured the imaginations of young viewers with their educational and entertaining content.

The decade was marked by significant events and political changes, and British television played a crucial role in reporting and analysing the news. Programs such as "Newsnight", "Question Time", and "This Week" provided in-depth coverage and insightful discussions on current affairs. It wasn't all serious though, British television in the 1980s excelled in political satire. Programs like "Spitting Image" and "Not the Nine O'Clock News" provided biting commentary on political figures and events, using humour to tackle social and political issues.

******

Channel 4 was launched on 2nd November 1982. It marked a significant development in the British broadcasting landscape, introducing a fresh and innovative approach to television programming. Channel 4 was established as a public service broadcaster, distinct from the existing BBC channels and the commercial ITV network. It was created with a specific remit to provide a diverse range of high-quality programming that catered to underrepresented audiences and tackled social issues. One of the distinctive features of Channel 4 was its funding model. It operated as a commercially funded but publicly owned broadcaster, with revenue generated through advertising. This allowed Channel 4 to have a degree of creative freedom and independence in its programming decisions. From its inception, Channel 4 aimed to offer alternative and provocative content that challenged the conventions of mainstream television. It became known for its groundbreaking and often controversial programming, pushing boundaries and tackling subjects that were considered taboo at the time. One of the early successes of Channel 4 was the youth-oriented music show "The Tube", which aired live performances by popular artists and became a platform for emerging musical talent. This show exemplified Channel 4's commitment to providing a platform for diverse and cutting-edge content.

Over the years, Channel 4 continued to introduce innovative programming that influenced British television. It featured groundbreaking comedies like "The Comic Strip Presents" and it also showcased thought-provoking dramas like "Brookside" and "Shameless", which delved into social issues and challenged traditional storytelling. Channel 4 also played a significant role in supporting independent and alternative filmmakers through its Film4 production company. It co-produced and distributed a range of critically acclaimed films, nurturing new talent and contributing to the British film industry. The launch of Channel 4 in Britain introduced a fresh and distinct voice to the television landscape. Its commitment to innovative programming, social commentary, and diverse representation has made it a vital and influential part of British broadcasting.

******

The Miners' Strike, which began in March 1984, was a year long industrial action initiated by the NUM in response to the government's plans to close 20 coal pits, which would result in the loss of thousands of mining jobs. The NUM hoped to force the government to reverse its pit closure plans and protect the future of the coal industry. Thatcher's government, however, was determined to confront the power of the unions and reshape the

British economy. The strike became a highly polarising and bitter confrontation, pitting the striking miners against the government, police, and other miners who continued to work during the strike. The government used various tactics to undermine the strike, including employing the police to maintain order and limiting the NUM's access to funds and resources.

The strike had a significant impact on the coal industry and mining communities. As the strike persisted, the government used stockpiled coal and imported coal to keep power stations running, reducing the strikers' bargaining power. Over time, the strike lost momentum, and many miners returned to work without achieving their objectives. The strike ultimately ended in March 1985, with the NUM conceding defeat. The closure of many coal mines proceeded, resulting in the loss of thousands of mining jobs and significant economic and social consequences for mining communities. The strike highlighted the declining influence of trade unions in shaping government policy and the increasing power of the Conservative government in implementing its economic agenda.

In the aftermath of the strike, the government introduced trade union reform through the Trade Union Act of 1984 and subsequent legislation. The reforms aimed to curb the power of trade unions, limit their ability to disrupt essential services, and promote greater transparency and democracy within unions. The Trade Union Act of 1984 introduced several significant changes. It required unions to hold secret ballots before undertaking industrial action, restricted secondary picketing, and increased the legal liability of unions for damages caused by strikes. The reforms were seen by the government as a necessary response to the perceived excessive power of trade unions and their ability to disrupt essential services and the economy. The trade union reforms of the 1980s had a lasting impact on labour relations in Britain. They significantly weakened the influence of trade unions, particularly in industries such as mining, and shifted the balance of power towards employers. The reforms were seen by critics as undermining workers' rights and reducing the collective bargaining power of unions, while supporters argued that they brought greater accountability and restored balance to labor relations.

******

Alternative comedy emerged as a response to the more mainstream and conservative style of comedy prevalent in the era, challenging social norms and pushing boundaries in terms of content and delivery. Alternative comedy was characterised by its emphasis on political and social commentary. Comedians tackled issues such as gender, race, class, and sexuality, offering satirical and thought-provoking perspectives on these subjects. Alternative comedians often adopted an anti-establishment stance, criticising institutions and authority figures. They challenged the status quo, making bold statements and subverting expectations through their comedy.

There was an emphasis on originality and innovation. Alternative comedy encouraged comedians to experiment with unconventional approaches to humour. It valued originality, encouraging performers to break away from traditional joke-telling formats and embrace new forms of expression. Comedians incorporated elements of performance art, blurring the lines between comedy, theatre, and music. Comedians incorporated sketch comedy, physicality, music, and visual effects into their acts, creating a multidimensional and immersive experience. The spirit of the comedy fostered a sense of collaboration and community among comedians. It often took the form of collective ventures, such as comedy clubs and performance groups, where artists could share ideas, support one another, and collaborate on projects.

Several influential comedians emerged during this era, shaping the landscape of alternative comedy. Some of the key figures include Alexei Sayle, Rik Mayall, Ade Edmondson, Dawn French, Jennifer Saunders, Ben Elton, and French & Saunders. Alternative comedy clubs, such as The Comedy Store in London, provided a platform for emerging comedians to perform their unique and often subversive material. These clubs became hubs for alternative comedy and helped to cultivate new talent. Alternative comedy gained wider exposure through television shows like "The Young Ones", "Blackadder", "The Comic Strip Presents" and "The Alternative Comedy Experience". These programs brought alternative comedy to a broader audience, showcasing its rebellious and unconventional spirit. The rise of alternative comedy in 1980s Britain marked a shift in comedic sensibilities and challenged traditional norms. It provided a platform for edgier, more socially aware humour, and set the stage for the continued evolution of comedy in the years to come.

******

"Tell Sid" was a prominent advertising campaign launched by the British government in the 1980s to encourage the public to invest in privatised companies. The campaign aimed to promote the sale of shares in state-owned enterprises, allowing individuals to become shareholders and participate in the free-market economy. The phrase "Tell Sid" became synonymous with the privatisation efforts of the Conservative government.

The campaign was part of a broader strategy of privatisation initiated by the Thatcher government. During the 1980s, several major industries, including telecommunications, gas, electricity, and water, were privatised. The goal was to reduce government control, increase competition, and promote the efficiency of these industries through private ownership and market forces. The "Tell Sid" campaign, launched in 1986, was designed to make privatisation more accessible and appealing to the general public. It sought to portray the sale of shares as an opportunity for ordinary citizens to become stakeholders in the economy and benefit from potential financial gains. The campaign featured a series of television and print advertisements that emphasised the potential profitability of investing in privatised companies.

The central character of the campaign was "Sid", a fictionalised representation of an average person considering investing in privatised companies. The advertisements used a friendly and relatable tone, urging viewers to "Tell Sid" about the opportunity to own shares and participate in the country's economic transformation. The campaign was successful in generating public interest and participation in share ownership. It appealed to the idea of widespread ownership and wealth creation, encouraging individuals to take an active role in the market economy. Many people who had never invested before saw the opportunity to become shareholders and potentially benefit from the success of privatised companies. The "Tell Sid" campaign helped to shift public perception and attitudes towards privatisation. It played a significant role in normalising the idea of private ownership and market-oriented reforms. The sale of shares to the public not only raised funds for the government but also dispersed ownership and created a sense of popular capitalism.

The impact of the "Tell Sid" campaign and the broader privatisation policies of the Thatcher government was significant. Privatisation resulted in the transformation of industries, increased competition, and changes in corporate governance. It also had social and political consequences, as it reshaped the relationship between the state, the public, and private enterprises.

******

The 1980s were a decade of sporting television firsts in Britain, with several notable milestones and memorable moments that shaped the sports broadcasting landscape. Among the significant television firsts during that time were the first 147 break in snooker, the first 9 dart finish in darts, and the first live league game in football.

The first 147 break in snooker on British television occurred 1982 during the Lada Classic. Steve Davis, one of the game's most dominant players, achieved this feat in his quarter-final match against John Spencer. The break involved potting all 15 reds with their respective colours, followed by all six colours in sequence, culminating in the black. This flawless performance by Davis captivated viewers and marked a historic moment in snooker history.

In terms of darts, the first televised 9 dart finish in Britain took place on 13th October 1984, during the MFI World Matchplay tournament. John Lowe, a renowned darts player, accomplished this remarkable feat. A 9 dart finish involves a player hitting the maximum possible score of 501 by throwing nine darts, using the fewest possible number of throws. Lowe's achievement of achieving a perfect leg in such a high-pressure environment was a groundbreaking moment for televised darts.

On 2nd October 1983, ITV made a significant television first by broadcasting a live top-flight football match for the first time since 1960. This marked a significant moment in British football broadcasting history and had a profound impact on the way football matches were televised in the country. The match in question featured Tottenham Hotspur against Nottingham Forest in the First Division, Tottenham won 2-1. Both teams were considered powerhouses in English football at the time, and the match generated considerable excitement among football fans. ITV's decision to broadcast a live top-flight football match came after a long hiatus since the last televised game in 1960. This move represented a shift in television coverage of football and opened up new possibilities for fans to watch their favourite teams in action from the comfort of their homes. The broadcast featured live commentary, expert analysis, and multiple camera angles, enhancing the viewing experience for football fans. It brought the excitement and drama of top-level football directly into people's living rooms, allowing them to follow the action as it unfolded.

The significance of this event cannot be understated, as it marked the beginning of a new era in football broadcasting in Britain. It provided fans with greater access to live football and contributed to the growing popularity and commercialisation of the sport. Since that groundbreaking broadcast in 1983, live top-flight football matches have become a staple of television programming, with multiple broadcasters competing for the rights to showcase the matches. These television firsts in the 1980s marked significant milestones in their respective sports and had a lasting impact on television broadcasting in Britain. The first 147 break in snooker, the first 9-dart finish in darts, and the first live league game in football showcased the excitement and drama of these sports, elevating their popularity and establishing them as must-watch events for fans across the country.

******

The fashion trends of this era reflected the socio-cultural changes and influences of the time, including the rise of the youth culture, the impact of music and subcultures, and the

increasing accessibility of global fashion through media and travel. One of the prominent fashion movements of the 1980s was the New Romantic movement, which emerged in the late 1970s but gained significant popularity in the early 1980s. New Romantics embraced a flamboyant and theatrical style, drawing inspiration from historical periods such as the Victorian and Edwardian eras. Men often wore frilly shirts, velvet jackets, and brocade waistcoats, while women embraced a more feminine look with ruffled blouses, lace dresses, and corsets. The movement was also associated with extravagant makeup, big hair, and accessories like wide-brimmed hats and fingerless lace gloves. The 1980s also saw the emergence of various mainstream fashion trends. One of the most iconic styles of the decade was the power dressing trend, popularised by influential women in politics and the corporate world. Power dressing emphasised sharp, tailored suits with padded shoulders, often in bold colours like red, electric blue, and fuchsia. This style represented a sense of empowerment and assertiveness for women in traditionally male-dominated fields. The decade also witnessed a fitness and aerobics craze, which influenced fashion trends like sportswear and neon coloured clothing. Tracksuits, leg warmers, and leotards became popular workout attire, with brands like Adidas and Nike leading the way. This trend spilled over into casual wear, with brightly coloured clothing, oversized sweatshirts, and graphic prints being popular choices.
Fashion icons of the 1980s included musicians like Madonna, Boy George, and David Bowie, whose distinctive styles influenced a generation. Their eclectic and daring fashion choices, along with the influence of music videos and MTV, pushed the boundaries of fashion and encouraged self-expression. Overall, fashion in 1980s Britain was characterised by a wide range of styles, from the glamorous and theatrical to the rebellious and edgy. It was a decade of bold experimentation,

reflecting the vibrant and dynamic spirit of the time. Many of the trends from the 1980s continue to inspire and influence fashion today, making it a truly iconic era in British fashion history.

******

Before the "Big Bang" in 1986, the financial markets in Britain were highly regulated and characterised by traditional practices. The London Stock Exchange, for example, operated under a system of fixed commissions and strict rules that limited competition and innovation. Foreign firms faced significant barriers to entry, and trading was conducted in a predominantly manual and closed manner. The Thatcher government recognised the need to modernise the financial sector to ensure its competitiveness on a global scale. The reforms were driven by the belief that reducing government intervention and promoting market forces would stimulate economic growth and increase London's prominence as a global financial centre. The key aspects of the "Big Bang" included the abolition of fixed commissions, the removal of restrictions on foreign ownership and trading, the introduction of electronic trading systems, and the liberalisation of financial services. These changes paved the way for increased competition, innovation, and international investment in the UK financial markets.

The deregulation of financial markets had several significant effects. Firstly, it led to a surge in foreign investment and the entry of international financial institutions into the UK. The removal of barriers allowed global banks and investment firms to establish a presence in London and participate in the UK financial market. This helped to solidify London's position as a leading global financial hub. Secondly, the "Big Bang" brought about a wave of technological advancements in the financial sector. Electronic trading systems replaced traditional open outcry trading, making transactions faster, more efficient, and accessible to a wider range of participants. This led to increased liquidity and trading volumes in the markets. Furthermore, the deregulation and liberalisation of financial services facilitated the growth of new financial products and services. This included the expansion of derivatives markets, the introduction of new trading instruments, and the development of innovative financing mechanisms. These developments helped to diversify the financial sector and cater to a broader range of client needs. The "Big Bang" also had social and cultural implications. It led to a significant shift in the composition of the financial industry, with larger firms and foreign institutions dominating the market. The traditional "old boys' network" was disrupted, and new players entered the scene, bringing with them a more meritocratic and internationalised culture.

However, the deregulation of financial markets and the "Big Bang" also raised concerns about potential risks and negative consequences. Critics argued that the increased competition and liberalisation led to a focus on short-term profits, excessive risk-taking, and market volatility. They also pointed out the growing income inequality and the concentration of wealth within the financial sector.

******

Before the Poll Tax, official named the Community Charge, local government in Britain was funded primarily through property-based taxes, such as the rates system. However, the Thatcher government believed that this system was unfair because it did not take into account the number of individuals living in a household or their ability to pay. In 1989, the government introduced the Community Charge as a replacement for the rates system. The Poll Tax was a flat-rate tax imposed on each adult resident in a local area, regardless of their income or property ownership. The idea behind this change was to create a system that was perceived as fairer and more equitable.

However, the implementation of the Poll Tax was met with widespread opposition and protests across the country. Critics argued that the tax placed a disproportionate burden on low-income households and disadvantaged individuals. Since the tax was based on the number of adults in a household rather than their income, it was seen as regressive and unfair. One of the key factors that fuelled opposition to the Poll Tax was its perceived impact on social inequality. The tax was seen as benefiting the wealthy while placing a heavier burden on the less affluent. This led to widespread unrest and demonstrations, culminating in the infamous "Poll Tax Riots" in March 1990, which took place in London and other major cities. The riots were marked by violent clashes between protesters and the police, resulting in injuries and property damage. The demonstrations reflected the deep-seated anger and frustration of many people who felt that the Poll Tax was unjust and disproportionately affected those already struggling financially.

The widespread opposition to the Poll Tax eventually led to its repeal. After Margaret Thatcher resigned as Prime Minister in 1990, her successor John Major introduced the Local Government Finance Act 1992, which replaced the Community Charge with the Council Tax system. The Council Tax introduced a more progressive structure based on property values, taking into account different tax bands and income-related exemptions. The introduction and subsequent repeal of the Poll Tax marked a significant setback for the Thatcher government, eroding public support and contributing to internal divisions within the Conservative Party. The controversy surrounding the Poll Tax was one of the factors that led to Thatcher's resignation as Prime Minister. What is more, the Poll

Tax played a role in shaping public attitudes towards taxation and social justice in Britain. It underscored the importance of fairness and equity in taxation policies and highlighted the need for a system that takes into account individuals' ability to pay.

1990s
Britpop, New Labour and The Third Way

Politically, the 1990s witnessed a shift in power from the Conservative Party to the Labour Party. In 1990, Margaret Thatcher resigned as Prime Minister, and her successor, John Major, faced challenges within his own party. The Labour Party, under the leadership of Tony Blair, embraced a centrist approach and sought to modernise its image. Blair's "New Labour" movement, which promised a harmonious blend of social justice and free-market economics, led to a landslide victory for the party in the 1997 general election. Economically, the 1990s brought both challenges and opportunities for Britain. The decade began with a recession, but the economy rebounded later, experiencing steady growth. The process of globalisation accelerated, with increased international trade and the expansion of financial services. London's financial sector, in particular, experienced significant growth, establishing the city as a global financial hub. The 1990s also saw the rise of the internet and the digital revolution. The World Wide Web became widely accessible, transforming communication, information sharing, and business practices. The dot com boom created opportunities for entrepreneurs and led to the emergence of new industries, while also experiencing a subsequent bust in the early 2000s. Socially, the 1990s witnessed diverse trends and changes. The decline of traditional manufacturing industries continued, leading to the restructuring of communities and rising inequality. The service sector grew, with an increasing focus on technology, finance, and creative industries. The job market shifted, placing greater emphasis on skills and education.

One significant social change of the 1990s was the increasing recognition and acceptance of diverse identities. The gay rights movement made significant strides, and the age of consent for same-sex relationships was equalised. The armed forces lifted the ban on gay individuals serving openly. The era also witnessed the repeal of Section 28, which restricted the promotion of homosexuality in schools.

Culturally, the 1990s was a vibrant and diverse period. British music experienced a renaissance, with the emergence of Britpop. Bands like Oasis, Blur, and Pulp gained international acclaim, and their music captured the spirit of the times. Electronic dance music, including genres like rave and techno, also grew in popularity, reflecting the club and party culture of the era. Fashion in the 1990s was characterised by a mix of grunge, minimalism, and eclectic styles. Influential designers like Alexander McQueen and John Galliano challenged conventions and pushed boundaries. High street fashion became more accessible and affordable, allowing for greater experimentation with personal style.

The peace process in Northern Ireland gained momentum during the 1990s. The Good Friday Agreement, signed in 1998, sought to bring an end to sectarian violence and establish a power-sharing government. This agreement laid the foundation for a more peaceful and stable Northern Ireland.

******

The launch of the Premier League in Britain marked a significant milestone in the history of English football. It transformed the landscape of the sport and had a profound impact on the way football was played, broadcast, and commercially operated. The Premier League was established on 29th February 1992, as a breakaway from the Football League First Division. The decision to form a new top-tier league was driven by several factors, including the desire to capitalise on the growing popularity and commercial potential of football. Before the launch of the Premier League, the top division in English football was known as the Football League First Division. However, clubs were increasingly concerned about falling behind other European leagues in terms of revenue, television coverage, and global appeal. There was a desire to revitalise English football and make it more competitive and attractive.

The restructuring of English football resulted in the formation of the Premier League, which consisted of the top 20 clubs. The inaugural season kicked off on 15th August 1992, with matches broadcast on Sky Sports, a satellite television network that secured the rights to televise the league. The Premier League brought several key changes and innovations to English football. It introduced a more lucrative revenue-sharing model, allowing clubs to benefit from increased television rights deals and sponsorship opportunities. This influx of money facilitated investments in infrastructure, player transfers, and the overall development of the clubs. The league also prioritised improving the match day experience for fans, with upgraded stadiums, enhanced facilities, and increased safety measures.

The Premier League's focus on commercial growth and fan engagement played a significant role in attracting global audiences and boosting the league's international appeal. The launch of the Premier League in Britain marked a turning point in football history, transforming English football into a global spectacle. It set new standards in terms of commercialisation, television coverage, and overall professionalism in the sport.

******

Manchester United's dominance of the early Premier League years is widely regarded as one of the most successful periods in English football history. Under the management of Sir Alex Ferguson, Manchester United established itself as a powerhouse, winning a string of Premier League titles and cementing its status as one of the most successful clubs in the country. The Premier League era began in the 1992-1993 season, and Manchester United wasted no time in making their mark. They clinched their first Premier League title in the inaugural season led by influential figures such as Eric Cantona, Ryan Giggs, and Paul Scholes, Manchester United showcased their attacking prowess and never-say-die mentality, securing the title by a 10-point margin over Aston Villa. This success marked the start of a remarkable period of dominance for Manchester United. They went on to win the Premier League in the following two seasons as well, completing a hat-trick of titles from 1993 to 1996. During this time, Ferguson built a strong squad with a winning mentality, blending experienced players with talented youngsters from the club's renowned youth academy. Manchester United's success continued into the late 1990s and early 2000s. They secured the Premier League title in the 1996-1997, 1998-1999, 1999-2000 and 2000-2001 seasons, becoming the first team to win three consecutive league titles since Liverpool in the 1980s.

The team was led by inspirational figures such as Roy Keane, David Beckham, and the prolific strike partnership of Andy Cole and Dwight Yorke.

The pinnacle of Manchester United's dominance came in the 1998-1999 season when they achieved an unprecedented treble. They won the Premier League title, the FA Cup, and the UEFA Champions League, becoming the first club in history to achieve such a feat. Their dramatic comeback victory in the Champions League final against Bayern Munich, with two injury-time goals, remains one of the most memorable moments in football history.

Overall, Manchester United won an impressive 13 Premier League titles between 1992 and 2013, firmly establishing themselves as the most successful club in the competition's history. Their dominance during the early years of the Premier League showcased the club's ability to consistently perform at the highest level and set new standards of excellence.

******

Music in 1990s Britain was a dynamic and transformative period, witnessing the emergence of various genres and movements that left a lasting impact on the music industry. One of the defining genres of 1990s British music was Britpop, which emerged in the mid-1990s as a response to the grunge movement from the United States. Britpop celebrated British culture and identity, with bands like Oasis, Blur, and Pulp leading the way. Britpop brought a sense of nostalgia for British music of the past, drawing inspiration from bands like The Beatles and The Kinks.

The 1990s also saw the resurgence of guitar-driven indie rock, with bands like Radiohead, The Stone Roses, and Manic Street Preachers making significant contributions. Radiohead's album "OK Computer" is widely regarded as a masterpiece of the era, blending alternative rock with experimental and atmospheric elements. The Stone Roses' self-titled debut album became a seminal work in the British indie scene, fusing elements of jangle pop and psychedelic rock. The Manic Street Preachers combined political and social commentary with their music, often delivering powerful and thought-provoking lyrics.

Another significant genre of the 1990s was electronic music, which experienced a surge in popularity and influenced various sub genres. The dance music scene flourished, with genres like acid house, rave, and techno gaining momentum. The Manchester-based band The Chemical Brothers were prominent figures in the electronic music scene, producing innovative and energetic tracks that dominated clubs and festivals. The popularity of electronic music also led to the rise of the "superclub" culture, with venues like the Ministry of Sound in London becoming legendary destinations for electronic music enthusiasts. In addition to these genres, the 1990s witnessed the rise of girl groups and pop acts that achieved massive commercial success. Bands like Spice Girls and All Saints captured the attention of a global audience with their infectious pop tunes and distinctive personas. Their music embraced themes of empowerment, female solidarity, and individuality, resonating with a generation of young fans. The 1990s in Britain also saw the emergence of influential solo artists, such as Robbie Williams, who achieved immense success after leaving the boy band Take That. Williams' pop-rock sound and charismatic stage presence made him one of the best-selling artists of the decade.

******

The UEFA Euro 1996 tournament held in England was a significant moment for both the England and Scotland national football teams. It was the first time the European Championship was hosted by England and marked a memorable campaign for both nations. England, as the host nation, entered the tournament with high expectations. Managed by Terry Venables, the team boasted a talented squad including notable players such as Alan Shearer and Paul Gascoigne. The tournament started with a group stage where England was drawn into Group A alongside Switzerland, the Netherlands, and Scotland.

England began their campaign with a 1-1 draw against Switzerland at Wembley Stadium on 8th June 1996. The team then faced their fierce rivals, Scotland, in a highly anticipated match on 15th June. Known in the tabloid press as the "Battle of Britain", the match took place at Wembley Stadium and was filled with tension and excitement. In a closely contested encounter, England managed to secure a 2-0 victory over Scotland. The goals were scored by Alan Shearer and Paul Gascoigne. Gascoigne's goal, in particular, remains one of the most iconic moments in English football history. Three days later England beat the Netherlands 4-1 to top the group and progress to the quarter finals. England faced Spain on 22nd June 1996 and won in a penalty shootout after a 0-0 draw. This set up a highly anticipated semi final clash with Germany, which ended in a heartbreak for England as they were eliminated after another penalty shootout, famously known for Gareth Southgate's missed penalty. On the other hand, Scotland had a challenging campaign at Euro 1996. Managed by Craig Brown, the Scottish team struggled to secure positive results in the group stage. Scotland drew 0-0 with the Netherlands, suffered the 2-0 defeat to England and lost 1-0 to Switzerland. They finished third in the group and were eliminated. Despite failing to progress past the group stage, Scotland's participation in Euro 1996 was significant for their passionate supporters and marked their return to a major international tournament after an absence of eight years.

******

John Major succeeded Margaret Thatcher as the Prime Minister in 1990 and led the country until 1997. His tenure was marked by both successes and difficulties, including economic issues, political divisions, and the changing landscape of European integration. One of the major challenges faced by the Major government was the state of the economy. The early 1990s saw a recession in Britain, partly caused by global economic factors but also exacerbated by domestic issues such as high interest rates and an overvalued housing market. Major's government had to implement economic policies to stabilise the economy and address issues such as inflation and unemployment.

One of the significant achievements of the Major government was the negotiation and signing of the Maastricht Treaty in 1992. This treaty led to the establishment of the European Union (EU) and laid the groundwork for further European integration. However, the Maastricht Treaty also sparked internal divisions within the Conservative Party, with some members strongly opposed to the idea of European integration. The issue of European integration and Britain's relationship with the EU became a contentious topic during Major's premiership. He faced challenges from both Eurosceptics within his own party and from the opposition Labour Party. The Conservative government was divided over the question of European integration, leading to rebellions and resignations by members of Parliament. Another significant event during Major's government was the signing of the Downing Street Declaration in 1993. This joint declaration with the Irish government outlined a framework for peace in Northern Ireland and played a crucial role in the subsequent Northern Ireland peace process. The Major government also implemented several domestic policies and reforms. It introduced the National Lottery in 1994, which aimed to fund various charitable causes and projects. Major's government also enacted reforms in education, health, and welfare, with initiatives such as the introduction of standardised testing in schools and the creation of the Jobseeker's Allowance.

However, the Major government faced political challenges, including allegations of corruption and scandals involving some Conservative politicians. The government also struggled to maintain public support, and the Conservative Party experienced electoral setbacks, including losses in by-elections and local elections. The 1997 general election proved to be a significant turning point for the Major government. The Conservative Party suffered a resounding defeat, losing to the Labour Party led by Tony Blair. The election result marked the end of Major's tenure as Prime Minister and brought about a change in the political landscape of Britain.

******

The rivalry between Oasis and Blur for the number one spot in the British music charts during the 1990s was a significant cultural phenomenon that captured the attention of the media and the public. Oasis, fronted by brothers Liam and Noel Gallagher, embodied a more rock 'n' roll and anthemic sound. They gained a reputation for their energetic live performances and their swaggering, working class image. Oasis' breakthrough album "Definitely Maybe" and their follow-up "What's the Story Morning Glory?" achieved enormous success and propelled them to the forefront of the Britpop movement. On the other hand, Blur, led by Damon Albarn, showcased a more eclectic and artful approach to their music. Their album "Parklife" became a defining record of the Britpop era, blending catchy melodies with observational lyrics that reflected everyday British life. Blur's subsequent albums, such as "The Great

Escape" and "Blur", further solidified their place in the Britpop landscape. The rivalry between Oasis and Blur reached its peak in 1995 when both bands released singles on the same day, aiming for the coveted number one spot on the charts. Oasis released "Roll with It", while Blur released "Country House". The media eagerly pitted the two bands against each other, creating a media frenzy around the competition. Ultimately, Blur's "Country House" won the chart battle and debuted at number one, beating Oasis' "Roll with It" which entered at number two. The Oasis vs. Blur rivalry not only focused on chart success but also represented wider cultural and social differences. Oasis was often associated with a working class, no nonsense attitude, while Blur was seen as more middle class and intellectual. The rivalry embodied the clash between the northern and southern regions of England and the contrasting cultural identities. Although the chart battle was a significant moment, both Oasis and Blur went on to achieve enduring success throughout the 1990s and beyond. They left a lasting impact on the Britpop movement, influencing subsequent generations of British musicians. Today, the Oasis vs. Blur rivalry remains an iconic chapter in British music history, symbolising a defining era in the 1990s and the cultural significance of the Britpop genre.

******

Britain had a notable presence at the Olympic Games throughout the 1990s. The decade saw British athletes achieve success in various sports, including athletics, rowing, cycling, and swimming. The 1992 Olympic Games in Barcelona, Spain. Britain sent a team of 371 competitors winning 20 medals including 5 gold, 3 silver and 12 bronze with significant success for British athletes. Linford Christie won the gold medal in the men's 100m and Sally Gunnell secured a memorable gold medal in the women's 400m hurdles. In rowing, Sir Steven Redgrave and Matthew Pinsent won in the men's coxless pair event. Steven Regrave's medal being the 3rd of his 5 gold medals at consecutive Olympics. Other gold medals were won by Chris Boardman in cycling and the men's coxed pair in rowing.

******

The Maastricht Treaty, signed in 1992, established the foundations for the EU by introducing new areas of cooperation and policy integration among member states. It created the framework for the Economic and Monetary Union (EMU), which aimed to establish a single currency, the Euro. The treaty also expanded the EU's competencies to include common foreign and security policies, as well as justice and home affairs. In Britain, the Maastricht Treaty sparked considerable debate and controversy.

The Conservative government led by Prime Minister John Major faced internal divisions within the party over the issue of European integration. Eurosceptic members of the Conservative Party, commonly referred to as "Eurosceptics", voiced concerns about the erosion of national sovereignty and the potential loss of control over key policy areas. The ratification of the Maastricht Treaty faced challenges in the British Parliament. The legislation implementing the treaty, known as the European Communities (Amendment) Act 1993, required parliamentary approval. It faced resistance from both Conservative Party rebels and opposition parties, leading to a series of intense debates and a significant number of rebellions during the bill's passage. Public opinion in Britain towards the Maastricht Treaty was also mixed, some segments of the population viewed European integration as a positive step towards peace, stability, and economic cooperation. Others, however, expressed concerns about the potential loss of sovereignty and the impact on national identity and democratic governance. The Maastricht Treaty also paved the way for a referendum on the issue of European integration in Britain. In 1997, the new Labour government led by Tony Blair made a campaign promise to hold a referendum on whether the UK should adopt the Euro. The referendum didn't happen. Despite the controversies and divisions, the Maastricht Treaty had a lasting impact on Britain's relationship with the EU. It laid the foundation for subsequent EU treaties and shaped the integration process in various policy areas. The treaty's provisions on the free movement of goods, services, capital, and people continue to be central to Britain's membership in the EU and subsequent debates on European integration.

******

The YBAs, or Young British Artists, were a prominent group of artists who emerged in Britain in the 1980s and 1990s and had a significant impact on the visual arts scene. Known for their provocative, conceptual, and often controversial artworks, the YBAs challenged traditional notions of art and gained international recognition for their innovative approaches. The term "Young British Artists" was coined by art critic Michael Corris in a 1992 Artforum article, and it became synonymous with the group of artists associated with the contemporary art scene in London during that time.

One of the most famous YBAs is Damien Hirst, whose work became emblematic of the movement. Hirst gained attention with his series of installations featuring preserved animals in formaldehyde, such as "The Physical Impossibility of Death in the Mind of Someone Living". Hirst's work explored themes of life, death, and the fragility of existence, often challenging the boundaries between art and science. Another notable YBA is Tracey Emin, known for her candid and confessional artwork. Emin's work often incorporates personal narratives, exploring themes of sexuality, identity, and vulnerability. Her installation "My Bed" caused a stir and became an iconic piece of YBA art, consisting of her unmade bed surrounded by personal belongings and debris. Other YBAs who made significant contributions to the art scene in the 1990s include Sarah Lucas, known for her provocative sculptures and installations that challenged gender stereotypes, and Chris Ofili, who gained attention for his vibrant and intricate paintings incorporating materials like elephant dung. The YBAs gained international recognition through exhibitions such as the seminal "Sensation" exhibition held at the Royal Academy of Arts in London in 1997. Curated by Charles Saatchi, the exhibition showcased works by various YBAs, attracting both critical acclaim and controversy. It featured artworks that explored themes of consumerism, British identity, and popular culture.

The YBAs were known for their entrepreneurial spirit and their ability to self-promote. They often organised their own exhibitions and events, creating a buzz around their work. Their artworks were often characterised by an irreverent and confrontational approach, challenging traditional notions of art and embracing new media and materials. The YBAs' impact on the art world extended beyond Britain, influencing contemporary art globally. Their innovative and often controversial works pushed boundaries and sparked conversations about the nature and purpose of art. While the YBA movement may have peaked in the 1990s, many of the artists associated with it continue to produce influential and thought-provoking work today.

******

Damien Hirst's artistic career began while studying at Goldsmiths, University of London, where he was part of the Young British Artists (YBAs) movement. He gained recognition for his installations, sculptures, and conceptual artworks that challenged traditional notions of art, often exploring themes of mortality, science, religion, and the fragility of life. One of Hirst's most famous and controversial works is "The Physical Impossibility of Death in the Mind of Someone Living". It features a preserved tiger shark suspended in a tank of formaldehyde, evoking questions about life, death, and the nature of art. This piece became emblematic of Hirst's use of unconventional materials and his exploration of the relationship between life and death.

Hirst's work often involves the use of animals, insects, and medical objects, such as butterflies, cows, pharmaceuticals, and human skulls. He became known for his "Spot Paintings", composed of meticulously arranged colourful dots, and his "Spin Paintings", created by spinning circular canvases while applying paint. In addition to his artistic endeavours, Hirst has also been involved in curating exhibitions, including the influential show "Freeze" in 1988, which showcased the works of his fellow Goldsmiths students. He has also collaborated with other artists, musicians, and fashion designers, further expanding his artistic reach. Throughout his career, Hirst has received numerous accolades and recognition for his contributions to contemporary art. He was awarded the prestigious Turner Prize in 1995, and his work has been exhibited in major art institutions worldwide, including the Tate Modern in London, the Guggenheim Museum in New York, and the Museum of Contemporary Art in Los Angeles. Hirst's art has often sparked debates and divided opinions, with critics questioning the commercialisation of his work and the artistic value of his concepts. Nevertheless, he remains a prominent figure in the art world, pushing boundaries and challenging conventions through his provocative and sometimes controversial creations.

Damien Hirst's impact on contemporary art extends beyond his artworks themselves. His entrepreneurial approach to the art market, including the establishment of his own studio, company, and art collection, has reshaped the relationship between artists, galleries, and the commercial aspects of the art world. Hirst's influence and legacy continue to resonate, and his works are held in prestigious collections worldwide. He has left an indelible mark on the art world, sparking conversations and pushing the boundaries of artistic expression.

******

The launch of the Rugby Super League in 1996 was a significant moment in the history of rugby league in the United Kingdom. It marked a new era for the sport, bringing about major changes in the structure, format, and commercialisation of professional rugby league. Before the formation of the Super League, rugby league in the UK operated under a traditional league structure, known as the Rugby Football League (RFL). However, in the early 1990s, there was a desire to modernise the game and create a more competitive and commercially viable product. The Super League was officially launched on 29th March 1996 in Paris to revitalise the sport and raise its profile. The first game saw Paris Saint Germain beat Sheffield Eagles 30-24. The competition was designed to be a breakaway from the existing RFL structure and featured a new format that emphasised entertainment, higher standards, and increased revenue opportunities.

Twelve teams were initially invited to join the Super League, which included established clubs from the traditional league structure as well as newly formed franchises. The participating teams included well-known clubs such as Wigan, Leeds, St Helens, Bradford Bulls, and many others. One of the key aspects of the Super League was its focus on attracting commercial partners and securing lucrative television deals. This allowed the sport to generate more revenue and invest in player development, infrastructure, and marketing efforts. The increased financial resources helped clubs attract talented players from around the world, elevating the overall quality of the competition. The Super League also introduced several innovations to enhance the spectator experience and make the sport more appealing to a wider audience. These included changes to the competition structure, such as a playoff system to determine the league champion, the introduction of a salary cap to ensure fair competition, and the adoption of a more structured and professional approach to club management.

The launch of the Rugby Super League brought about a transformation in the landscape of rugby league in the UK. It ushered in a new era of professionalism, commercialisation, and higher standards, contributing to the growth and development of the sport. The competition continues to be a cornerstone of British rugby league, attracting passionate fans, driving financial investment, and providing a platform for players to showcase their skills at the highest level.

******

In the early 1990s, the Labour Party was struggling to gain electoral success. It had experienced consecutive general election defeats in 1979, 1983, 1987 and 1992, which led to a period of introspection and ideological reevaluation within the party. This period of reflection culminated in the election of Tony Blair as the leader of the Labour Party in 1994. Blair and his supporters sought to redefine the Labour Party's identity and shed its traditional left-wing image. They believed that the party needed to appeal to a wider spectrum of voters and adopt a more pragmatic, centrist approach to policies. This rebranding effort became known as "New Labour".

One of the key elements of New Labour's strategy was to distance itself from the more radical policies associated with the party's past, such as nationalisation and extensive state intervention. Instead, New Labour emphasised a commitment to market-oriented policies, economic stability, and social justice. The rise of New Labour was also accompanied by a significant rebranding effort. The party adopted a more modern and media savvy approach to campaigning, utilising marketing techniques and spin doctors to present a more polished and professional image. Blair, with his charismatic and telegenic personality, played a crucial role in reshaping the party's public perception and connecting with voters.

The rise of New Labour in the 1990s fundamentally reshaped the political landscape in Britain. It brought about a modernisation of the Labour Party, a shift towards centrist policies, and a focus on electoral appeal. While the New Labour project had its successes, it also faced criticism for abandoning certain traditional principles and failing to address inequality and social issues to the satisfaction of all supporters.

******

British cinema in the 1990s experienced a resurgence and showcased a wide range of films that garnered critical acclaim and commercial success. The decade witnessed the emergence of talented filmmakers, the exploration of diverse genres, and the portrayal of social issues relevant to British society. One of the defining films of the 1990s was "Trainspotting", directed by Danny Boyle and based on the novel by Irvine Welsh.

"Trainspotting" became a cultural phenomenon, highlighting the talent of British actors like Ewan McGregor and introducing a distinctive visual style and a memorable soundtrack.

British cinema in the 1990s also explored social and political issues. "Secrets & Lies", directed by Mike Leigh, delved into themes of race, identity, and family dynamics. The film received critical acclaim and won the Palme d'Or at the Cannes Film Festival, solidifying Leigh's reputation as a master of character-driven dramas. Ken Loach, known for his socially conscious films, continued to make an impact during this decade. "My Name Is Joe" tackled issues of poverty, addiction, and community in Glasgow, while "Raining Stones" shed light on the struggles of working class families. Loach's films often highlighted the inequalities and challenges faced by ordinary people in British society.

Another significant film from the 1990s was "Four Weddings and a Funeral", directed by Mike Newell and written by Richard Curtis. This romantic comedy achieved both critical and commercial success, catapulting Hugh Grant to stardom. The film's witty dialogue, charming characters, and quintessentially British setting resonated with audiences around the world. The 1990s also witnessed the success of British period dramas. "Sense and Sensibility", directed by Ang Lee and based on the novel by Jane Austen, showcased the talents of British actresses Emma Thompson and Kate Winslet. The film received critical acclaim and multiple Academy Award nominations, including a win for Emma Thompson's screenplay. In addition to these films, the 1990s marked the debut of several British directors who would go on to make significant contributions to cinema in subsequent years. Directors like Christopher Nolan, Guy Ritchie, and Sam Mendes emerged during this period, showcasing their distinct styles and storytelling abilities.

******

The decade witnessed the emergence of talented writers who made significant contributions to contemporary literature. One of the defining novels of the 1990s was "Trainspotting" by Irvine Welsh. Set in Edinburgh, Scotland, the novel captured the gritty reality of drug addiction through its vivid and often shocking portrayal of a group of heroin addicts. "Trainspotting" utilised a unique narrative style, incorporating Scottish dialect and stream-of-consciousness writing, which contributed to its raw and powerful impact. The novel's success led to a highly acclaimed film adaptation directed by Danny Boyle in 1996. Salman Rushdie, an acclaimed British-Indian author, released "The Moor's Last Sigh" in 1995. The novel explored themes of identity, multiculturalism, and the complex history of India. Rushdie's rich storytelling and his ability to blend history and mythology with contemporary issues continued to captivate readers during this decade.

Another notable work from the 1990s was "Captain Corelli's Mandolin" by Louis de Bernières. Set on the Greek island of Cephalonia during World War II, the novel depicted the complex relationships and experiences of its characters against the backdrop of war. It was celebrated for its evocative writing style, memorable characters, and exploration of love, loss, and the effects of conflict. Jeanette Winterson, known for her innovative and experimental writing, published "Written on the Body" in 1992. The novel challenges conventional notions of gender and identity through its exploration of a love affair between two unnamed individuals. Winterson's lyrical prose and unconventional narrative structure made "Written on the Body" a standout work of the 1990s.

The 1990s also saw the rise of the "lad lit" genre, which focused on the lives and experiences of young men. Nick

Hornby's "High Fidelity" and Irvine Welsh's "Marabou Stork Nightmares" are examples of this genre. These novels delved into themes of masculinity, relationships, and personal growth, often with a humorous and self reflective tone. Overall, British literature in the 1990s was characterised by a diverse range of voices and genres. It reflected the changing social and cultural landscape of the time, tackling issues such as addiction, identity, multiculturalism, and the complexities of human relationships.

******

Damon Hill achieved the remarkable feat of winning the Formula One World Championship in 1996. He followed in the footsteps of his father, the legendary Graham Hill, becoming the first son of a World Champion to win the title himself. Damon Graham Devereux Hill was born on 17th September 1960, in Hampstead, London. Growing up in a racing family, he had a passion for motorsport from an early age. However, his journey to the top of Formula One was not a straightforward one.

Hill began his racing career in the 1980s, competing in various lower formulae and making his way up the ranks. He worked as a test driver for Williams before In 1993 becoming Williams' full-time driver alongside the reigning World Champion Alain Prost. He quickly established himself as a formidable competitor, showcasing his talent and determination on the track. Despite facing tough competition from his teammate and other top drivers, Hill consistently delivered strong performances, earning his first Grand Prix victory at the 1993 Hungarian Grand Prix.

The 1994 season was a tumultuous one for Hill. Tragedy struck the Williams team when his teammate Ayrton Senna was fatally injured during the San Marino Grand Prix. Hill assumed the role of the team leader and, despite the immense pressure and tragedy, continued to perform admirably, winning six races that season. However, due to a combination of retirements and incidents, he narrowly missed out on the championship, finishing as the runner-up to Michael Schumacher.

Hill's perseverance finally paid off in 1996 when he secured the Formula One World Championship. Driving for Williams-Renault, he put together a remarkable season, winning eight out of the sixteen races and consistently outperforming his rivals. Hill's calm and composed approach, combined with his natural talent, allowed him to secure the championship with two races to spare. The 1996 championship victory made Damon Hill the first son of a World Champion to become a World Champion himself, creating a unique and special legacy in Formula One history. After his championship triumph, Hill continued to compete in Formula One for several more seasons, driving for various teams, including Jordan and Arrows. Although he did not reach the same level of success as he did with Williams, Hill remained a respected figure in the sport, admired for his sportsmanship and dedication.

******

The 1997 General Election in Britain was a watershed moment in British political history. It marked a significant turning point, ending 18 years of Conservative Party rule and bringing the Labour Party, under the leadership of Tony Blair, to power with a landslide victory. The election was held on 1st May 1997 and saw a high level of public interest and engagement. It was preceded by a period of intense media scrutiny and a sense of anticipation for potential change after years of Conservative government.

The Labour Party, led by Tony Blair, campaigned on a platform of modernisation, social justice, and economic stability. Blair sought to present Labour as a moderate, centrist party, distancing it from its traditional left-wing image and appealing to a broad range of voters. The party's campaign focused on issues such as education, healthcare, crime, and improving public services. On the other hand, the Conservative Party, led by Prime Minister John Major, faced internal divisions and voter fatigue after nearly two decades in power. The party struggled to present a unified message and faced criticism for economic issues, such as the recession in the early 1990s and the perceived impact of Conservative policies on public services.

The election results were a resounding victory for Labour. The party won 418 seats, giving them a comfortable majority in the House of Commons. The Conservatives, in contrast, won only 165 seats, their worst electoral performance since 1906. The Liberal Democrats, led by Paddy Ashdown, made some gains, increasing their number of seats to 46. However, their performance fell short of expectations, and they remained a minor party in terms of parliamentary representation.

The 1997 General Election saw a significant voter turnout, with around 71% of eligible voters casting their ballots. The result marked a seismic shift in British politics, reflecting a desire for change and an appetite for a fresh approach to governance. The 1997 General Election is often remembered for its symbolism of a new era in British politics. It represented a break from the Thatcherite and Conservative dominance of the previous years, ushering in a period of New Labour and a more centrist approach to governance.

******

The "Third Way" was a political ideology that emerged within the Labour Party under the leadership of Tony Blair and the New Labour Movement. The Third Way sought to position itself as an alternative to both traditional left-wing socialism and right-wing conservatism, presenting a centrist approach to governance. The term "Third Way" originated from the belief that there was a need to move beyond the ideological divides of the past and find a new path that incorporated elements of both market-oriented capitalism and social justice. It emphasised the importance of economic efficiency, individual responsibility, and social cohesion.

In the context of British politics, the Third Way emerged in the 1990s as a response to the perceived failures of traditional left-wing policies and the need to adapt to changing global circumstances. Tony Blair, along with key figures such as Peter Mandelson and Gordon Brown, played a crucial role in shaping and promoting the Third Way agenda. The Third Way advocated for market-oriented economic policies that embraced globalisation and sought to create a competitive, entrepreneurial economy. It aimed to balance economic growth with social justice and emphasised the importance of investment in education, technology, and infrastructure. It sought to address social inequalities and promote social justice through progressive policies. It emphasised the importance of providing equal opportunities and reducing poverty and social exclusion. Initiatives such as the introduction of a minimum wage, investment in public services, and welfare reforms were central to the Third Way agenda. The Third Way aimed to reform the welfare state to make it more efficient and responsive to the changing needs of society. It sought to strike a balance between providing a safety net for those in need and encouraging self-reliance and individual responsibility. It emphasised the role of the private sector in delivering public services. It promoted partnerships between the government and private entities to improve service delivery and increase efficiency. The Third Way took a tough stance on law and order, advocating for policies that prioritised crime prevention, community policing, and rehabilitation. It sought to address the underlying causes of crime, such as poverty and social exclusion.

The Third Way in British politics brought about substantial changes in areas such as education, healthcare, welfare, and the economy. However, the Third Way also faced criticism from both the left and the right, with some arguing that it led to a dilution of traditional left-wing values and a lack of ideological clarity. Ultimately, the Third Way represented an attempt to modernise and adapt left-wing politics to a changing global landscape. It sought to combine elements of market-oriented capitalism with a commitment to social justice, aiming to find a middle ground that appealed to a broad range of voters.

******

Television in 1990s Britain experienced significant changes, both in terms of the emergence of new genres and the transformation of existing ones. The decade witnessed the introduction of innovative programming, the expansion of cable and satellite television, and the rise of iconic shows that captured the attention of audiences.

Reality television emerged as a significant genre in 1990s Britain, revolutionising the television landscape and captivating audiences with its unscripted and often voyeuristic format. The 1990s saw the birth of several influential reality TV shows that paved the way for the genre's future success. In 1999, the show "Big Brother" made its debut and became a cultural phenomenon. Based on a Dutch concept, "Big Brother" featured a group of contestants living together in a house rigged with cameras, with their every move monitored and broadcast to the public. The show popularised the concept of reality TV as a social experiment, with viewers voting to evict or save contestants. "Big Brother" generated immense public interest and controversy, making household names out of its participants and sparking debates about privacy, ethics, and the impact of reality TV on society. Another significant reality TV show of the 1990s was "Changing Rooms". The show, which aired from 1996 to 2004, focused on home improvement and interior design. In each episode, two sets of neighbours swapped homes and redecorated a room with the help of a professional designer. "Changing Rooms" appealed to audiences' fascination with home improvement and DIY projects, and it inspired a wave of similar shows in the following years. Reality TV in the 1990s brought ordinary people into the spotlight, creating a new breed of celebrity and changing the dynamics of fame. It blurred the lines between reality and entertainment, captivating audiences with the drama, conflicts, and emotional moments of real people's lives. Sitcoms continued to be a popular genre during the 1990s. Shows like "Only Fools and Horses", "Absolutely Fabulous", and "The Vicar of Dibley" entertained audiences with their comedic writing and memorable characters. These sitcoms often reflected the changing social dynamics and cultural shifts of the era.

The 1990s also saw the emergence of cult TV series that gained a dedicated following. "The X-Files", imported from the United States, became a huge hit in Britain, captivating viewers with its blend of science fiction, conspiracy theories, and supernatural mysteries. The show's popularity highlighted the increasing globalisation of television and the cross-cultural appeal of certain programs. British dramas also thrived during the 1990s. "Cracker", starring Robbie Coltrane, explored the psychological complexities of a criminal profiler, while "Prime Suspect", starring Helen Mirren, followed the career of a determined female detective. Both shows received critical acclaim for their writing, performances, and their ability to tackle gritty and realistic subject matter.

The 1990s also marked the introduction of satellite and cable television, which brought a wider range of channels and programming options to British viewers. Channels like Sky One, BBC Four, and Channel 5 offered new content, including international imports, documentaries, and niche programming catering to specific interests. Another significant development in 1990s British television was the increased coverage of live events and sports. Major sporting events like the FIFA World Cup and the Olympic Games received extensive coverage, bringing viewers together to witness memorable sporting moments. It's important to note that the 1990s also marked the transition from analog to digital television broadcasting, paving the way for technological advancements and increased viewing options seen in subsequent decades.

******

In the 1990s, the United Kingdom underwent a significant constitutional transformation with the introduction of devolution for Scotland, Wales, and Northern Ireland. Devolution granted these regions a degree of self-governance and allowed them to have their own legislative bodies and decision-making powers within specified areas. This marked a shift towards a more decentralised system of governance and aimed to address regional disparities and promote local democracy.

The devolution process began with Scotland, where a pre legislative referendum was held on 11th September 1997, resulting in overwhelming public support for the creation of a Scottish Parliament. The Scotland Act 1998 was subsequently passed by the UK Parliament, establishing the devolved Scottish Parliament with powers over various policy areas, including health, education, and justice. The Scottish Executive, later renamed the Scottish Government, was formed to exercise executive functions. In Wales, a similar referendum was held on 18th September 1997 also resulted in majority support for the establishment of a devolved assembly. The Government of Wales Act 1998 created the National Assembly for Wales, which initially had limited powers.

In Northern Ireland, the devolution process was more complex due to the ongoing peace process and the Troubles. The Good Friday Agreement of 1998 played a significant role in facilitating the establishment of devolved institutions in Northern Ireland. The Northern Ireland Assembly and the power-sharing executive, consisting of both unionist and nationalist parties, were established on 2nd December 1999. However, due to political disagreements and periods of suspension, the assembly faced significant challenges in its early years. Devolution for Scotland, Wales, and Northern Ireland brought about several benefits and challenges. Proponents argued that it empowered local communities, allowed for more tailored policies to address regional needs, and promoted a sense of regional identity and pride. Devolution also provided opportunities for greater public participation and accountability in decision-making. However, devolution also raised questions about the balance of powers between the devolved administrations and the UK government. The division of responsibilities and financial arrangements between the UK and devolved institutions remained topics of ongoing debate. Additionally, concerns were raised about the potential for divergence in policies and priorities among the different regions, leading to tensions within the UK. The introduction of devolution in the 1990s marked a significant change in the UK's constitutional arrangements, recognising the unique circumstances and demands of Scotland, Wales, and Northern Ireland. It aimed to address calls for greater regional autonomy and has since shaped the political landscape and decision-making processes in these regions.

******

The Good Friday Agreement was the result of intensive negotiations involving various parties, including the British and Irish governments, as well as political representatives from Northern Ireland. The agreement was named after the day it was signed, which was 10th April 1998. One of the crucial aspects of the agreement was the establishment of a power-sharing executive in Northern Ireland. This meant that political parties representing both unionist and nationalist communities would share power in a devolved government. The executive would be composed of a First Minister and a Deputy First Minister, elected by the Northern Ireland Assembly. The Good Friday Agreement also outlined a series of principles to address the complex issue of decommissioning paramilitary weapons. It called for the decommissioning of all paramilitary arms by the participating groups, which included loyalist and republican organisations. A new Independent International Commission on Decommissioning was established to oversee this process.

In addition to political aspects, the Good Friday Agreement addressed human rights issues and established bodies to promote equality and address past grievances. The agreement created the Northern Ireland Human Rights Commission and the Equality Commission for Northern Ireland, which were tasked with upholding and promoting human rights and equality within the region. What is more, the agreement acknowledged the relationship between Northern Ireland and the Republic of Ireland. It recognised the right of the people of Northern Ireland to identify as Irish, British, or both, and it outlined mechanisms for cross-border cooperation and consultation between the British and Irish governments.

The Good Friday Agreement was approved in referendums on 22nd May 1998 held in both Northern Ireland and the Republic of Ireland, receiving overwhelming support from voters. Its implementation faced challenges and setbacks, including periods of political deadlock and sporadic violence. However, the agreement provided a framework for peaceful political processes and encouraged dialogue and reconciliation among the communities in Northern Ireland. The Good Friday Agreement has had a significant impact on Northern Ireland's political landscape. It has contributed to a more stable and peaceful environment, with political institutions and power-sharing arrangements being established and sustained. The agreement also paved the way for increased cross-border cooperation between Northern Ireland and the Republic of Ireland, fostering a more positive relationship between the two.

******

The British reaction to the disappointing results at the 1996 Olympic Games in Atlanta was a mixture of disappointment, introspection, and a call for improvements in the country's sporting system. The overall performance of the British team fell below expectations, leading to discussions and debates about the state of British sport and the need for reforms. The British team finished the Atlanta Games with just one gold medal, won by rower Steve Redgrave and rowing partner Matthew Pinsent in the men's coxless pair event. This low medal count and the failure to achieve success in some traditionally strong sports led to disappointment and frustration among fans, athletes, and sports officials.

The media and public reaction to the results were critical, with many questioning the funding, training, and overall support provided to British athletes. There were discussions about the structure of British sport and whether changes needed to be made to improve performance on the international stage. The poor results in Atlanta prompted the British Olympic Association (BOA) to conduct a review of the country's performance and identify areas for improvement. The review led to the establishment of a lottery-funded program called "World Class Performance" aimed at providing financial support and resources to elite athletes.

Additionally, there were calls for better coordination and collaboration between sports bodies, coaches, and athletes to enhance training and development programs. The need to invest in grassroots sports and talent identification was also highlighted as crucial for long-term success. The disappointing performance at the 1996 Olympics served as a wake-up call for British sport, sparking a renewed focus on high-performance programs and strategic planning. The subsequent years saw increased funding and support for Olympic sports in the UK, leading to improved results in future Olympic Games.

The reaction to the bad results in 1996 ultimately fuelled a determination to create a stronger sporting system in Britain, with a focus on talent development, coaching, infrastructure, and funding. These efforts would later bear fruit as British athletes achieved significant success in subsequent Olympic Games, including the record-breaking performance at the London 2012 Olympics. Overall, the disappointing results at the 1996 Olympics prompted a critical evaluation of British sport and a commitment to making the necessary changes to improve future performance. The reaction to the setback played a crucial role in reshaping the country's sporting landscape and setting the stage for future success on the Olympic stage.

******

The handover of Hong Kong was a significant event in modern history, it marked the end of British colonial rule and the transfer of sovereignty over Hong Kong to the People's Republic of China. The background of the handover can be traced back to the history of Hong Kong and the negotiations between the British and Chinese governments. Hong Kong was a British colony for over 150 years, starting from the First Opium War in 1842 when the Qing Dynasty ceded Hong Kong Island to the British. Over time, the territory expanded with the addition of the Kowloon Peninsula and the New Territories. Under British rule, Hong Kong developed into a major international trading and financial hub, experiencing rapid economic growth and becoming a global centre of commerce.

In the early 1980s, as the expiration date of the lease for the New Territories approached, negotiations between the British and Chinese governments began to determine the future status of Hong Kong. The Chinese government insisted on the principle of "one country, two systems", which meant that Hong Kong would be returned to Chinese sovereignty but would maintain a high degree of autonomy and its own legal, economic, and political systems for 50 years. The negotiations resulted in the signing of the Sino-British Joint Declaration in 1984. The declaration outlined the terms of the handover and guaranteed the preservation of Hong Kong's existing way of life, including its legal system, freedoms, and capitalist economy. It also established the Basic Law, which would serve as Hong Kong's mini-constitution after the handover. In the years leading up to the handover, there were concerns and uncertainties about how the transition would unfold and how the Chinese government would uphold the promised autonomy and freedoms in Hong Kong. Some residents of Hong Kong were anxious about their future and potential changes under Chinese rule, leading to an increase in emigration to other countries.

On 1st July 1997, the handover ceremony took place, with Prince Charles representing the British Crown and President Jiang Zemin representing China. The British flag was lowered, and the Hong Kong Special Administrative Region (HKSAR) was established. Tung Chee-hwa became the first Chief Executive of the HKSAR, serving as the region's leader under Chinese sovereignty. Following the handover, Hong Kong retained its own legal system based on common law, separate from mainland China's legal framework. It also maintained its free-market economy and continued to be a major global financial centre. However, concerns about the erosion of political freedoms and the degree of autonomy granted to Hong Kong have persisted over the years, leading to political tensions and protests in more recent times.

The handover of Hong Kong represents a significant milestone in the history of both China and Britain. It marked the end of British colonial rule and the return of Hong Kong to Chinese sovereignty. The handover also highlighted the complexities of managing the transition from colonialism to a new political and governance system, raising questions about the preservation of civil liberties, democratic values, and the relationship between Hong Kong and mainland China.

******

As the clock struck midnight on 31 December 1999, a wave of anticipation and excitement swept across the nation as Britons bid farewell to the old century and welcomed the dawn of a new millennium. In cities and towns across the country, people gathered in public squares, parks, and iconic landmarks to mark the occasion. The atmosphere was electric, as individuals from all walks of life came together to share in the anticipation of the new millennium. The festivities were infused with a sense of historical significance, as the turn of the millennium was seen as a unique moment to reflect on the past and embrace the possibilities of the future.

London, the vibrant heart of the nation, was a focal point for the celebrations. The iconic River Thames became a focal point, with thousands of people lining its banks to witness a magnificent firework display lighting up the night sky. The London Eye, a newly erected landmark, provided a stunning backdrop to the spectacle, offering panoramic views of the city and its illuminated skyline. The revelry extended to Trafalgar Square, where crowds gathered to sing, dance, and revel in the spirit of unity and camaraderie.

Across the rest of the country, cities and towns hosted their own festivities, each with their unique flair and traditions. Edinburgh's Hogmanay celebration, renowned for its exuberance, attracted visitors from near and far. The streets of the Scottish capital were filled with revellers, who participated in the traditional torchlight procession, enjoyed live music performances, and joined hands to form the world's largest rendition of the traditional Scottish dance, the "Strip the Willow". In Manchester, the spirit of the occasion was captured in the dazzling Millennium Dome, a temporary structure erected in Exchange Square. The dome housed an array of interactive exhibits and artistic installations, inviting visitors to reflect on the past century's achievements and ponder the possibilities of the future. The city's streets came alive with music, street performances, and a vibrant carnival atmosphere that radiated joy and optimism. Throughout the country, private parties, street celebrations, and community events created a tapestry of jubilation and togetherness. Families and friends gathered in homes, pubs, and village halls, sharing laughter, food, and drinks as they counted down the seconds to midnight. The clinking of glasses and the chorus of "Auld Lang Syne" reverberated in every corner, symbolising the bonds of friendship and the cherished traditions that unite the nation.

The celebrations on 31 December 1999 not only marked the transition to a new millennium but also reflected the zeitgeist of the times. It was a moment to look back on the challenges and achievements of the past century and to embrace the possibilities and aspirations of the future. The festivities showcased the resilience, creativity, and spirit of the British people, who came together in a shared sense of optimism and unity. In the aftermath of the celebrations, as the new millennium dawned, the nation embarked on a new chapter in its history. The optimism and enthusiasm that permeated the celebrations would continue to shape the years to come, as Britain navigated the challenges and opportunities of the 21st century.

Printed in Great Britain
by Amazon